PENGUIN CLASSICS

ON THE NATURE OF THE UNIVERSE

TITUS LUCRETIUS CARUS must have been born soon after 100 BC and was probably already dead when his poem was given to the world in 55 BC. Almost nothing is known about his life. He was a Roman citizen and a friend of Gaius Memmius, an eminent Roman statesman, and his poem was read and admired by Cicero. It is doubtful if there is any truth in the story preserved by St Jerome and immortalized by Tennyson that he died at his own hand after being driven mad by a love philtre.

RONALD LATHAM also translated *The Travels of Marco Polo* for the Penguin Classics. Born in Northumberland in 1907, he graduated from Balliol College, Oxford, being appointed Lecturer in Latin at Queen's University, Belfast. From 1934 until 1967, with the exception of the war years, he was an Assistant Keeper of the Public Records. Ronald Latham was an O.B.E. and a Fellow of the Society of Antiquaries. His other publications include *In Quest of Civilization, Finding Out About the Normans*, and he edited the *Revised Medieval Latin Word List from British and Irish Sources*, in the British Academy Series. He was also the original editor of the *Oxford Dictionary of Medieval Latin from British Sources*. He died in 1992.

JOHN GODWIN is Head of the Classics Faculty at Shrewsbury School. He was born in 1955 and educated at St Bede's College, Manchester, University College, Oxford, and the University of Kent at Canterbury. He is a Fellow of the Royal Society of Arts and sits on the Council of the Classical Association. He has published editions of Book Four (1986) and Book Six (1991) of *On the Nature of the Universe*.

LUCRETIUS

ON THE NATURE OF
THE UNIVERSE

TRANSLATED BY R. E. LATHAM
REVISED WITH AN INTRODUCTION AND
NOTES BY JOHN GODWIN

PENGUIN BOOKS

PENGUIN BOOKS

Published by the Penguin Group
Penguin Books Ltd, 27 Wrights Lane, London w8 5tz, England
Penguin Putnam Inc., 375 Hudson Street, New York, New York 10014, USA
Penguin Books Australia Ltd, Ringwood, Victoria, Australia
Penguin Books Canada Ltd, 10 Alcorn Avenue, Toronto, Ontario, Canada m4v 3b2
Penguin Books (NZ) Ltd, Private Bag 102902, NSMC, Auckland, New Zealand

Penguin Books Ltd, Registered Offices: Harmondsworth, Middlesex, England

This translation first published 1951
This revised translation, with a new introduction and notes, published 1994
5 7 9 10 8 6

Translation copyright 1951 by R. E. Latham
Revisions, introduction and notes copyright © John Godwin, 1994

The moral right of the editor has been asserted

Typeset by Datix International Ltd, Bungay, Suffolk
Printed in England by Clays Ltd, St Ives plc
Filmset in 10/12 pt Monophoto Garamond

CONTENTS

REVISER'S PREFACE

R. E. Latham's excellent translation of Lucretius was first published in 1951 and is still the best translation on the market. This revision has been undertaken for two reasons: first to bring it more into line with what is now the generally agreed text of Lucretius and second to provide more assistance and background information to the reader than was available in the first edition. The textual revision is necessary in the light of the research that continues to be devoted to the corruptions and gaps in the manuscript readings, which has advanced a long way over the last forty years: the places where I have disagreed with the Oxford Classical Text of Lucretius are listed and (briefly) discussed in Appendix D. Gaps in the text that have been filled by proposed emendations are enclosed in angle brackets (⟨⟩). Material that is suspected of being interpolated into the text is enclosed in square brackets ([ ]).

The extra critical apparatus is required because the Penguin Classics series is increasingly being used as a textbook in courses in classical civilization, philosophy and ancient history, and the student who is attempting to come to grips with the detail and the context of this text without knowing much – or any – Latin needs considerable help in the notes, introduction and appendices. The footnotes are brief and are not intended to be a substitute for the detailed commentaries that exist on this text; the introduction attempts to cover the background and the problems of the poem in a brief and readable compass; points that I considered to merit further discussion – but that would have held up the argument of the introduction – are relegated to a series of appendices at the end of the volume. At no point do I claim to have covered all the answers – or even all the questions – and the serious student is referred to the bibliography for further reading.

No editor of Lucretius is an island, and one of the reasons for producing this revision is to give the student a digest of recent scholarship in accessible form, which will, I hope, justify my plundering the ideas and discoveries of the many scholars working in this field. In particular this revision owes a great deal to the kind assistance and time of Desmond Costa, Chris Emlyn-Jones and David West, who all read parts of the typescript and saved me from many mistakes. Those that remain are all my own.

JOHN GODWIN
Shrewsbury, March 1993

INTRODUCTION

This book should carry a warning to the reader: it is intended to change your life. Many authors believe that their writing will make a real impact on its audience, but few imagine the sort of conversion that this poet sets as his ambition. The reader is badgered to pay attention like an inattentive child, to drink the sour medicine in order to be cured of fear and ignorance. It is, he keeps telling us, well worth the effort. Imagine, Lucretius would say, waking up one day and finding that the fear of death and all your insatiable appetites for power and pleasure had all evaporated. Imagine feeling contented and secure in a sound understanding of the universe and its physical laws such that life could spring no more unpleasant surprises, no bogeymen from the dark corners of our ignorance could attack us now that the whole universe was floodlit with knowledge of the laws of nature. Imagine being free of ambition for power, for money, for love, even for life itself. You could forgo any or all of these things without shedding a tear. You would enjoy life as it presented itself to you without hankering after more than you have been given. You would be untouchably serene, contented, wise. By the end of this book, Lucretius states, you too could have a life like this.

This poem is not, then, a dry philosophical treatise written to show off abstruse clever ideas. Still less is it just a jaded poet stuck for a subject showing that he can expound Greek philosophy in Latin verse. And yet this was very much the view of Lucretius that prevailed in some circles until recently – that of a rather lacklustre hack droning on about physics. There *is* a great deal of argument and technical detail in the poem, and some of it is difficult, but the primary purpose of the composition is ethical rather than simply scientific. The exact nature of this ethical purpose will be examined later; but let us first look at the theory expounded here, Epicureanism.

EPICUREANISM

Early Greek philosophy had for centuries been asking questions about the universe: its composition and its purpose, if any. The apparent unity of a universe composed of diverse heterogeneous elements had to be explicable in some way, and one solution was to urge that everything was in reality different forms of the same thing: hence many of the Presocratic thinkers of the sixth and early fifth centuries BC tried to find this single substance out of which everything was ultimately made, such as air (Anaximenes), or water (Thales), or fire (Heraclitus), or perhaps a combination of the primary elements earth, air, fire and water (Empedocles). Then in the later fifth century two thinkers emerged with an idea that has dominated our understanding of the world right until this century. Their names were Democritus and Leucippus, and the theory they propounded formed the basis of Epicurean philosophy: Epicurus adopted their broad line of argument and developed it into a more complete scientific and ethical approach to life, known as the Atomic theory.

In essence, the theory is very simple. Everything that exists is made up of matter and empty space. Matter is composed of tiny invisible and indivisible elements called 'atoms' (the Greek word *atomos* means 'indivisible'), which are the building-blocks of everything we see around us, ourselves included. The enormous variety of phenomena we see and are is caused by the different combinations these atoms enter into. The indivisible nature of atoms is 'proved' by the continued existence of matter – if there were not some level beyond which matter could not be divided any further, then everything would have dissolved into nothing long ago (1.540–50). These atoms are always flying off the surface of objects and forming fresh compounds, and they cannot themselves be destroyed, although the compounds they make can be broken up (e.g., at death). The atoms go on for ever making new 'bodies' of matter. Thus food atoms are ingested into the body in compounds whose component atoms are separated out, some absorbed into the compound which is our physical body, others discarded as waste. Empty space must also exist to give the atoms room to move at all, and also to explain the different weights and densities of matter: a lump of lead has more atoms and less space than a lump of wood, and hence is heavier and denser. This empty space is without limit – for what can limit nothingness? – and hence the universe is infinite. The number of different atomic shapes and sizes is finite – otherwise some would be big enough to be visible – but the number of individual atoms of each size and shape is infinite throughout an infinite universe.

These atoms move all the time. To form material compounds they have to collide and stick together. Now, free-flying atoms fall naturally downwards, which makes the likelihood of collision remote, as all atoms would be flying in the same direction at the same time. It might have been thought that heavier atoms would fall faster and so fall on top of the lighter atoms as they all descended, but Epicurus was quick to point out that all objects of whatever weight descend at the same speed. He therefore invented his theory of the 'swerve' (*clinamen*) to account for atomic collisions: atoms falling downwards swerve on occasion from the straight vertical path to one side or another, and so collide. This theory is scientifically vulnerable – it cannot be proved because there is no causal explanation for the swerve. It was, however, essential in Lucretius' account to explain the phenomenon of free will.

This last point demonstrates very aptly that Lucretius did not simply admire these ideas as beautiful hypotheses – he used them as a foundation for a whole philosophy of life. Now there seems little point in advocating radical change in the way we think and feel if the scientific theory being propounded precludes the existence of free will. A mechanistic view of human nature as being helplessly and inexorably obedient to the laws of cause and effect would leave us incapable of self-improvement, just as my car cannot mend its own puncture. The dance of the atoms appears random, the effects of their collisions are dictated by their construction and nature, and we are as atomic a compound as the humblest brick. How, then, is it possible to maintain that we have moral choice over our actions, and that we can exercise volition both in thought and deed, when we are undeniably the victims of external atomic forces? The mechanistic determinism of Democritus left no room for moral responsibility or simple human choice, yet our subjective experience of volition is evidence in itself that atoms are not always compelled to a certain course of movement by the laws of nature. 'Both the brave man's and the coward's heart beat faster when the enemy's tanks begin to move forward, but only the coward deserts his post on the gun.' (D. J. Furley, *Two Studies in the Greek Atomists* (1967) 222) It is sometimes asserted that Epicurus invented the swerve to counter Democritus' unappealing determinism – it would be fairer to say that he observed free will in action and sought to find an explanation for it in his atomic theory. Far from being a tender-minded refusal to accept the grim truth about ourselves, it represents a brave attempt to solve a problem that remains largely unsolved to this day. If he failed, have we done so much better?

There is nothing tender-minded about Epicurus' attitude towards death, where his thorough-going materialism leaves no room for any form of personal survival of death. The body obviously dies and rots. What we call the spirit or soul consists, on Epicurean principles, of superfine atoms that receive and transmit sensory signals and that hold together the unity of bodily self-consciousness and sensation. These atoms are none the less material and will disperse on death along with the rest of us: the spirit is seen as on the one hand a collection of atoms collected in the breast, which is the seat of our thoughts and emotions (*animus*), and on the other hand a network of sensory receivers and transmitters spread throughout the body (*anima*). The spirit is never any form of incorporeal soul that might – as in Pythagorean thought – leave the tomb of the body at death and carry on an independent happier existence. The Epicurean soul may have what we call spiritual aspects – self-awareness, volition, pleasure, etc. – but these are inseparable from the body and can both influence and be influenced by bodily events such as drunkenness and sickness. Like the music of the violin, when the bow and the instrument are damaged or destroyed, the music stops. Once again, however, the teachings of Epicurus and Lucretius go beyond a mere statement of brute fact, and the long final section of the third book of this poem is a protracted rhetorical diatribe against the fear of death. Lucretius intends his poetry to remove fear, not to instil new irrational terrors of non-existence that, he believed, are as futile as they are groundless.

One of the principal difficulties with Epicureanism is its theory of perception, which seems to involve Epicurus in self-contradiction. The philosophy of materialism states that everything in the world is made of matter and that nothing can exist which is non-material, except the vacuum of empty space. Now if that is true, then all our perceptions must be some sort of material effect caused by some sort of material cause: all perceptions are therefore in some sense *real*, even imagined sensations without any obvious external stimulus. Epicurus went further than this, however, to argue that all perceptions are *true*, which lays him wide open to criticism. Quite apart from obvious illusions like the oar appearing bent under the surface of the water or the square tower looking round from a distance (4. 436–42: 353–63), there are visions of the dead that appear to us in sleep, which would seem to contradict the statement that we do not survive death. Can Epicurus have it both ways? Can he both assert that visions of the dead are real atomic constructs from real dead people, but also that these dead people no longer exist as people? Before answering this, let us examine the mechanics of sense as interpreted by Epicureanism.

'*For touch and nothing but touch (by all that men call holy!) is the essence of all our bodily sensations.*' (2.434–5) All perceptions are caused by contact between the object perceived and the sense-organs of the perceiver. Sound-atoms enter your ears, make the eardrum vibrate and thus stimulate the 'spirit', surface atoms can emanate from the surface of objects and enter the nostrils or establish direct contact with the skin in touch or the tongue in taste. So far, so good – but what of sight? Epicurus postulates that atoms are constantly leaving the surface of all objects, and that these leave the surface as complete coherent images or 'films' which preserve both the shape and appearance of the object. When a 'film' of something enters our eyes, it touches our organs of sight, stimulates the 'spirit' and so we see it. These organs of sight are simply receivers of sensory stimuli, with no power to assess and interpret the sense-data they receive: this is left to the 'spirit' – we would call it the mind – whose judgement can be mistaken without thereby impugning the reliability of the sense-organs. This lets the senses off the hook in both the above difficulties: the bent oar is only apparently bent, the mind receiving multiple images (of water and of oar) which it clearly fails to interpret separately and correctly. The ghosts of the dead, on the other hand, either really are atomic remains of the dead person emitted during life and still flitting about, or they are images of living people whom the brain mistakes for the dead people they resemble.

It can seem that Book Four of the poem was begun solely to counter the apparent objection to the mortality of the soul posed by the appearance of ghosts – but if so Lucretius soon went far beyond this limited exercise. The enemy soon turns out to be the Sceptic rather than the Spiritualist. The Sceptics refused to accept any sense-perception as reliable in the light of the obvious unreliability of such sense-experiences as dreams, hallucinations, optical illusions etc. Knowledge – certainty, that is – is not available to us, and so we cannot be sure of anything, no matter how persuasive the empirical evidence seems at the time. Diogenes Laertius in his *Life of Pyrrho* (9.62) reports that the great Sceptic Pyrrho 'faced all risks – traffic, precipices, dogs' and was saved from harm only by his less Sceptical friends. The Atomist tradition was steeped in Scepticism – Democritus asserted that 'in reality we know nothing' (KRS fr. 117, pp. 410–11), and Epicurus' own teacher Nausiphanes was given to Scepticism (Diogenes Laertius 9.64, Rist p. 4). The group of teachers and thinkers known to us as the Sophists practised Scepticism in virtually all aspects of philosophy: epistemological, theological and moral, with even the Academy of Plato being 'converted' to Scepticism when Arcesilaus of Pitane became its head. Scepticism found its greatest statement in the figures first of Aenesidemus – who probably originated the famous 'Ten Modes of Scepticism' – and then of Sextus Empiricus, whose writings are the major statement of the Sceptical position in the ancient world. (See on this Annas and Barnes, *The Modes of Scepticism passim*.)

One example of the conflict between Epicureanism and Scepticism will serve to illustrate the problem. If, as Epicurus argued, all sensation is material and atomically determined, then we ought to be able to expect similar sensations to produce predictably similar results, just as sufficiently high temperatures always boil water or melt ice. Why, then, does the same food taste pleasant to one person and sour to another? Why does the tower look round from here, but square from there? We have no grounds for preferring situation 1 to situation 2, so it becomes impossible to decide whether the food is 'really' sour and the tower is 'really' square. All that Epicurus can do in this case is to repeat that in the latter case the mind is clearly misinterpreting the veracious sense-data received by the eyes; and in the former case there must be atomic differences in the different organs of taste – just as different species show violently different reactions to the same food (4.633–72). As with the swerve, so here it seems that Epicurus was working from the manifest variety of sense-experience and sought to explain it in terms that would accommodate the diversity of phenomena without invalidating the Atomic theory itself. Lucretius the poet, of course, had further reasons for wanting to show the contribution that the mind makes to the understanding of the world. Our senses may be as irrational as the camera, but the mind has the power to interpret, to understand and to wonder at the range of phenomena presented to it – and none can show this so well as the poet.

Apparitions of the gods merit separate discussion. It was common in antiquity to see Epicurus as an atheist (Cicero, *On the Nature of the Gods* 2.75–6), and Lucretius is a tireless campaigner against foolish and violent forms of religious worship such as human sacrifice (1.80–101). Epicurus developed a subtle theology in which the gods are disinterested beings (this easily passed for atheism in popular imagination), and he certainly spoke out against the foolish beliefs of 'the masses' (*Letter to Menoeceus* 123–4). The gods exist, he appears to have claimed, dwelling in 'spaces between the worlds' (*intermundia, metakosmia*), and their atomic bodies are in some way as deathless as the atoms out of which they are composed: all atoms are eternal, but they are the only example of atomic compounds that can constantly regenerate themselves and thus not disintegrate with age and death. As with most things in Epicureanism, however, the ethical implications are of enormous importance, and it is here that both Epicurus and Lucretius display an unorthodox attitude towards personal and public religious practice. On the one hand, they both opposed the fear of the angry, bullying gods who were thought to throw thunderbolts, punish men with sterility and demand human sacrifice to make the wind blow (6.379–422: 4.1233–41: 1.80–101). The Epicurean gods, on the contrary, are ideals of contentment and serenity who by definition cannot be bothered with human beings and their petty problems. The argument runs as follows:

> The gods by definition live a life of serenity.
> If they bother about our lives they cannot be serene.
> ∴ they cannot bother about us.

The anthropomorphic gods who dwell on Olympus, fighting and loving each other and using human conflict as entertainment differ completely from the tranquil beings so memorably conjured up in Lucretius' account:

> The majesty of the gods is revealed and those quiet habitations, never shaken by storms nor drenched by rain-clouds, nor defaced by white drifts of snow that a harsh frost congeals. A cloudless ether roofs them, and laughs with radiance lavishly diffused. All their wants are supplied by nature, and nothing at any time cankers their peace of mind. (3.18–24. cf. 2.1093–4)

The gods therefore pass from being the objects of our superstitious fear and grovelling self-abasement to becoming the paradigms of a happiness that we ourselves could obtain, the role models of that Epicurean serenity which is the goal of both the philosophical system and the poem that expounds it. True contemplation of the gods and the universe will help us to calm our minds and emulate divine happiness to the point where we can both understand everything – and thus see with the eyes of a god – and also guarantee our happiness by a total contentment with the pleasure available to us within the limitations imposed on us by nature itself (see 5.1161–1240, 6.68–79). Fear is bred of ignorance and is thus dispelled by knowledge of the truth; the gods are a part of the universe but have no more personal malice against us than do raindrops or daisies; when enlightened by knowledge we can become serene and finally *dignam dis degere vitam* ('lead a life worthy of the gods' 3.322). The perfect example of this life is of course Epicurus himself, who in the fulsome proem to Book Five is praised as a god for precisely this reason: he was as content as the blessed gods although enjoying none of their immortal advantages.

All this is a fascinating chapter in the history of philosophy and science, no doubt, but it does not explain why anybody should get excited about atoms. It is hard to see why people should wish to surrender the lively gods of myth and legend for these faceless, idle bon viveurs, especially since the removal of divine intervention in the world removes one possible means of controlling nature in the form of religious observance and leaves man a helpless victim before the random devastation of atomic collisions. Furthermore, what has been said so far does not account for the popularity of Epicureanism in Rome over two centuries after Epicurus' death. To understand this we need to look in more detail at Epicurus' ethical and political attitudes and set them in the context of late-republican Rome.

Epicurus' moral philosophy is often called Hedonist, in that he asserted that men are driven, in making their choices, by considerations of pleasure rather than any altruistic or disinterested motives. Put starkly in these terms it is easy to see why so many people in the ancient and in the modern world have visualized Epicureans as living a life of gluttony and debauchery, totally given over to the pleasures of the flesh and without any scruples when it came to moral responsibility. It will quickly become clear that this is far from being the case.

Epicurus asserts that the pursuit of pleasure and the avoidance of pain are the driving forces behind our volitional and appetitive behaviour: given the 'atomic' nature of our minds and bodies and the non-existence of anything other than matter and void, it is difficult to see how he could have found room in his atomic universe for such abstract entities as justice or freedom. He clearly needed a word to describe physical well-being and the desire for what we instinctively seek, both mentally and physically, and used pleasure to refer to this. However, his definition of the term embraces a far wider range of feelings than simply the unqualified satisfaction of our bodily appetites: the pursuit of pleasure may indeed induce us to deny pleasure, as some pleasures may end up causing us great pain in the long term. Similarly, some pain may be worth pursuing in order to preserve life or to preclude greater pain later – having a tooth extracted when it is going to cause agonies of toothache, or undergoing unpleasant military duty rather than suffering the pain of social ostracism and a court martial, for example. Furthermore, pleasure is essentially the removal of the pain of need and is therefore limited to the satisfaction of the bodily appetite: once the desire has been satisfied – the gaping chasm filled by food, for instance (4.858–69) – the pleasure cannot then be increased but only varied. This basic instinctive pleasure, produced by action to satisfy need such as the ingestion of food or the ejaculation of sperm, is called 'kinetic' pleasure and is what most people would immediately think of in this sort of discussion. Epicurus however insisted on adding the notion of what he called 'katastematic' pleasure, which is the pleasure of contentment and serenity, the absence of both need and desire, the equilibrium of tranquillity. Far from being an afterthought, this sort of pleasure was elevated into the highest goal of our life, a state for which Epicurus devised the term 'ataraxia' (serenity). It is thus far superior to the animal pursuit of food and sex – being a transcendence of these basic needs – and is the mark of the true philosopher. Kinetic pleasure, after all, is temporary and involves pain: the pleasure of eating will soon be followed by the pain of hunger, and the sexual appetite, Lucretius informs us, is totally insatiable (4.1089–96). Katastematic pleasure lasts longer and involves no pain.

In all this it is vital to recognize which pleasures are healthy and susceptible of satisfaction and which are not. Epicurus divided pleasures into three categories:

1. those which are natural and necessary
2. those which are natural but not necessary
3. those which are neither natural nor necessary.

In the first category are the pleasures without which we cannot survive – food, drink, warmth, all of which can be satisfied from the natural world around us, and most of which involve ingestion. Those in the second category are the ones that produce change in the sense-organs themselves – most obviously sexual pleasure, which is natural but only necessary for the survival of the species: nobody ever died of lack of sex – and these are to be satisfied in moderation only and must be watched carefully. The third class of pleasures are luxuries, addictions to pleasures that are totally unnecessary as they satisfy no real need of the body but represent unhealthy mental desires and fixations, as well as involving us in unnecessary pain when the pleasure of their enjoyment becomes the pain of their withdrawal. This is most easily seen in the cases of food and sex: if the appetite is cultivated to the point where it needs special conditions to be satisfied – such that bread will no longer suffice but we must have caviar – then we have not increased our pleasure but rather worsened our pain. Similarly, the romantic attachment to one person, instead of the recommended promiscuity (4.1065–6), will produce the pain of sexual deprivation when that person is not willing or available. The apparent 'cultivation' of pleasure in this way only serves to diminish it, whereas the wise man will remain content with what is easily available – the 'little that is enough' (as, for instance at 5.1119) – and will not develop appetites that cannot easily be satisfied. What goes for the body also goes for the mind: greed for money and power is also unnecessary and insatiable and the wise man will eliminate it altogether. Lucretius depicts the ambitious politician as Sisyphus rolling his rock up the hill only to see it roll back down again in a mockery of his futile efforts (3.995–1002), and the yearning lover as a thirsty man dreaming that he is drinking when his gaping mouth is of course imbibing nothing at all (4.1097–101).

In general, then, the greater the need we have, the greater the pain: and so we reach the paradox that 'poverty . . . is great wealth and unlimited wealth is great poverty' (*Vatican Sayings* 25). Lucretius expresses it well:

> if a man would guide his life by true philosophy, he will find ample riches in a modest livelihood enjoyed with a tranquil mind. Of that little he need never be beggared (5. 1117–19).

The man who can find pleasure in simple things will always be satisfied, and the fastidious bon viveur will have less pleasure and more pain than the humblest of the poor.

This does, however, raise serious questions about the social duty of the wise man and his attitude towards his fellow men. The traditional Epicurean advice seems to advocate a thoroughly selfish policy whereby the wise man will remove himself from the public arena and pursue his own serenity without caring about other people except in so far as they can make him even more serene. Everything will serve as a means to the end of his personal pleasure – or else be discarded. The austere Epicurean concept of self-sufficiency ('autarkeia') enjoins the avoidance of all attachments and so can easily be taken for a recipe for quietist refusal to get involved in the sufferings and needs of others; the traditional Epicurean advice to 'live in secret' (λάθε βιώσας) would appear to reject all forms of political and social involvement as damaging to the precious peace of the wise man, and the famous opening lines of the second book of this poem can easily be read as smug *Schadenfreude* as the poet looks down on the sufferings of less enlightened people. There are clearly problems here, but – while I hold no brief for Epicureanism – there is another side to the moral case.

Then neighbours began to form mutual alliances, wishing neither to do nor to suffer violence among themselves. They appealed on behalf of their children and womenfolk, pointing out with gestures and inarticulate cries that it is right for everyone to pity the weak . . . (5.1019–23)

This evolutionary theory of social values was not the first or the only answer to the question of their origin. Lucretius' contemporary Cicero believed that social values were innate and natural in man, a vital part of his make-up without which the race would never have survived, and thus more than simply a means to the end of pleasure. The Epicurean theory of the 'social contract' contrasts strongly also with the traditional legends of a Golden Age of blissful social harmony degenerating to silver, then to bronze and then to iron, as the earth becomes less fruitful and men less virtuous. (See Hesiod, *Works and Days* 109–201, Aratus, *Phaenomena* 96–136, Ovid, *Metamorphoses* 1.89–150.) One could set up the two sides of the argument in stark terms, progress versus degeneration, things getting better versus things getting worse, Utopia in the present or the future versus Utopia in the past. Lucretius, however, does not fit so easily into either category.

For on the one hand, he shows us that early man had a life of pain and hardship: it was cold, the diet was not appealing, ignorance was widespread. The comforts of life – fire, clothes, laws, the arts, etc. – being man-made, came only with a long process of trial and error, the odd flash of inspiration in the dark ages of primitivism. And yet, on the other hand, the poet has more than a touch of sentimental romanticizing of the past: man lived in accordance with nature in those days, luxuries which would enervate and corrupt simply did not exist, and men were bigger and stronger then (5.925ff.) than the puny people of today. Nobody ploughed the land, but everybody was content with what nature provided free of charge. People must have been killed now and then by wild beasts – but they did not send thousands into battle to kill each other as they do now. People may have drunk poisonous substances by accident – but now they give them to others deliberately. Scratch the fifth book of this poem and the noble savage is not far below the surface, a man living a life in many ways closer to the ideals of Epicurus than the 'civilized' counterpart of today racked with worry and disease. So how, then, does Epicureanism add to the 'progress' of humanity?

In the first place, there is the Epicurean stress on friendship. This is not innate in man – early man was a lone wolf who only came together with others when it dawned on him that there was greater safety in numbers – but became the overriding ethical good for the wise man:

> Of all the things that wisdom acquires for the blessedness of life, the greatest by far is the possession of friendship. (Epicurus, *Key Doctrines* 27)

Such friendship marked the advance of man from his earlier bestial state:

> (Epicurus) says that you should be more concerned at inspecting with whom you are eating and drinking, than what you eat and drink. For feeding without a friend is the life of a lion and a wolf. (Seneca, *Letters* 19.10)

and was not simply the means to the end of more selfish pleasure – note the paradox that:

> Epicureans say that it is more pleasurable to confer a benefit than to receive one. (Plutarch, *Against Epicurean Happiness* 1097A)

We can thus see how the negative, defensive-alliance understanding of friendship developed into a more positive set of aspirations as the moral benefits of society were appreciated. It does, however, remain fairly clear that the friends in question are fellow-Epicureans, and that the famous idyllic Garden of Epicurus was open only to sympathizers and not to the unenlightened rabble. Contact with the rest of humanity will benefit the wise if it converts more people to Epicureanism and thus provides for more serenity (cf. Cicero, *Letters to his Friends* 15.19.2), and there are Epicurean texts from the ancient world that imagine the perfect state of a world totally converted to Epicureanism

(Diogenes of Oenoanda NF 21). Such apocalyptic dreaming may have been comforting, but the reality was of course different. The world has never been the contented trouble-free paradise of enlightenment that Epicurus would have liked, and certainly not the Roman world.

Writing when Julius Caesar was dictator, Cicero tells us that Epicureanism has 'taken over the whole of Italy' (*Tusculan Disputations* 4.7). By then the Greek Epicurean Siro had already established his 'little garden' of followers (including perhaps the young Virgil) and in Herculaneum disciples of Epicureanism were flocking to the school of a man of undoubted literary refinement, whom Cicero praises for his elegant and beautiful poetry, Philodemus. The prose treatises of Amafinius were extremely popular, and Lucretius composed his epic – though we do not know what success (if any) greeted his *magnum opus*. In order to understand the appeal of Epicureanism in the last century before Christ it is only necessary to glance at the political and social turmoil in Rome.

In the 80s BC the dictator Sulla had taken over the city and massacred hundreds of its citizens, and after his death the political life of the capital became increasingly dominated by corruption and violence as army commanders struggled for power and popular politicians such as Clodius moved their gangs onto the streets. Civil war in 49 BC between Pompey and Caesar ended with the suspension of republican rights in the dictatorship of Caesar, a tyranny from which the tyrant's assassination on the Ides of March 44 only offered a brief respite before plunging Rome back into civil disarray with the rival claims for power of Republicans such as Cassius, Caesar's consul Mark Antony, Caesar's heir Octavian and the pirate Sextus Pompeius. Throughout the hundred or so years from 133 to 27 BC the 'little man' in Rome came to have less and less say in the running of the state, and by the time of Lucretius even the old nobles who had formerly held massive power in the Senate were increasingly helpless in the face of the tyranny of the armed forces and their ruthless commanders. If ever there was a society susceptible to the attractions of Epicurus' serene garden, it was this one; the pastoral idyll was irresistibly alluring to the urban citizens who had seen their lives ruined and their streets flow with blood, and the anti-political stance of 'live secretly' was corroborated by the corruption and futility of government in Rome. The old ideal of service to the state and duty to society – embodied in that generation perfectly in the figure of Marcus Porcius Cato Uticensis, who committed suicide rather than see his free republic become the slave of Caesar (see *Oxford Classical Dictionary* s. v. Cato 5) – was hard to justify when men of integrity fell like flies before the unscrupulous power plays of the generals. It is in this context that the cynical caricatures of politics and society in Lucretius are to be seen (3.59ff., 995–1002). The sentiments expressed there deriding the folly and corruption of political ambition become something of a literary cliché in that and the succeeding generations – Sallust (*Cat* 10), Horace, Virgil, Tibullus, Propertius and Tacitus all in their different ways express distaste for the ways of contemporary politics and politicians – and most of them were not card-carrying Epicureans, either. We should not, however, underestimate the extent to which Lucretius was challenging the world in which he lived and the ethos in which he had grown up. The whole history of the Roman people was one of ambition, expansion and power, and the Roman ideal of success was to enjoy the *gloria* that came with a distinguished Senatorial career, the acclamation of the people and the respect of one's peers. No Roman could fail to be shocked by Lucretius' assertion (5.1129–30): 'far better to lead a quiet life in subjection than to long for sovereign authority and lordship over kingdoms'. The very idea was monstrous to a people whose whole political ethic, at home and abroad, was later articulated by Virgil as: 'Roman, remember that ruling the nations by force is your role . . .' (*Aeneid* 6.851). There had always been people who regarded philosophy as childish or politically useless – cf. e.g. Plato *Gorgias* 484c4–485e2, *Theaetetus* 173cd – but the Roman patriarchal republic was here being presented with a philosophy that regarded women as equals and monarchy as the best – as that involving the least political activity – system for the wise man to live under. Such people were a threat to Roman values in fundamental ways: in religious observance, in refusal to join the race for power and curry favour, in denying the god-given destiny of the Roman people and so on. There is a nice parallelism between Lucretius' physics and his politics: just as his atoms are passively moved by other atoms, so also wise people are prepared to accept passively whatever happens to them, the wise man even being capable of happiness when being tortured to death. Virgil's echo of Lucretius' lines (*Aeneid* 6.851) is surely not accidental, and Cicero's assessment of Epicureanism 'taking over' Italy (*Tusculan Disputations* 4.6–7) is perhaps a cry from the heart of a man seeing Roman values under serious threat. Once again, this innocent-seeming philosophical poet expounding the nature of atoms was to the Romans of his day ethical dynamite.

LUCRETIUS AND THE DIDACTIC EPIC

Lucretius of course was more a poet than a pamphleteer, and no introduction to this great work would be complete without some account of his poetry and the tradition in which he was writing.

Unlike some writers in the ancient world, we know almost nothing about Lucretius the man except from the occasional autobiographical aside delivered in the poem itself. We have no extant *Life* as we do in the case of other poets such as Virgil and Horace, and the tiny remarks that we do possess are of dubious value and interpretation. There is the infamous statement of St Jerome, for instance, which simply says, under the year 94 BC:

> The poet Titus Lucretius Carus was born. A love-potion drove him mad, and he composed, in the intervals of his insanity, several books which Cicero corrected. He committed suicide aged 43.

Then there is a brief but interesting remark in a letter from Cicero to his brother: 'The poems of Lucretius contain, as you say in your letter, many flashes of inspiration and also much poetic skill' (*Letters to his brother Quintus* 2.9). A more poignant testimony to the man comes in the lines from Virgil's second *Georgic* (490–92) where he pays tribute to his didactic predecessor, clearly referring to 3.25–7 of the poem:

> Happy is he who has discovered the causes of things and has cast beneath his feet all fears, unavoidable fate and the din of the devouring Underworld.

As M. F. Smith argues in the Introduction to his Loeb text of the poem, this is excellent evidence to fire against St Jerome's insanity theory: Virgil would have been a heartless sarcastic cynic to write these sublime lines about a man who in fact had taken his life in deranged depression. More than that we simply cannot say and must content ourselves with the poem itself, the best and only evidence for the achievement of the poet.

So what kind of poetry is this? The verse is composed in hexameter metre (with six stresses to the line, each metrical stress being followed by either two short syllables or one long) as was all Greek and Latin epic poetry, and its length also puts it into the category of epic. This is not, however, a tale of war (like Homer's *Iliad*) or a hero and his homecoming (like Homer's *Odyssey*), or both (like Virgil's *Aeneid*): if Homer is the father of narrative epic, we must look elsewhere for the origin of the genre perfected in this poem. Its first exponent in Greek is Hesiod, a poet living in Boeotia in about 700 BC who claimed inspiration from the Muses as he tended sheep on Mount Helicon; they gave him the 'divine voice' to sing of 'things that will be and things that have already been.' (*Theogony* 31–2), and he went on in that poem to tell of the birth and legends of the gods. His other major surviving work is the *Works and Days*, addressed to his brother Perses, in which he gives practical advice and moral exhortation. Both poems fall under the broad heading of Wisdom literature (see M. L. West's magisterial commentary on *Works and Days* pp. 3–25 for an examination of the genre in a wide range of cultures) and were the inspiration for later philosophical poetry. In the sixth century Xenophanes satirized the anthropomorphic gods of contemporary worship in this sort of verse and also wrote a hexameter poem *On Nature* (KRS 163–80, Barnes 82–3). In the following century both Parmenides and Empedocles wrote philosophical poems in hexameters (KRS 241–62, 282–321). Prose literature grew in stature with the achievements of men such as Herodotus, Thucydides, Plato and Aristotle, but the genre of the didactic (educational, instructive) epic enjoyed a resurgence in the so-called Hellenistic period, after the death of Alexander the Great, when the centres of Greek culture were no longer exclusively in Greece. Aratus (*c.* 315–240 BC) was a poet in the court of King Antigonus Gonatas of Macedonia and composed didactic poetry on such topics as anatomy, pharmacology and (most famously) astronomy: his *Phainomena* was later translated into Latin by Cicero (among others), who clearly admired it enormously. Later Nicander of Colophon (second century BC) produced didactic poetry with such unattractive titles as *Venomous Reptiles*, *Antidotes to Poisons* and *Things changed into other things* (*Metamorphoses*). Now Aratus quarried the prose treatise of the astronomer Eudoxus for the raw factual material for his transforming poetic skill, and Nicander also will have used prose manuals, creating poetry out of prose and versifying a subject of which they themselves had little or no direct knowledge. The term metaphrast was coined to describe this sort of indirect poetry, produced often as *tours de force* to demonstrate the consummate technical mastery of the art of verse-writing required to translate dry and complex subjects into clever lines of verse. The style of the metaphrast can be the main interest in the verse, the pleasure consisting in the appreciation of clever verbal tricks and neatness of expression, and the ironic awareness of the gap between the ostensible audience of peasants or sailors being 'instructed' and the real audience of the urban sophisticates being 'entertained'. Nobody seriously imagines real farmers having Nicander's *Venomous Reptiles* on their bookshelves in case a snake bites them – nor can we seriously see Virgil's contemporary farmers ploughing the land with the *Georgics* tucked into their tunics. The all-important question is then whether Lucretius is primarily a clever poet who randomly chose Epicureanism as his vehicle but whose purpose is to entertain and impress, or whether we need to take his words at face value and accept that he intends to change our minds and our lives.

Contemporaries are not much help here, alas. We know little about Lucretius and cannot tell, for instance, whether he belonged to an Epicurean circle. We know little about the addressee of the poem, Memmius – on whom see Appendix B. We do know of other didactic poems from this period with similar-sounding titles – and the title 'On Nature' (περὶ φύσεως, de rerum natura) was by now conventional after the work of Xenophanes, Empedocles etc.: an *Empedoclea* by a Sallust (not the historian), and a *De Rerum Natura* by Egnatius – but we cannot say whether they were 'sincere' or 'metaphrastic'. Ultimately we cannot be certain of Lucretius' own degree of 'sincerity', but the following points deserve to be made.

In the first place, the poem is of a scale and a size that makes it more than a mere *jeu d'esprit*. It is ambitious and perfectionist, unfinished in the form in which we have it but still full of flashes of imagination and original *aperçus* as well as a thorough knowledge of Epicurean theory. This poet, in other words, has done more than simply translate Epicurus into Latin and make it scan: he has breathed his own life into it, amplifying his master's ideas with corrections and illustrations of his own and giving the whole thing a contemporary Roman flavour – e.g., in the famous diatribe against the folly of romantic love at the end of Book Four. This argues for a degree of creative originality in Lucretius well beyond the limited word-wizardry of the metaphrast.

We have to be careful here, however. Scholars often polarize the argument into two sides, the poet versus the philosopher, and then take sides themselves as to whether Lucretius is really the one or the other. There is even the theory that Lucretius himself was in two minds about many of his doctrines and that on occasions the poet in him revealed his true feelings, denied or suppressed in the 'philosophy', a theory first put forward by Patin as 'l' anti-Lucrèce chez Lucrèce' (on which see Appendix A). The poet's own words would suggest that the poetry is the honey round the cup of Epicurus' medicine, a means to the end of persuading us to drink unattractive truths about the world rather than the end in itself (see 1.933–50); we need also to remember that, ever since Ennius, Roman poets had prized the quality of learning, or erudition (*doctrina*) in their poetry, ensuring that most subsequent poetry would be intellectual and allusive – especially allusive to the work of other poets – rather than simply emotion recollected in tranquillity. When Lucretius therefore uses phrases, ideas and whole passages from a vast range of earlier writers (both Greek and Roman), he is keeping true to this tradition of 'learned' poetry. (See Kenney 'Doctus Lucretius' *Mnemosyne* 23 (1970) 366–92.) It does not mean that the whole poem is there just to parade a collection of quotations culled from other sources; but it does show us a writer familiar with virtually every genre available to the ancients. If he chose Epicureanism as his theme, it was not because that was all he knew about.

The choice of Epicureanism was astonishingly apt for a poet of his gifts. In the first place, the dogmatic stress on the primacy of the senses – and our capacity to see the truth if we will only open our eyes and *look* – is ideal for a poet who will use his verse to paint the real world before the eyes of our mind with clarity and sharpness of perception. Through his eyes we see everyday sights such as rainstorms (6.256–61), leaps of historical imagination such as the description of early man (5.925–1447) and social behaviour such as that of mourners (3. 894–911) or the impotent husband (4.1233–9) or the pathetic lover (4.1121–91) satirized and dramatized with merciless accuracy. In the second place, Epicureanism is primarily an ethical theory based on a scientific reading of the world: but the physics is also invested with an emotional interest of its own. For the poet who found ideas exciting, who could invest cerebral concepts with emotional significance, this philosophy was perfect. Time after time he applies the facts to the values he will infer, the physics to the ethics. It is not enough to say that we are mortal and leave it at that: he goes on to show us how we ought to behave in the face of inexorable and eternal death. Not content with showing us the mechanics of the production and emission of sperm from the body, he shows us how to conduct our sex lives. Most controversial of all, he tells us the facts behind the spread of diseases and then concludes the whole poem with a bleak and stark vision of a city dying of the plague. (On the problems of the ending see Appendix E.) Nowhere does Lucretius hide behind the objectivity of scientific inquiry and refuse to face the human consequences of his teachings: on the contrary, his scientific teaching is there primarily to provide the understanding of the physics of the universe which will in turn show us that the lifestyle he enjoins is a rational and necessary response to the world of proven facts. The artist's eye for detail convinces the audience of the accuracy of his observation, the mixture of logical argumentation and rhetorical diatribe hammers the theories home against all opposition, and the indefinable emotional effects of the poetry make it the ideal medium for this instructor of minds and converter of souls.

The poetry is, however, not just turned on for the purple passages: nor is it applied like a final coat of colour to a drab wall of physics – 'poetry cannot be spread on things like butter', in Santayana's famous remark (*Three Philosophical Poets* (1922) 16). Lucretius intended to smear *everything* with the honey of the Muses (4.9), not simply the flourishes or the similes. This is, of course, impossible for any translation to bring out, and the reader without the Latin can only receive a faint impression of the poetic effects at work in the original. One device which I have tried to reproduce in the translation, however, is metaphor, and this is a device which Lucretius uses to devastating effect. Not just the brief metaphors such as sleep 'fettering our limbs in pleasant slumber' (4.453), but also sustained metaphors such as the following:

At other times a violent squall of wind falls upon a cloud already pregnant with a full-grown thunderbolt. The wind rips open the cloud, and in that moment out drops that fiery whirlwind which is what we in our traditional language call a thunderbolt. (6.295–7)

Here the violence of the wind is clearly compared to that of a particularly savage Caesarean section on a pregnant woman ripping the child (the whirlwind) out of her womb and causing it to drop (be born) and then receive its name. Besides the metaphor of childbirth there is here also perhaps an implicit myth of ironic intent: the thunderbolt falls out fully armed with fire, as Athena was born fully armed out of the head of Zeus. Yet the poet has been arguing all along that thunderbolts are not sent by Zeus, despite what popular superstition thinks – Lucretius thus uses the hint of a mythical allusion to point up an ironic contrast between the rationalism of the theory being explained and the 'poetic' legends the theory will displace. (This account will not fully explain the prelude to the poem, however, on which see Appendix A. On implicit myth – a notion not accepted by all scholars – see Lyne *Further Voices in Virgil's Aeneid* 139–40.) Then there are the fuller masterpieces of sustained writing such as the opening to the second book: a dominant metaphor of the wise man looking down from a high and safe vantage point onto the struggles of his less enlightened fellows: ships on the stormy sea, then battle on land are adduced as metaphors of futile stress. The metaphors are both of men being attacked by threatening violence – so what better to depict the invulnerability of the philosopher than metaphors of being 'fortified' and 'elevated' as if in a high and stout citadel? The poet returns to struggling mankind (lines 10–13) with a caricature: explicit social comment and implicit myth (Sisyphus is perhaps suggested in the futile attempt to scale the heights – see now D. P. Fowler, 'Lucretius and Politics' in Griffin and Barnes, *Philosophia Togata* 140 n.79). The term 'caricature' does not seem out of place here for this mixing of imagery in a way that is both critical and amusing: for other examples, see the ludicrous figures of the gods practising their marksmanship with thunderbolts (6.396–405) and the Sceptic philosopher standing on his head (4.471–2). The poet then waxes rhetorical with all the exclamatory force of a Cicero ('O joyless hearts of men! O minds without vision! . . .') before going back into social criticism of the rich and gilded luxuries that can never make us happy contrasted with the easy life of those content with the free pleasures of nature, the 'pleasures' in both cases being spelled out in graphic detail. The poet continues his harangue with Roman colour (troops on the Campus Martius), rhetorical questions fired at the patron by name, the personification of the fears that terrorize us as 'stalking unabashed among princes and potentates', and he rounds off the section with the familiar simile of the unenlightened being like children frightened in the dark. This is poetry of a rare degree of sophistication and interest – but it is also, as Lucretius intended it, not aimed solely at the scholar. This is a book which can be read by *everyone* – and this, in the last analysis, is the clinching reason for thinking that the poem is not simply an ironic entertainment for the salon, but a work that speaks from conviction and passion.

BIBLIOGRAPHY

The purpose of this bibliography is to indicate to the curious and the studious where further help and discussion can be obtained on the detailed questions provoked by this poem. Exhausting as it may appear, it makes no claims to being exhaustive, and most individual items will suggest further reading in their own bibliographies. Lucretius is an encyclopedic writer whose work raises questions in many different spheres, and people read him both for philosophical and for literary reasons: I have therefore tried to list items that are of interest in both fields. The more accessible items I have marked with an asterisk, and in the case of less accessible items I have occasionally indicated where an informative review can be found.

WORKS OF REFERENCE

The Oxford Classical Dictionary (2nd edition, Oxford 1970)
*Robert Graves *The Greek Myths* (2 vols., Harmondsworth 1955)

TEXTS

The most accessible text of Epicurus is to be found in Diogenes Laertius, *Lives of Eminent Philosophers* vol. 2 (Loeb Classical Library, with facing English translation by R. D. Hicks, London and Cambridge, Mass., 1925). The best text of Epicurus is Arrighetti: *Epicuro, Opere* (2nd edition, Torino 1973), with Italian translation and notes. Still useful is Bailey's *Epicurus: The Extant Remains* (Oxford 1926), with translation and commentary.

For the texts of the Presocratic philosophers, see: Kirk, Raven and Schofield: *The Presocratic Philosophers* (2nd edition, Cambridge 1983, usually abbreviated to KRS), with English translation and full discussion. The standard edition of all the known fragments is still H. Diels: *Die Fragmente der Vorsokratiker* (6th edition, revised W. Kranz, Berlin 1952) (usually abbreviated to D–K). All the main texts relating to Hellenistic philosophy are to be found, with full text, translation and commentary, in Long and Sedley: *The Hellenistic Philosophers* (2 vols., Cambridge 1987). The most accessible text of Sextus Empiricus is still to be found in the Loeb Classical Library (edited by R. G. Bury, 4 vols. 1933–49), and the most accessible English edition of the main Sceptic texts with full discussion is to be found in J. Annas and J. Barnes: *The Modes of Scepticism* (Cambridge 1985).

Most other ancient texts referred to in the Introduction, Notes and Appendices are available in English versions. The Penguin Classics series includes translations of all works mentioned except the following, which are available in the Loeb Classical Library series with English translation facing the original text.

Aratus *Phaenomena* (in: Callimachus: *Hymns*)
Aristotle *Physics, Metaphysics, On Coming into Being, Natural History, On the Movements of Animals, Meteorology, On the Heavens.*
Callimachus *Aetia, Hecale* etc.
Cicero *Brutus, For Flaccus, Letters to his Friends, Letters to his brother Quintus, On Divination, On Duties, On the Nature of the Gods, Prior Academics, Tusculan Disputations, Verrine Orations*
Diodorus Siculus
Ennius (in: *Remains of Old Latin* vol. I)
Galen *On Temperaments*
Homeric Hymns in: Hesiod & Homeric Hymns
Lucian *Conversations of Prostitutes*
Plato *Axiochus, Cratylus*
Pliny *Natural History*
Plutarch *Against Epicurean Happiness* (in: *Moralia* vol. XIV)
On hearing poets (in: *Moralia* vol. I)
Seneca *Natural History*
Suetonius *On Grammarians*

Theognis (in: *Greek Elegy and Iambus* vol. I)
Theophrastus *Characters*
Vitruvius *On Architecture*

The two texts not published by Penguin and/or Loeb are as follows:

Aetius in: Diels *Doxographi Graeci* (1879) 273–444

Nicander *Fragments* ed. A. S. F. Gow and A. F. Scholfield, Cambridge 1953

MAJOR EDITIONS OF LUCRETIUS' *DE RERUM NATURA*

Editio Aldina (Avancius) Venice 1500
Editio Juntina (Candidus) Florence 1512
Lambinus, D. (Paris 1563–4, 1565, 1570; Frankfurt 1583)
Lachmann, K. (Berlin 1850)
Munro, H. A. J. (Cambridge 1864, 1866, 1873, 1886)
Giussani, C. (Torino 1896–8)
Bailey, C. (Oxford Classical Text, 1900, 1922) (*OCT*)
Leonard-Smith (Madison 1942)
Bailey, C. (3 vols. Oxford 1947)
Ernout-Robin (Budé, 2nd edition, Paris 1962)
Martin, J. (Teubner, 5th edition, Leipzig 1963)
Smith, M. F. (Loeb Classical Library, London and Cambridge, Mass. 1975)
Müller, K. (Zurich 1975)

EDITIONS OF SINGLE BOOKS OF *DE RERUM NATURA*

Book 1, edited by P. Michael Brown (Bristol 1984)
Book 3, edited by R. Heinze (Leipzig 1897)
Book 3, edited by E. J. Kenney (Cambridge 1971)
Book 4, edited by J. Godwin (Warminster 1986)
Book 5, edited by C. D. N. Costa (Oxford 1985)
Book 6, edited by J. Godwin (Warminster 1991)

ON THE GENERAL PHILOSOPHICAL BACKGROUND, SEE:

Barnes, J. *The Presocratic Philosophers* (2nd edition, London 1982)
Long, A. A. *Hellenistic Philosophy* (2nd edition, London 1986)
  (reviewed by R. B. Todd, *Phoenix* 29 (1975) 295–9)

ON EPICUREANISM IN PARTICULAR, SEE ALSO:

Bailey, C. *The Greek Atomists and Epicurus* (Oxford 1928)
de Witt, N. W. *Epicurus and his Philosophy* (Minneapolis 1954)
Diano, C. *Scritti Epicurei* (Florence 1974)
Frischer, B. *The Sculpted Word: Epicureanism and philosophical
  recruitment in Ancient Greece* (Berkeley/Los Angeles 1982)
Gigon, O. 'Zur Psychologie Epikurs' in: *Aspects de la Philosophie
  Hellénistique* (Fondations Hardt Entretiens) 32 (1986) 67–98
*Jones, H. *The Epicurean Tradition* (London 1989)
Momigliano, A: review of Farrington: *Science and Politics in the
  Ancient World*: *Journal of Roman Studies* 31 (1941) 149–57
Paratore, E. 'La Problematica sull'epicureismo a Roma' in
  Aufstieg und Niedergang der römischen Welt (ed. Temporini)
  vol. I. 4 (1973) 116–204
Rist, J. M. *Epicurus, an Introduction* (Cambridge 1972)
Schmid, W. *Epicuro e l'epicureismo cristiano* (Brescia 1984)
Sedley, D. 'Epicurus and his professional rivals' *Études sur
  l'épicurisme antique*: *Cahiers de Philologie* I (1976) 121–59

ON THE HISTORY OF THE GENRE OF DIDACTIC EPIC, SEE:

*Cox, A. 'Didactic Poetry' in (ed.) J. Higginbotham *Greek and
  Latin Literature, a Comparative Study* (London 1969) 124–61
Pöhlmann, E. 'Charakteristika des römischen Lehrgedicts' in
  Aufstieg und Niedergang der römischen Welt (ed. Temporini)
  vol. I. 3, 814–901

ON HELLENISTIC LITERATURE, SEE:

Fraser, P. M. *Ptolemaic Alexandria* (Oxford 1972)
*Hutchinson, G. O. *Hellenistic Poetry* (Oxford 1988)

Clausen, W. 'Callimachus and Roman Poetry' *Greek, Roman and Byzantine Studies* 5 (1964) 181–96

FOR ROMAN LITERATURE AND ITS SOCIAL SETTING, SEE:

Griffin, J. *Latin Poets and Roman Life* (London 1985)

*Ogilvie, R. M. *Roman Literature and Society* (Harmondsworth 1980)

Rawson, E. *Intellectual Life in the Late Roman Republic* (London 1985)

ON THE NEW POETS, SEE:

Granarolo, J. 'L'époque néotérique ou la poésie romaine d'avant-garde au dernier siècle de la République (Catulle excepté)' in *Aufstieg und Niedergang der römischen Welt I*.3 278–360

*Quinn, K. *The Catullan Revolution* (London 1969)

GENERAL ACCOUNTS OF THE WORK OF LUCRETIUS INCLUDE:

Bergson, H. *The Philosophy of Poetry: the genius of Lucretius* (New York 1959)

Bignone, E. *Storia della letteratura latina* vol. 2, chs. 6–8 (Florence 1945)

Bollack, M. *La Raison de Lucrèce* (Paris 1978)

Boyancé, P. *Lucrèce et l'Épicurisme* (Paris 1963)

Clay, D. *Lucretius and Epicurus* (Ithaca 1983)

*Dalzell, A. 'Lucretius' in: Kenney, E. J. (ed.) *The Cambridge History of Classical Literature* vol. 2, part 2, 33–55

Dudley, D. R. (ed.) *Lucretius* (London 1965)

*Kenney, E. J. *Lucretius* (*Greece and Rome New Surveys in the Classics* no. 11 (1977))

Masson, J. *Lucretius, Epicurean and Poet* (2 vols., London 1907–9)

*Minadeo, R. *The Lyre of Science* (Michigan 1969)

Nichols, J. H. *Epicurean Political Philosophy: the De Rerum Natura of Lucretius* (Ithaca and London 1976)

Perelli, L. *Lucrezio Poeta dell'angoscia* (Florence 1969)

Regenbogen, O. *Lukrez, seine Gestalt in seinem Gedicht* (Leipzig 1932)

*Santayana, G. *Three Philosophical Poets* (Cambridge, Mass. 1910)

*Segal, C. *Lucretius on Death and Anxiety: Poetry and Philosophy in De Rerum Natura* (New Jersey 1990)

*Sikes, E. E. *Lucretius: poet and philosopher* (Cambridge 1936)

Traglia, A. *Sulla formazione spirituale di Lucrezio* (Rome 1948)

MORE SPECIFIC ITEMS ON LUCRETIUS INCLUDE:

Ackermann, E. *Lukrez und der Mythos* (Wiesbaden 1979), reviewed by E. J. Kenney in *Classical Review* 31 (1981) 19–21

Amory, A. '*Obscura de re lucida carmina*: Science and Poetry in *De Rerum Natura*', *Yale Classical Studies* 21 (1969) 143–68

Arragon, R. F. 'Poetic Art as a Philosophic Medium for Lucretius' *Essays in Criticism* 11 (1961) 371–89

Brown, R. D. 'Lucretius and Callimachus' *Illinois Classical Studies* 7 (1982) 77–97

Classen, C. J. 'Poetry and Rhetoric in Lucretius' *Transactions of the American Philological Association* 99 (1968) 77–118

— *Probleme der Lukrezforschung* (Hildesheim 1986)

Clay, D. 'The Sources of Lucretius' Inspiration' *Études sur l'épicurisme antique (Cahiers de Philologie)* 1 (1976) 205–27

Deutsch, R. E. *The Pattern of Sound in Lucretius* (Diss. Bryn Mawr 1939)

Ferrero, L. *Poetica Nuova in Lucrezio* (Florence 1949)

Friedländer, P. 'The pattern of sound and atomistic theory in Lucretius' *American Journal of Philology* 62 (1941) 16–33

Gillis, D. J. 'Pastoral Poetry in Lucretius' *Latomus* 26 (1967) 339–62

Kenney, E. J. 'Doctus Lucretius' *Mnemosyne* 23 (1970) 366–92

Mayer, R. 'The Epic of Lucretius' *Papers of the Leeds International Latin Seminar* 6 (1990) 35–43

Minadeo, R. 'The Formal Design of the *de rerum natura*' *Arion* 4 (1965) 444–61

Minyard, J. D. *Lucretius and the Late Republic* (Leiden 1985)

Müller, G. 'Die Finalia der sechs Bücher des Lukrez' in *Lucrèce* (Fondations Hardt Entretiens) 24 (1977) 197–231

Sallmann, K. G. *Die Natur bei Lukrez* (Bonn, 1962)

Schiesaro, A. *Simulacrum et imago: gli argomenti analogici nel De Rerum Natura* (Pisa 1990)

Schrijvers, P. H. *Horror ac Divina Voluptas, Études sur la poétique et la poésie de Lucrèce* (Amsterdam 1970), reviewed by E. J. Kenney in *Classical Review* 22 (1972) 348–51

— 'Le Regard sur l'invisible. Étude sur l'emploi de l'analogie dans l'oeuvre de Lucrèce' in *Lucrèce* (Fondations Hardt Entretiens) 24 (1978)

Snyder, J. M. *Puns and poetry in Lucretius' de rerum natura* (Amsterdam, 1980), reviewed by D. A. West in *Classical Review* 31 (1981)

Sykes Davies, H. 'Notes on Lucretius' *Criterion* 11 (1931–2) 25–42

Townend, G. B. 'The Original Plan of Lucretius' *de rerum natura*' *Classical Quarterly* 29 (1979) 101–11

West, D. *The Imagery and Poetry of Lucretius* (Edinburgh 1969)

— 'Lucretius' Methods of Argument' *Classical Quarterly* 25 (1975) 94–116

ON THE PARTICULAR TOPIC OF THE 'ANTI-LUCRÈCE CHEZ LUCRÈCE', SEE:

Kinsey, T. E. 'The Melancholy of Lucretius' *Arion* 3 (1964) 115–30

Patin, H. J. G. *Études sur la poésie latine* (Paris 1883) vol. i, 117–37

ON THE DETAILS OF THE TOPICS CONTAINED IN BOOKS ONE AND TWO, THE FOLLOWING ARE OF IMPORTANCE:

Avotins, I. 'The question of *mens* in Lucretius 2.289' *Classical Quarterly* 29 (1979) 95–100

— 'On some Epicurean and Lucretian arguments for the infinity of the universe' *Classical Quarterly* 33 (1983) 421–7

Brown, R. D. 'Lucretian ridicule of Anaxagoras' *Classical Quarterly* 33 (1983) 146–60

Capelle, W. 'Das Problem der Urzeugung bei Aristoteles und

Theophrast und in der Folgezeit', *Rheinisches Museum* 98 (1955) 150–80

Englert, W. G. *Epicurus on the swerve and voluntary action* (Atlanta, Georgia 1987)

Fowler, D. P. 'Lucretius on the *clinamen* and "free will" (2.251–93)' in: *ΣΥΖΗΤΗΣΙΣ. Studi sull'epicureismo greco e latino offerti a Marcello Gigante* (2 vols. Naples 1983) 329–52

Furley, D. J. 'Lucretius and the Stoics' *Bulletin of the Institute of Classical Studies* 13 (1966) 13–33

— *Two Studies in the Greek Atomists* (Princeton 1967)

— 'The Greek Theory of the Infinite Universe' *Journal of the History of Ideas* 42 (1981) 571–85

Gottschalk, H. B. 'Lucretius 1.983' *Classical Philology* 70 (1975) 42–4

Kleve, K. 'Philosophical Polemics in Lucretius' in *Lucrèce* (Fondations Hardt Entretiens) 24 (1978) 39–75

— 'id facit exiguum clinamen' *Symbolae Osloenses* 15 (1980) 27–30

Müller, G. *Die Darstellung der Kinetik bei Lukrez* (Berlin, 1959)

Saunders, T. J. 'Free will and the atomic swerve in Lucretius' *Symbolae Osloenses* 49 (1984) 37–59

Schmidt, J. *Lukrez und die Stoiker. Quellen und Untersuchungen zu De Rerum Natura* (Marburg 1975)

Vlastos, G. 'Minimal Parts in Epicurean Atomism' *Isis* 56 (1965) 121–47

ON THE PROLOGUES OF THE DIFFERENT BOOKS, AND LUCRETIUS' ATTITUDE TO POETRY, SEE:

Canfora, L. 'I proemi del *de rerum natura*' *Rivista di Filologia e di Istruzione Classica* 110 (1982) 63–77

Cox, A. S. 'Lucretius and his message: a study in the prologues of the *de rerum natura*' *Greece and Rome* 18 (1971) 1–16

Elder, J. P. 'Lucretius 1.1–49' *Transactions of the American Philological Association* 85 (1954) 88–120

Giancotti, F. *Il Preludio di Lucrezio* (Messina 1959)

Segal, C. 'Poetic Immortality and the Fear of Death: the second proem of the *De Rerum Natura*' *Harvard Studies in Classical Philology* 92 (1989) 193–212

Waszink, J. H. 'Lucretius and Poetry' *Mededelingen der konin-klijke Nederlandse Akademie van Wetenschafpen* (Afd. Letterkunde) N.S. 17 (1954) 243–57

ON MEMMIUS, SEE ESPECIALLY:

Boyancé, P. 'Lucrèce et son disciple' *Revue des Études anciennes* 52 (1950) 212–33

Gruen, E. S. 'The consular elections for 53 BC' in: J. Bibauw *Hommages à Marcel Rennard* (Brussels 1969)

Holland, L. A. *Lucretius and the Transpadanes* (Princeton 1979) 101–15

Roller, D. W. 'Gaius Memmius: Patron of Lucretius' *Classical Philology* 65 (1970) 246–8

Townend, G. 'The Fading of Memmius' *Classical Quarterly* 28 (1978) 267–83

Wiseman, T. P. 'The Two Worlds of Titus Lucretius' in *Cinna the Poet and other Roman Essays* (Leicester, 1974) 11–43

ON THE EPICUREAN VIEW OF THE SOUL, SEE:

Kerferd, G. B. 'Epicurus' doctrine of the soul' *Phronesis* 16 (1971) 80–96

ON THE DIATRIBE AGAINST THE FEAR OF DEATH, SEE:

Furley, D. J. 'Nothing to us?' in M. Schofield and G. Striker, (eds.) *The Norms of Nature: studies in Hellenistic ethics* (Cambridge/Paris 1986) 75–91

Stork, T. *Nil igitur mors est ad nos: Der Schlussteil des dritten Lukrezbuches und sein Verhältnis zur Konsolationsliteratur* (Bonn 1970)

Wallach, B. P. *Lucretius and the Diatribe against the Fear of Death: DRN 3.830–1094* (Leiden 1976)

ON THE THEORY OF PERCEPTION AND THE REFUTATION OF SCEPTICISM, SEE:

Annas J. and J. Barnes *The Modes of Scepticism* (Cambridge 1985)

Asmis, E. 'Lucretius' explanation of moving dream figures at 4.768–76' *American Journal of Philology* 102 (1981) 138–45

— *Epicurus' Scientific Method* (Ithaca/London 1984)

Barigazzi, A. 'Epicure et le Scepticisme' *Association Guillaume Budé: Actes de congrès* (1969) 286–93

Burnyeat, M. 'The upside-down back-to-front sceptic of Lucretius 4.472' *Philologus* 122 (1978) 197–206

Gigante, M. *Scetticismo e Epicureismo* (Naples 1981), reviewed by D. P. Fowler in *Oxford Studies in Ancient Philosophy* 2 (1984) 237–67

Glidden, D. K. '*Sensus* and sense-perception in the *de rerum natura*' *California Studies in Classical Antiquity* 12 (1981) 155–81

Schoenheim, U. 'The place of *tactus* in Lucretius' *Philologus* 110 (1966) 71–87

Schrijvers, P. H. 'La Pensée d'Epicure et de Lucrèce sur le sommeil' *Études sur l'épicurisme antique (Cahiers de Philologie)* I (1976) 231–59

— 'Die Traumtheorie des Lukrez' *Mnemosyne* 33 (1980) 128–51

Sedley, D. 'On Signs' in *Science and Speculation* ed. Barnes, Burnyeat, Brunschwig and Schofield (Cambridge 1982) 239–72

Striker, G. 'Epicurus on the truth of sense impressions' *Archiv für Geschichte der Philosophie* 59 (1977) 125–42

Taylor, C. C. W. 'All perceptions are true' in (ed.) Schofield, Burnyeat and Barnes *Doubt and Dogmatism* (Oxford 1980) 105–24

ON LUCRETIUS' TREATMENT OF SEX AND LOVE, SEE:

Barone, C. 'Le spese e le illusioni degli amanti (L. 4. 1123–30)' *Studi Urbinati di Storia, Filosofia e Letteratura* 52 (1978) 75–90

Betensky, A. 'Lucretius and Love' *Classical World* 73 (1980) 291–9

*Brown, R. D. *Lucretius on Love and Sex* (Leiden 1987)

Fitzgerald, W. 'Lucretius' cure for love in the *de rerum natura*' *Classical World* 78 (1984) 73–86

Goar, R. J. 'On the end of Lucretius' fourth book' *Classical Bulletin* 47 (1971) 75–7

Rosivach, V. J. 'Lucretius 4.1123–40' *American Journal of Philology* 101 (1980) 401–3

Taladoire, B. A. 'Lucrèce devant l'amour' *Annales de la Faculté des Lettres et Sciences Humaines de Nice* 21 (1974) 231–5

Traina, A. '*Dira Libido* (sul linguaggio lucreziano dell'Eros)' *Studi di Poesia Latina in onore di A. Traglia* (ed. Di Storia) (Rome 1979) vol. 2, 259–76

ON THE EPICUREAN VIEW OF PLEASURE, SEE:

Gosling, J. C. B. and C. C. W. Taylor *The Greeks on Pleasure* (Oxford 1982) 345–413

Rist, J. M. 'Pleasure: 360–300 BC' *Phoenix* 28 (1974) 167–79

ON THE GODS IN EPICUREANISM AND THE ANTI-TELEOLOGICAL ARGUMENT OF THE POEM, SEE:

Farrington, B. *The Faith of Epicurus* (London 1967)

Festugière, A. J. (transl. C. W. Chilton) *Epicurus and his Gods* (Oxford 1955)

Lemke, D. *Die Theologie Epikurs* (Munich 1973)

Solmsen, F. 'Epicurus and cosmological heresies' *American Journal of Philology* 72 (1951) 1–23

ON THE HISTORY AND NATURE OF LANGUAGE, SOCIETY AND POLITICS AND LUCRETIUS' VIEWS ON PROGRESS, SEE:

Blickman, D. R. 'Lucretius, Epicurus and Prehistory' *Harvard Studies in Classical Philology* 92 (1989) 157–91

Edelstein, L. *The Idea of Progress in Classical Antiquity* (Baltimore 1967)

Fowler, D. P. 'Lucretius and Politics' in M. Griffin and J. Barnes (eds.) *Philosophia Togata – Essays on Roman Philosophy and Society* (Oxford 1989) 120–50

Furley, D. J. 'Lucretius the Epicurean. On the History of Man' in *Lucrèce* (Fondations Hardt Entretiens) 24 (1977) 1–27

*Kenney, E. J. 'The Historical Imagination of Lucretius' *Greece and Rome* 19 (1972) 12–24

*Long, A. A. 'Pleasure and Social Utility – the virtues of being Epicurean' in H. Flashar and O. Gigon (eds.) *Aspects de la Philosophie Hellénistique* (Fondations Hardt Entretiens) 32 (1986) 283–324

Merlan, P. 'Lucretius – Primitivist or Progressivist?' *Journal of the History of Ideas* 11 (1950) 364–8

Monti, R. C. 'Lucretius on Greed, Political Ambition and Society: *DRN* 3.59–86' *Latomus* 40 (1981) 48–66

Phillipson, R. 'Die Rechtsphilosophie der Epikureer' in: *Studien zu Epikur und den Epikureern* (Hildesheim 1983) 27–89

Robin, L., 'Sur la conception épicurienne du progrès' *Revue de Métaphysique et de Morale* 23 (1916) 697–719

Schmid, W., 'Lucretius Ethicus' in *Lucrèce* (Fondations Hardt Entretiens) 24 (1978) 123–65

Schrijvers, P. H. 'La pensée du Lucrèce sur l'origine de la vie' *Mnemosyne* 27 (1974) 245–61

— 'La pensée de Lucrèce sur l'origine du langage' *Mnemosyne* 27 (1974) 337–64

ON THE PLAGUE AT THE END OF BOOK SIX, SEE:

Bright, D. F. 'The Plague and the Structure of the *De Rerum Natura*' *Latomus* 30 (1971) 607–32

Commager, H. S. Jr, 'Lucretius' Interpretation of the Plague' *Harvard Studies in Classical Philology* vol. LXII (1957), 105–18

ON THE HISTORY OF THE TEXT OF LUCRETIUS, SEE
ESPECIALLY:

Cini, G. F. 'La posizione degli "Italici" nello stemma lucreziano'
Atti e Memorie dell'Accademia Toscana La Colombaria 41
(1976) 115–69

Reeve, M. D. 'The Italian Tradition of Lucretius' *Italia Medio-
evale e Umanistica* 23 (1980) 27–48

Reynolds, L. D. *Texts and Transmission: a Survey of the Latin
Classics* (Oxford 1983)

Richter, W. *Textstudien zu Lukrez* (Munich 1974)

ON THE NATURE OF
THE UNIVERSE

SYNOPSIS

BOOK ONE

INTRODUCTION

EXISTENCE OF ATOMS

EXISTENCE OF EMPTY SPACE

EVERYTHING IS COMPOSED OF THESE TWO, MATTER AND SPACE

ATOMS CANNOT BE DESTROYED (483–634)

BOOK TWO

THREE GENERAL STATEMENTS

BOOK THREE

INTRODUCTION

MIND AND SPIRIT

MORTALITY OF THE SOUL

CONCLUSION

BOOK FOUR

INTRODUCTION

VISION

OTHER SENSES

BOOK FIVE

BOOK SIX

THE EARTH AND ITS WONDERS

EPIDEMIC DISEASES

BOOK ONE
MATTER AND SPACE

Mother of Aeneas and his race, delight of men and gods, life-giving Venus,[1] it is your doing that under the wheeling constellations of the sky all nature teems with life, both the sea that buoys up our ships and the earth that yields our food. Through you all living creatures are conceived and come forth to look upon the sunlight. Before you the winds flee, and at your coming the clouds forsake the sky. For you the inventive earth flings up sweet flowers. For you the ocean levels laugh, the sky is calmed and glows with diffused radiance. When first the day puts on the aspect of spring, when in all its force the fertilizing breath of Zephyr is unleashed,[2] then, great goddess, the birds of air give the first intimation of your entry; for yours is the power that has pierced them to the heart. Next the wild beasts and farm animals alike run wild, frisk through the lush pastures and swim the swift-flowing streams. Spellbound by your charm, they follow your lead with fierce desire. So throughout seas and uplands, rushing torrents, verdurous meadows and the leafy shelters of the birds, into the breasts of one and all you instil alluring love, so that with passionate longing they reproduce their several breeds.

Since you alone are the guiding power of the universe and without you nothing emerges into the shining sunlit world to grow in joy and loveliness, yours is the partnership I seek in striving to compose these lines *On the Nature of the Universe*[3] for my noble Memmius.[4] For him, great goddess, you have willed outstanding excellence in every field and everlasting fame. For his sake, therefore, endow my verse with everlasting charm.

Meanwhile, grant that this brutal business of war by sea and land may everywhere be lulled to rest. For you alone have power to bestow on mortals the blessing of quiet peace. In your bosom Mars himself, supreme commander in this business of brutality, flings himself down at times, laid low by the irremediable wound of love. Gazing upward, his neck a pros-

trate column, he fixes hungry eyes on you, great goddess, and
gluts them with love. As he lies outstretched, his breath hangs
upon your lips. Stoop, then, goddess most glorious, and enfold
him at rest in your hallowed bosom and whisper with those lips
sweet words of prayer, beseeching for the people of Rome
untroubled peace. In this evil hour of my country's history, I
cannot pursue my task with a mind at ease, as an illustrious
scion of the house of Memmius cannot at such a crisis[5] withhold
his service from the common weal. ⟨I beg you for peace⟩ since
it is essential to the very nature of deity that it should enjoy
immortal existence in utter tranquillity, aloof and detached
from our affairs. It is free from all pain and peril, strong in its
own resources, exempt from any need of us, indifferent to our
merits and immune from anger.

For what is to follow, my Memmius, lay aside your cares and
lend undistracted ears and an attentive mind to true reason. Do
not scornfully reject, before you have understood them, the
gifts I have marshalled for you with zealous devotion. I will set
out to discourse to you on the ultimate realities of heaven and
the gods. I will reveal those *atoms* from which nature creates all
things and increases and feeds them and into which, when they
perish, nature again resolves them. To these in my discourse I
commonly give such names as the 'raw material', or 'generative
bodies', or 'seeds' of things. Or I may call them 'primary
particles', because they come first and everything else is com-
posed of them.

When human life lay grovelling in all men's sight, crushed to
the earth under the dead weight of superstition whose grim
features loured menacingly upon mortals from the four quarters
of the sky, a man of Greece[6] was first to raise mortal eyes in
defiance, first to stand erect and brave the challenge. Fables of
the gods did not crush him, nor the lightning flash and the
growling menace of the sky.[7] Rather, they quickened the keen
courage of his heart, so that he, first of all men, longed to
smash the constraining locks of nature's doors. The vital vigour
of his mind prevailed. He ventured far out beyond the flaming

74 ramparts of the world and voyaged in mind throughout infinity. Returning victorious, he proclaimed to us what can be and what cannot: how the power of each thing is limited, and its boundary-stone sticks buried deep. Therefore superstition in its turn lies crushed beneath his feet, and we by his triumph are lifted level with the skies.

80 One thing that worries me is the fear that you may fancy yourself embarking on an impious course of philosophy, setting your feet on the path of sin. Far from it. More often it is this very superstition that is the mother of sinful and impious deeds. Remember how at Aulis[8] the altar of the virgin goddess was foully stained with the blood of Iphigeneia by the leaders of the Greeks, the patterns of chivalry. The headband was bound about her virgin tresses and hung down evenly over both her cheeks. Suddenly she caught sight of her father standing sadly in front of the altar, the attendants beside him hiding the knife and her people bursting into tears when they
91 saw her. Struck dumb with terror, she sank on her knees to the ground. Poor girl, at such a moment it did not help her that she had been first to give the name of father to a king. Raised by the hands of men, she was led trembling to the altar. Not for her the sacrament of marriage and the loud chant of Hymen. It was her fate in the very hour of marriage to fall a sinless victim to a sinful rite, slaughtered to her greater grief by a father's hand, so that a fleet might sail under happy auspices. Such are the heights of wickedness to which men have been driven by superstition.
102 You yourself, if you surrender your judgement at any time to the blood-curdling declamations of the prophets, will want to desert our ranks. Only think what phantoms they can conjure up to overturn the tenor of your life and wreck your happiness with fear. And not without cause. For, if men saw that a term was set to their troubles, they would find strength in some way to withstand the hocus-pocus and intimidations of the prophets. As it is, they have no power of resistance, because they are haunted by the fear of eternal punishment after death. They know nothing of the nature of the spirit. Is it born, or is it

implanted in us at birth? Does it perish with us, dissolved by death, or does it visit the murky depths and dreary sloughs of the Underworld? Or is it transplanted by divine power into other creatures, as described in the poems of our own Ennius,[9] who first gathered on the delectable slopes of Helicon[10] an evergreen garland destined to win renown among the nations of Italy? Ennius indeed in his immortal verses proclaims that there is also a Hell, which is peopled not by our actual spirits or bodies but only by shadowy images, ghastly pale. It is from this realm that he pictures the ghost of Homer,[11] of unfading memory, as appearing to him, shedding salt tears and revealing the nature of the universe.

I must therefore give an account of celestial phenomena, explaining the movements of sun and moon and also the forces that determine events on earth. Next, and no less important, we must look with keen insight into the make-up of spirit and mind: we must consider those alarming phantasms that strike upon our minds when they are awake but disordered by sickness, or when they are buried in slumber, so that we seem to see and hear before us men whose dead bones lie in the embraces of earth.

I am well aware that it is not easy to elucidate in Latin verse the obscure discoveries of the Greeks. The poverty of our language[12] and the novelty of the theme often compel me to coin new words for the purpose. But your merit and the joy I hope to derive from our delightful friendship[13] encourage me to face any task however hard. This it is that leads me to stay awake through the quiet of the night, studying how by choice of words and the poet's art I can display before your mind a clear light by which you can gaze into the heart of hidden things.

This dread and darkness of the mind cannot be dispelled by the sunbeams, the shining shafts of day, but only by an understanding of the outward form and inner workings of nature. In tackling this theme, our starting-point will be this principle: *Nothing is ever created by divine power out of nothing.* The reason why all mortals are so gripped by fear is that they see all sorts of things happening on the earth and in the sky with no

154 discernible cause, and these they attribute to the will of a god. Accordingly, when we have seen that nothing can be created out of nothing, we shall then have a clearer picture of the path ahead, the problem of how things are created and occasioned without the aid of gods.

First then, if things were made out of nothing, any species could spring from any source and nothing would require seed.[14] Men could arise from the sea and scaly fish from the earth, and birds could be hatched out of the sky. Cattle and other farm animals and every kind of wild beast, multiplying indiscriminately, would occupy cultivated and waste lands alike. The same fruits would not grow constantly on the same trees, but they would keep changing: any tree might bear any fruit. If each species were not composed of its own generative bodies, why should each be born always of the same kind of mother? Actually, since each is formed out of specific seeds, it is born and emerges into the sunlit world only from a place where there exists the right material, the right kind of atoms. This is why everything cannot be born of everything, but a specific power of generation inheres in specific objects.

Again, why do we see[15] roses appear in spring, grain in summer's heat, grapes under the spell of autumn? Surely, because it is only after specific seeds have drifted together at their own proper time that every created thing stands revealed, when the season is favourable and the life-giving earth can safely deliver delicate growths into the sunlit world. If they were made out of nothing, they would spring up suddenly after varying lapses of time and at abnormal seasons, since there would of course be no primary bodies that could be prevented by the harshness of the season from entering into generative unions. Similarly, there would be no need of any lapse of time for the accumulation of seed in order that things might grow. Tiny tots would turn suddenly into young men, and trees would shoot up spontaneously out of the earth. But it is obvious that none of these things happens since, as is natural, everything grows gradually from a specific seed and retains its specific character. It is a fair inference that each is increased and nourished by its own raw material.

161

172

182

14

Here is a further point. Without seasonable showers the earth cannot send up gladdening growths. Lacking food, animals cannot reproduce their kind or sustain life. This points to the conclusion that many elements are common to many things, as letters are to words,[16] rather than to the theory that anything can come into existence without atoms.

192

Or again, why has not nature been able to produce men on such a scale that they could ford the ocean on foot or tear down high mountains with their hands or prolong their lives over many generations?[17] Surely because each thing requires for its birth a particular material that determines what can be produced. It must therefore be admitted that nothing can be made out of nothing, because everything must be generated from a seed before it can emerge into the unresisting air.

201

Lastly, we see that tilled plots are superior to untilled, and their fruits are improved by cultivation. This is because the earth contains certain atoms that we rouse to productivity by turning the fruitful clods with the ploughshare and stirring up the soil. But for these, you would see great improvements arising spontaneously without any aid from our labours.

212

The second great principle is this: *nature resolves everything into its component atoms and never reduces anything to nothing.* If anything were perishable in all its parts, anything might perish all of a sudden and vanish from sight. There would be no need of any force to separate its parts and loosen their links. In actual fact, since everything is composed of indestructible seeds, nature obviously does not allow anything to perish till it has encountered a force that shatters it with a blow or creeps into chinks and unknits it.

223

If the things that are banished from the scene by age are annihilated through the exhaustion of their material, from what source does Venus bring back the several races of animals into the light of life? And, when they are brought back, where does the inventive earth find for each the special food required for its sustenance and growth? From what fount is the sea replenished by its native springs and the streams that flow into it from afar? From where does the ether draw nutriment for the

232 stars? For everything consisting of a mortal body must have been exhausted by the long day of time, the illimitable past. If throughout this bygone eternity there have persisted bodies from which the universe has been perpetually renewed, they must certainly be possessed of immortality. Therefore things cannot be reduced to nothing.

240 Again, all objects would regularly be destroyed by the same force and the same cause were it not that they are sustained by imperishable matter more or less tightly fastened together. Why, a mere touch would be enough to bring about destruction supposing there were no imperishable bodies whose union could be dissolved only by the appropriate force. Actually, because the fastenings of the atoms are of various kinds while their matter is imperishable, compound objects remain intact until one of them encounters a force that proves strong enough to break up its particular constitution. Therefore nothing returns to nothing, but everything is resolved into its constituent 250 bodies.

Lastly, showers perish when father ether has flung them down into the lap of mother earth.[18] But the crops spring up fresh; the branches on the trees burst into leaf; the trees themselves grow and are weighed down with fruit. Hence in turn man and beast draw nourishment. Hence we see flourishing cities blest with children and every leafy thicket loud with new broods of songsters. Hence in lush pastures cattle wearied by their bulk fling down their bodies, and the white milky juice oozes from their swollen udders. Hence a new generation frolic 261 friskily on wobbly legs through the fresh grass, their young minds tipsy with undiluted milk. Visible objects therefore do not perish utterly, since nature repairs one thing from another and allows nothing to be born without the aid of another's death.

Well, Memmius, I have taught you that things cannot be created out of nothing nor, once born, be summoned back to nothing. Perhaps, however, you are becoming mistrustful of my words, because these atoms of mine are not visible to the eye. Consider, therefore, this further evidence of *bodies whose*

existence you must acknowledge though they cannot be seen. First, wind, 270
when its force is roused, whips up waves, founders tall ships
and scatters clouds. Sometimes scouring plains with hurricane
force it strews them with huge trees and batters mountain
peaks with blasts that hew down forests. Such is wind in its
fury, when it whoops aloud with a mad menace in its shouting.
Without question, therefore, there must be invisible particles of
wind that sweep sea, that sweep land, that sweep the clouds in 279
the sky, swooping upon them and whirling them along in a
headlong hurricane. In the way they flow and the havoc they
spread they are no different from a torrential flood of water
when it rushes down in a sudden spate from the mountain
heights, swollen by heavy rains, and heaps together wreckage
from the forest and entire trees. Soft though it is by nature, the
sudden shock of oncoming water is more than even stout
bridges can withstand, so furious is the force with which the
turbid, storm-flushed torrent surges against their piers. With a
mighty roar it lays them low, rolling huge rocks under its 289
waves and brushing aside every obstacle from its course. Such,
therefore, must be the movement of blasts of wind also. When
they have come surging along some course like a rushing river,
they push obstacles before them and buffet them with repeated
blows; and sometimes, eddying round and round, they snatch
them up and carry them along in a swiftly circling vortex. Here
then is proof upon proof that winds have invisible bodies, since
in their actions and behaviour they are found to rival great
rivers, whose bodies are plain to see.

Then again, we smell the various scents of things though we 298
never see them approaching our nostrils. Similarly, we do not
look upon scorching heat nor can we grasp cold in our eyes
and we do not see sounds. Yet all these must be composed of
physical bodies, since they are able to impinge upon our senses.
For nothing can touch or be touched except bodies.

Again, clothes hung out on a surf-beaten shore grow moist.
Spread in the sun they grow dry. But we do not see how the
moisture has soaked into them, nor again how it has been
dispelled by the heat. It follows that the moisture is split up
into minute parts which the eye cannot possibly see.

311 Again, in the course of many annual revolutions of the sun a ring is worn thin next to the finger with continual rubbing. Dripping water hollows a stone. A curved ploughshare, iron though it is, dwindles imperceptibly in the furrow. We see the cobblestones of the highway worn by the feet of many wayfarers. The bronze statues by the city gates show their right hands worn thin by the touch of travellers who have greeted 319 them in passing. We see that all these are being diminished, since they are worn away. But to perceive what particles drop off at any particular time is a power grudged to us by our ungenerous sense of sight.

To sum up, whatever is added to things gradually by nature and the passage of days, causing a cumulative increase, eludes the most attentive scrutiny of our eyes. Conversely, you cannot see what objects lose by the wastage of age – sheer sea cliffs, for instance, exposed to prolonged erosion by the mordant brine – or at what time the loss occurs. It follows that nature 328 works through the agency of invisible bodies.

On the other hand, things are not hemmed in by the pressure of solid bodies in a tight mass. This is because *there is vacuity*[19] *in things*. A grasp of this fact will be helpful to you in many respects and will save you from much bewildered doubting and questioning about the universe and from mistrust of my teaching. Well then, by vacuity I mean intangible and empty space. If it did not exist, things could not move at all. For the distinctive action of matter, which is counteraction and obstruc- 338 tion, would be in force always and everywhere. Nothing could move forward, because nothing would give it a starting-point by receding. As it is, we see with our eyes at sea and on land and high up in the sky that all sorts of things in all sorts of ways are on the move. If there were no empty space, these things would be denied the power of restless movement – or rather, they could not possibly have come into existence, embedded as they would have been in motionless matter.

Besides, there are clear indications that things that pass for solid are in fact porous. Even in rocky caves a trickle of water seeps through, and every surface weeps with brimming drops.

Food percolates to every part of an animal's body. Trees grow   350
and pour forth their fruit in season, because their food is
distributed throughout their length from the tips of the roots
through the trunk and along every branch. Noises pass through
walls and fly into closed buildings. Freezing cold penetrates to
the bones. If there were no vacancies through which the
various bodies could make their way, none of these phenomena
would be possible.

Again, why do we find some things outweigh others of equal   357
volume? If there is as much matter in a ball of wool as in one of
lead, it is natural that it should weigh as heavily, since it is the
function of matter to press everything downwards, while it is
the function of space on the other hand to remain weightless.
Accordingly, when one thing is not less bulky than another but
obviously lighter, it plainly declares that there is more vacuum
in it, while the heavier object proclaims that there is more
matter in it and much less empty space. We have therefore
reached the goal of our diligent enquiry: there is in things an   369
admixture of what we call vacuity.

In case you should be misled on this question by the idle
imagining of certain theorists,[20] I must anticipate their argu-
ment. They maintain that water yields and opens up liquid
ways to the scaly bodies of fish that push against it, because
they leave spaces behind them into which the yielding water
can flow together. In the same way, they suppose, other things
can move by mutually changing places, although every place
remains filled. This theory has been adopted utterly without
warrant. For how can the fish advance till the water has given   379
way? And how can the water retire when the fish cannot move?
There are thus only two alternatives: either all bodies are
devoid of movement, or you must admit that things contain an
admixture of vacuity whereby each is enabled to make the first
move.

Lastly, if two broad bodies suddenly spring apart from
contact, all the intervening space must be void until it is
occupied by air. However quickly the air rushes in all round,
the entire space cannot be filled instantaneously. The air must
occupy one spot after another until it has taken possession of

391 the whole space. If anyone supposes that this consequence of such springing apart is made possible by the condensation of air,[21] he is mistaken. For condensation implies that something that was full becomes empty, or vice versa. And I contend that air could not condense so as to produce this effect; or, at any rate, if there were no vacuum, it could not thus shrink into itself and draw its parts together.

398 However many pleas you may advance to prolong the argument, you must end by admitting that there is vacuity in things. There are many other proofs that I could scrape together into the pile in order to strengthen conviction; but for an acute intelligence these small clues should suffice to discover the rest for yourself. As hounds often smell out the lairs of a mountain-ranging quarry screened in thickets, when once they have got on to the right trail, so in such questions one thing will lead on to another, till you can succeed by yourself in tracking down the truth to its lurking places and dragging it forth. If you
411 grow weary and relax from the chase, there is one thing, Memmius, that I can safely promise you: my honeyed tongue will pour from the treasury of my breast such generous draughts, drawn from inexhaustible springs, that I am afraid slow plodding age may creep through my limbs and unbolt the bars of my life before the full flood of my arguments on any single point has flowed in verse through your ears.

To pick up the thread of my discourse, all nature as it is in itself consists of two things – bodies and the vacant space in which
421 the bodies are situated and through which they move in different directions. The existence of bodies is vouched for by the agreement of the senses. If a belief resting directly on this foundation is not valid, there will be no standard to which we can refer any doubt on obscure questions for rational confirmation. If there were no place and space, which we call vacuity, these bodies could not be situated anywhere or move in any direction whatever. This I have just demonstrated. It remains to show that *nothing exists that is distinct both from body and from vacuity* and could be ranked with the others as a third substance. For whatever *is* must also be something. If it offers resistance

to touch, however light and slight, it will increase the mass of
body by such amount, great or small, as it may amount to, and
will rank with it. If, on the other hand, it is intangible, so that
it offers no resistance whatever to anything passing through it,
then it will be that empty space which we call vacuity. Besides,
whatever it may be in itself, either it will act in some way, or
react to other things acting upon it, or else it will be such that
things can be and happen in it. But without body nothing can
act or react; and nothing can afford a place except emptiness
and vacancy. Therefore, besides matter and vacuity, we cannot
include in the number of things any third substance that can
either affect our senses at any time or be grasped by the
reasoning of our minds.

You will find that anything that can be named is either a
property or an accident of these two. A *property* is something
that cannot be detached or separated from a thing without
destroying it, as weight is a property of rocks, heat of fire,
fluidity of water, tangibility of all bodies, intangibility of
vacuum. On the other hand, servitude, poverty and riches,
freedom, war, peace and all other things whose advent or
departure leaves the essence of a thing intact, all these it is our
practice to call by their appropriate name, *accidents*.

Similarly, time by itself does not exist; but from things
themselves there results a sense of what has already taken place,
what is now going on and what is to ensue. It must not be
claimed that anyone can sense time by itself apart from the
movement of things or their restful immobility.

Again, when men say it *is* a fact that Helen[22] was ravished or
the Trojans were conquered, we must not let anyone drive us
to the admission that any such factual event *exists* independently
of any object, on the ground that the generations of men of
whom these events were accidents have been swept away by the
irrevocable lapse of time. For we could put it that whatever has
taken place is an accident of a particular tract of earth or of the
space it occupied. If there had been no matter and no space or
place in which things could happen, no spark of love kindled
by the beauty of Tyndareus' daughter[23] would ever have glowed

21

474   inside the breast of Phrygian Paris to light that dazzling blaze of pitiless war; no Wooden Horse, unmarked by the sons of Troy, would have set the towers of Ilium aflame through the midnight issue of Greeks from its womb. So you may see that events cannot be said to *be* by themselves like matter or in the same sense as space. Rather, you should describe them as accidents of matter, or of the place in which things happen.

483   *Material objects are of two kinds, atoms and compounds of atoms. The atoms themselves cannot be swamped by any force, for they are preserved indefinitely by their absolute solidity.* Admittedly, it is hard to believe that anything can exist that is absolutely solid. The lightning stroke from the sky penetrates closed buildings, as do shouts and other noises. Iron glows white-hot in the fire, and rocks crack in savage scorching heat. Hard gold is softened and melted by heat; and the ice of bronze is liquefied by flame. Both heat and piercing cold seep through silver, since we feel both alike when a cooling shower of water is poured into a
495 goblet that we hold ceremonially in our hands. All these facts point to the conclusion that nothing is really solid. But sound reasoning and nature itself drive us to the opposite conclusion. Pay attention, therefore, while I demonstrate in a few lines that there exist certain bodies that are absolutely solid and indestructible, namely those atoms which according to our teaching are the seeds of prime units of things from which the whole universe is built up.

   In the first place, we have found that nature is twofold, consisting of two totally different things, matter and the space
505 in which things happen. Hence each of these must exist by itself without admixture of the other. For, where there is empty space (what we call vacuity), there matter is not; where matter exists, there cannot be a vacuum. Therefore the prime units of matter are solid and free from vacuity.

   Again, since composite things contain some vacuum, the surrounding matter must be solid. For you cannot reasonably maintain that anything can hide vacuity and hold it within its body unless you allow that the container itself is solid. And what contains the vacuum in things can only be an accumulation

of matter. Hence matter, which possesses absolute solidity, can   518
be everlasting when other things are decomposed.

Again, if there were no empty space, everything would be
one solid mass; if there were no material objects with the
property of filling the space they occupy, all existing space
would be utterly void. It is clear, then, that there is an alterna-
tion of matter and vacuity, mutually distinct, since the whole is
neither completely full nor completely empty. There are there-   527
fore solid bodies, causing the distinction between empty space
and full. And these, as I have just shown, can be neither
decomposed by blows from without nor invaded and unknit
from within nor destroyed by any other form of assault. For it
seems that a thing without vacuum[24] can be neither knocked to
bits nor snapped nor chopped in two by cutting; nor can it let
in moisture or seeping cold or piercing fire, the universal
agents of destruction. The more vacuum a thing contains
within it, the more readily it yields to these assailants. Hence, if
the units of matter are solid and without vacuity, as I have   540
shown, they must be everlasting.

Yet again, if the matter in things had not been everlasting,
everything by now would have gone back to nothing, and the
things we see would be the product of rebirth out of nothing.
But, since I have already shown that nothing can be created out
of nothing nor any existing thing be summoned back to noth-
ing, the atoms must be made of imperishable stuff into which
everything can be resolved in the end, so that there may be a
stock of matter for building the world anew. The atoms,
therefore, are absolutely solid and unalloyed. In no other way   550
could they have survived throughout infinite time to keep the
world renewed.

Furthermore, if nature had set no limit to the breaking of
things, the particles of matter in the course of ages would have
been ground so small that nothing could be generated from
them so as to attain from them in the fullness of time to the
summit of its growth. For we see that anything can be more
speedily disintegrated than put together again. Hence, what the
long day of time, the bygone eternity, has already shaken and
loosened to fragments could never in the residue of time be

561 reconstructed. As it is, there is evidently a limit set to breaking, since we see that everything is renewed and each according to its kind has a fixed period in which to grow to its prime.

Here is a further argument. Granted that the particles of matter are absolutely solid, we can still explain the composition and behaviour of soft things – air, water, earth, fire[25] – by their intermixture with empty space. On the other hand, supposing
571 the atoms to be soft,[26] we cannot account for the origin of hard flint and iron. For there would be no foundation for nature to build on. Therefore there must be bodies strong in their unalloyed solidity by whose closer clustering things can be knit together and display unyielding toughness.

If we suppose that there is no limit set to the breaking of matter, we must still admit that material objects consist of particles which throughout eternity have resisted the forces of destruction. To say that these are breakable does not square with the fact that they have survived throughout eternity under
584 a perpetual bombardment of innumerable blows.[27]

Again, there is laid down for each thing a specific limit to its growth and its tenure of life, and the laws of nature ordain what each can do and what it cannot. No species is ever changed, but each remains so much itself that every kind of bird displays on its body its own specific markings. This is a further proof that their bodies are made of changeless matter. For, if the atoms could yield in any way to change, there would be no certainty as to what could arise and what could not, at what point the power of everything was limited by an immov-
597 able frontier post; nor could successive generations so regularly repeat the nature, behaviour, habits and movements of their parents.

To proceed with our argument, there is an ⟨ultimate point in visible objects that represents the smallest thing that can be seen. So also there must be an⟩ ultimate point in objects that lie below the limit of perception by our senses. This point is without parts and is the smallest thing that can exist. It never has been and never will be able to exist by itself, but only as one primary part of something else. It is with a mass of such parts, solidly jammed together in formation, that matter is filled

up. Since they cannot exist by themselves, they must needs   607
stick together in a mass from which they cannot by any means
be prized loose. The atoms, therefore, are absolutely solid and
unalloyed, consisting of a mass of least parts[28] tightly packed
together. They are not compounds formed by the coalescence
of their parts, but bodies of absolute and everlasting solidity.
To these nature allows no loss or diminution, but guards them
as seeds for things. If there are no such least parts, even the   615
smallest bodies consist of an infinite number of parts, since they
can always be halved and their halves halved again without
limit. On this showing, what difference will there be between
the whole universe and the very least of things? None at all.
For, however endlessly infinite the universe may be, yet the
smallest things will equally consist of an infinite number of
parts. Since true reason cries out against this and denies that the
mind can believe it, you must needs give in and admit that
there are least parts which themselves are partless. Granted that
these parts exist, you must needs admit that the atoms they   627
compose are also solid and everlasting. But, if all things were
compelled by all-creating nature to be broken up into these
least parts, nature would lack the power to rebuild anything
out of them. For partless objects cannot have the essential
properties of generative matter – those varieties of attachment,
weight, impetus, impact and movement on which everything de-
pends.

For all these reasons, *those who have imagined that the raw material
of things is fire and the universe consists of fire alone have evidently
wandered far from the truth*. Of these the first champion to plunge   637
into the fray was Heraclitus,[29] illustrious for the darkness of
his speech, though rather among the lighter-witted of the
Greeks than among those who are earnest seekers after truth.
For fools are more impressed and intrigued by what they detect
under a screen of riddling words, and accept as true what
pleasantly tickles their ears and all that is dyed with a smart
sound.[30] I should like to know how things can be so manifold
if they are created out of nothing but sheer fire. It would not
help if hot fire were condensed or rarefied, so long as the

649 particles of fire retained the same nature that fire possesses as a whole. Its heat would simply be fiercer as its parts were more concentrated, milder as they were dispersed and dissipated. There is no further effect that you could attribute to such causes – no possibility that the infinite variety of things could result from variations in the density or rarity of fire. Even these variations in density could not occur unless we allow in things

657 an intermixture of vacuity. But, because these theorists see that many things run counter to their theories, they dodge the issue and decline to leave any pure vacuum in things. Shunning the steep, they lose the true path. They do not see that without vacuity everything would be condensed and would become one body, which could not throw off anything at high speed from itself as blazing fire throws off light and heat, so that you can see that its parts are not solidly compacted.

If, on the other hand, they think that there is some other way in which fires in combination can be quenched and change their

667 substance, then obviously – if they do not shrink from any implication of this view – the fieriness must be completely annihilated and whatever emerges must be a new creation out of nothing.[31] For, if ever anything is so transformed as to overstep its own limits, this means the immediate death of what was before. It follows that they must leave something intact, or you would find everything reduced to nothing and the stock of things reborn and reinvigorated from nothing. As it is, there are certain definite bodies that always keep the same nature, and it is by the withdrawal or advent of these and their

678 reshuffling that things change their nature and material objects are transformed. And these primary bodies cannot be fiery. So long as they possessed and retained a fiery nature, it would make no odds if some of them were detached and withdrawn and others tacked on and some were reshuffled. Whatever they created would still be simply fire. The truth, as I maintain, is this: there are certain bodies whose impacts, movements, order, position and shapes produce fires. When their order is changed, they change their nature. In themselves they do not resemble fire or anything else that can bombard our senses with particles or impinge on our organs of touch.[32]

To say, as Heraclitus does, that everything is fire, and   690
nothing can be numbered among things as a reality except fire,
seems utterly crazy. On the basis of the senses he attacks and
unsettles the senses – the foundation of all belief and the only
source of his knowledge of that which he calls fire.[33] He
believes that the senses clearly perceive fire, but not the other
things that are in fact no less clear. This strikes me as not only
pointless but mad. For what is to be our standard of reference?   700
What can be a surer guide to the distinction of true from false
than our own senses? What grounds have we for taking every-
thing else and leaving fire, any more than for taking away
everything else and leaving some other thing? Either procedure
appears equally insane.

For this reason those who have thought that fire is the raw
material of things and the universe can consist of fire and those
who have made *air*[34] the starting-point for the growth of things
or have supposed that *water*[35] by itself could form everything or
that *earth*[36] could create all things and be transformed into their   711
natures – all these have evidently wandered far from the truth.

Not less mistaken are those who make the elements two-fold, coupling
air with fire and earth with water, *and those who think that
everything can grow from four elements*, fire and earth and air and rain.
Conspicuous among these is Empedocles[37] of Acragas, born in the
three-cornered confines of that Isle round which surges the
Ionian deep, rushing far into creeks and dashing up salt spray
from its grey-green billows. The sea that parts it from Aeolian[38]
shores runs headlong through its narrow channel. Here is   722
deadly Charybdis.[39] Here the rumbling of Etna's[40] flames is a
warning that it is rallying its wrath that once again its force
may spew out fires bursting in a torrent from its throat, to
bring its flashing flames back up to the sky. This great country
is acknowledged to have many claims to the admiration of
mankind and the attention of sight-seekers. But, for all its
surfeit of good things and its ample garrison of men, it has
surely held nothing more glorious than this man, nothing
holier, nothing more wonderful, nothing more precious.
Indeed, the songs that took shape in his divine breast proclaim

732 in ringing tones such glorious discoveries that he scarcely seems a scion of mortal stock. Empedocles and those lesser men of whom we have spoken above, who rank far and away below him, have certainly made many excellent and divine discoveries and uttered oracles from the inner sanctuary of their hearts with more sanctity and far surer reason than those the Delphic prophetess pronounces, drugged by the laurel fumes, from Apollo's tripod. Yet among the very foundations of things they have come to grief. Great as they were, great has been their fall.

740

Their first error is this: they postulate movement while banishing empty space from the universe, and they admit the existence of soft and flimsy things − air, sun, water, earth, animals, vegetables − without allowing their bodies an intermixture of vacuity.

Secondly, they acknowledge no limit to the splitting of things, no rest from crumbling, no smallest unit of matter, although we see that every object has an ultimate point that seems to our senses to be the smallest, from which you may infer that the things you cannot perceive have also an ultimate point which actually is the smallest.[41] Besides, since they rank as elements soft things that we perceive to be neither birthless nor deathless, the universe ought by now to have returned to nothing and whatever exists ought to be a new creation and growth out of nothing, both of which suppositions you already know to be false. Furthermore, these supposed elements are in many ways hurtful and lethal to one another, so that they will either be destroyed on contact or will rush apart, as when a storm has gathered we see lightning flashes, rainclouds and winds rush apart.

749

761

Again, if everything is created from four things and resolved into them, why should we say that these are the elements of things rather than the reverse − that other things are the elements of these? For one gives birth to another continually, and they interchange their colours and their entire natures throughout the whole of time. If, on the other hand, you believe that particles of fire and earth, airy wind and watery moisture, combine without changing their natures in combination, then nothing can be created from them, either animate or (like a tree) with inanimate body. For each element in a composite assemblage will betray its own nature; air will appear mixed with earth, and fire will remain side by side with moisture. But in fact the elements, in giving birth to things, must contribute a nature that is hidden and viewless,[42] so that nothing may show that conflicts with the thing created and prevents it from being distinctively itself.

774

These authors[43] trace everything back to the sky and its fires. First they make fire transform itself into the winds of air; hence is born rain, and from rain is created earth. Then the process is reversed: first from earth is born moisture, then comes air, then fire. And things never cease to interchange, migrating from heaven to earth, from earth to the starry firmament. This is something elements ought never to do. For it is essential that something should remain immutable, or everything would be reduced to nothing. For, if ever anything is so transformed that it oversteps its own limits, this means the immediate death of what was before.[44] Therefore, since the substances just mentioned enter into interchange, they must needs consist of other substances that cannot be altered, so that you may not find everything reduced to nothing. You ought rather to postulate bodies possessed of such a nature that, if they happen to have created fire, they only need a few subtractions and additions and some change of order and movement to make gusty air. In this way we can account for any change from one thing to another.

781

793

'But,' you say, 'observation clearly shows that all growing things do grow up into the gusty air out of the earth and it is from the earth that they draw their food. And, unless an auspicious season gives free play to the rain, so that trees reel beneath the dissolving clouds, and unless the sun in turn provides fostering warmth, there can be no growth of crops, trees, or animals.' Yes, and unless we ourselves were sustained by dry food and fluid juices, our bodies would waste away till every bit of life had escaped from all our sinews and bones. There can be no doubt that we are fed and sustained by certain specific things, other things by others, and so forth.[45] Obviously,

803

815 it is because there are in things many elements common to many commingled in many ways that various things draw their food from various sources. It often makes a big difference in what combinations and positions the selfsame elements occur, and what motions they mutually pass on or take over. For the same elements compose sky, sea and lands, rivers and sun, crops, trees and animals, but they are moving differently and in different combinations. Consider how in my verses,[46] for instance, you see many letters common to many words; yet you must admit that different verses and words differ in substance and in audible sound. So much can be accomplished by letters through mere change of order. But the elements can bring more factors into play so as to create things in all their variety.

823

Now let us look into the theory of Anaxagoras,[47] which the Greeks call *homoeomeria*: the poverty of our native language will not let me translate the word, but the thing itself can be expressed readily enough. Understand, then, that in speaking of the *homoeomeria* of things Anaxagoras means that bones are formed of minute miniature bones, flesh of minute miniature morsels of flesh, blood by the coalescence of many drops of blood; gold consists of grains of gold; earth is a conglomeration of little earths, fire of fires, moisture of moistures. And he pictures everything else as formed in the same way. At the same time he does not admit any vacuum in things, or any limit to the splitting of matter, on both of which counts he seems to me guilty of the same error as the others.[48] Add to this that he makes the elements too frail, if indeed we can allow the name of 'elements' to bodies that have the same nature as the things themselves, that suffer and decay no less than they do and are not reined in by any force in their race to destruction. For which of these things will withstand violent assault, so as to escape extinction in the very jaws of death? Will fire or water or air? Which of these? Blood or bones? Nothing, I maintain, will escape, where everything is as perishable as those objects that we see vanishing from before our eyes under stress of some force or other. In proof of the impossibility of such annihilation and regrowth from nothing, I appeal to the evidence already adduced.

834

848

Again, since food builds up and nourishes our bodies, our 859
veins and bones and blood ⟨and sinews must be composed of
matter unlike themselves.⟩

Alternatively, if it is alleged that all foods are of mixed substance
and contain little morsels of sinews and bones and veins and
drops of blood, it must be supposed that all food, whether solid
or fluid, consists of unlike matter, namely of a mixture of bones 866
and sinews, pus and blood. Similarly, if the material of all the
things that grow out of the earth occurs in the earth, earth
must consist of unlike matter that rises out of it. Turn to other
phenomena, and the same words will hold good. If flame,
smoke and ashes lurk unseen in wood, then wood must consist
of unlike matter that rises out of it. Furthermore, all the
material atoms that the earth feeds and makes to grow ⟨must
consist of things unlike themselves – and they in their turn
must also contain things unlike themselves.⟩

Here there is left some scanty cover for escaping detection, 875
and Anaxagoras avails himself of it. He asserts that there is in
everything a mixture of everything, but all the ingredients
escape detection except the one whose particles are most numer-
ous and conspicuous and stand in the front line. This is far
removed from the truth. Otherwise it would naturally happen
that corn, when it is crushed by the dire force of the grindstone,
would often show some trace of blood, and that blood would
exude when we crush between stones any of those things that
derive material from our bodies. Similarly, grass and water
ought often to emit sweet drops of the same flavour as the milk 887
in the udders of fleecy ewes. When clods of soil are crumbled,
finely divided particles of different plants and grains and leaves
ought to become visible, lurking among the soil. When sticks
are snapped, ashes and smoke ought to be revealed, and tiny
hidden fires. But observation plainly shows that none of these
things happens. It is clear therefore that one sort of thing is not
intermingled with another in this way, but there must be in
things a mixture of invisible seeds that are common to many
sorts.

'But,' you may object, 'it often happens in mountainous

898 country that nearby tops of tall trees are rubbed together by the force of strong south winds till suddenly they blossom out[49] into a blaze of flame.' Agreed. And yet there is no fire embedded in the wood. What it does contain is a multitude of seeds of heat, which start a conflagration in the forest only when they have been concentrated by rubbing. If there were ready-made flame concealed in the wood, the fires could not be hidden for any length of time; they would spread havoc through the

906 woodland and burn the trees to ashes. Now do you see the point of my previous remark, that it makes a great difference in what combinations and positions the same elements occur and what motions they mutually pass on and take over, so that with a little reshuffling the same ones may produce forests and fires? This is just how the words themselves are formed, by a little reshuffling of the letters, when we pronounce 'forests' and 'fires' as two distinct utterances.[50]

If you cannot account for what you see happen without inventing particles of matter with the same sort of nature as the

917 whole objects, there is an end of your elements altogether; you will have to postulate particles that shake their sides with uproarious guffaws and bedew their cheeks with salt tears.

And now pay special attention to what follows and listen more intently. I am well aware how full it is of obscurity. But high hope of fame has struck my heart with its holy staff and in so doing has implanted in my breast the sweet love of the Muses. That is the spur that lends my spirit strength to pioneer through pathless tracts of their Pierian realm where no foot has

926 ever trod before.[51] What joy it is to light upon virgin springs and drink their waters. What joy to pluck new flowers and gather for my brow a glorious garland from fields whose blossoms were never yet wreathed by the Muses round any head. This is my reward for teaching on these lofty topics, for struggling to loose men's minds from the tight knots of superstition and shedding on dark material the bright beams of my song that irradiate everything with the sparkle of the Muses. My art is not without a purpose. Physicians, when they wish to treat children with a nasty dose of wormwood, first smear the

rim of the cup with the sweet yellow fluid of honey. The   938
children, too young as yet for foresight, are lured by the
sweetness at their lips into swallowing the bitter draught. So
they are tricked but not trapped, for the treatment restores
them to health. In the same way our doctrine often seems
unpalatable to those who have not handled it, and the masses
shrink from it.[52] That is why I have tried to administer my
philosophy to you in the dulcet strains of poesy, to touch it with   947
the sweet honey of the Muses. My object has been to engage
your mind with my verses while you gain insight into the
nature of the universe and the pattern of its architecture.[53]

Well then, since I have shown that there are completely solid
indestructible particles of matter flying about through all eter-
nity, let us unroll[54] whether or not there is any limit to their
number. Similarly, as we have found that there is a vacuum, the
place or space in which things happen, let us see whether its
whole extent is limited or whether it stretches far and wide into
immeasurable depths.   958

Learn, therefore, that *the universe is not bounded in any direction.*
If it were, it would necessarily have a limit somewhere. But
clearly a thing cannot have a limit unless there is something
outside to limit it, so that the eye can follow it up to a certain
point but not beyond. Since you must admit that there is
nothing outside the universe, it can have no limit and is
accordingly without end or measure. It makes no odds in
which part of it you may take your stand: whatever spot
anyone may occupy, the universe stretches away from him just
the same in all directions without limit. Suppose for a moment   968
that the whole of space were bounded and that someone made
his way to its uttermost boundary and threw a flying dart.[55] Do
you choose to suppose that the missile, hurled with might and
main, would speed along the course on which it was aimed? Or
do you think something would block the way and stop it? You
must assume one alternative or the other. But neither of them
leaves you a loophole. Both force you to admit that the
universe continues without end. Whether there is some obstacle
lying on the boundary line that prevents the dart from going
farther on its course or whether it flies on beyond, it cannot in

980 fact have started from the boundary. With this argument I will pursue you. Wherever you may place the ultimate limit of things, I will ask you: 'Well then, what does happen to the dart?' The upshot is that the boundary cannot stand firm anywhere, and final escape from this conclusion is precluded by the limitless possibility of running away from it.

987 Further, if all the space in the universe were shut in and confined on every side by definite boundaries, the supply of matter would already have accumulated by its own weight at the bottom,[56] and nothing could happen under the dome of the sky – indeed, there would be no sky and no sunlight, since all the available matter would have settled down and would be lying in a heap throughout eternity. As it is, no rest is given to the atoms, because there is no bottom where they can accumulate and take up their abode. Things go on happening all the time through ceaseless movement in every direction; and atoms of matter bouncing up from below are supplied out of the

998 infinite. Lastly it is a matter of observation that one thing is limited by another. The hills are demarcated by air, and air by the hills. Land sets bounds to sea, and sea to every land. But the universe has nothing outside to limit it. There is therefore a limitless abyss of space, such that even the dazzling flashes of the lightning cannot traverse it in their course, racing through an interminable tract of time, nor can they even shorten the distance still to be covered. So vast is the scope that lies open to things far and wide without limit in any dimension.

The universe is restrained from setting any limit to itself by nature, which compels body to be bounded by vacuum and vacuum by body. Thus nature either makes them both infinite in alternation, or else one of them, if it is not bounded by the other, must extend in a pure state without limit. ⟨Space, however, being infinite, so must matter be. Otherwise⟩ neither sea nor land nor the bright zones of the sky nor mortal beings nor the holy bodies of the gods[57] could endure for one brief hour of time. The supply of matter would be shaken loose from combination and swept through the vastness of the void in isolated particles; or rather, it would never have coalesced to form anything, since its scattered particles could never have been driven into union.

1010

Certainly the atoms did not post themselves purposefully in due order by an act of intelligence, nor did they stipulate what movements each should perform.[58] As they have been rushing everlastingly throughout all space in their myriads, undergoing a myriad changes under the disturbing impact of collisions, they have experienced every variety of movement and conjunction till they have fallen into the particular pattern by which this world of ours is constituted. This world has persisted many a long year, having once been set going in the appropriate motions. From these everything else follows. The rivers replenish the thirsty sea with profuse streams of water. Incubated by the sun's heat, the earth renews its fruits, and the brood of animals that springs from it grows lustily. The gliding fires of ether sustain their life. None of these results would be possible if there were not an ample supply of matter to bounce up out of infinite space in replacement of all that is lost. Just as animals deprived of food waste away through loss of body, so everything must decay as soon as its supply of matter goes astray and is cut off.[59]

Whatever world the atoms have combined to form, impacts from without cannot preserve it at every point. By continual battering they can hold back part of it till others come along to make good the deficiency. But they are compelled now and then to bounce back and in so doing to leave ample space and time for the atoms to break free from combination. It is thus essential that there should be great numbers of atoms coming up. Indeed, the impacts themselves could not be maintained without an unlimited supply of matter from all quarters.

There is one belief,[60] Memmius, that you must beware of entertaining – *the theory that everything tends towards what they call 'the centre of the universe'*. On this theory, the world stands fast without any impacts from without, and top and bottom cannot be parted in any direction, because everything has been tending towards the centre – if you can believe that anything rests upon itself. Whatever heavy bodies there may be under the earth must then tend upwards and rest against the surface upside down, like the images of things which we now see reflected in water. In the same way they would have it that animals walk

1021

1029

1041

1052

1061 about topsy-turvy and cannot fall off the earth into the nether quarters of the sky any more than our bodies can soar up spontaneously into the heavenly regions. When they are looking at the sun, we see the stars of night; so they share the hours with us alternately and experience nights corresponding to our days. But this is an idle fancy of fools who have got hold of the wrong end of the stick. There can be no centre in infinity. And, even if there were, nothing could stand fast there rather than flee from it. For all place or space, at the centre no less than elsewhere, must give way to heavy bodies, no matter in what direction they are moving. There is no place to which bodies can come where they lose the property of weight and stand still in the void. And vacuum cannot support anything but rather must allow it free passage, as its own nature demands. Therefore things cannot be held in combination by this means through surrender to a craving for the centre.

1072

Besides, they do not claim that all bodies have this tendency towards the centre, but only those of moisture and earth – the waters of the deep and the floods that pour down from the hills and in general whatever is composed of a more or less earthy body. But according to their teaching the light breaths of air and hot fires are simultaneously wafted outwards away from the centre. The reason why the encircling ether twinkles with stars and the sun feeds its flames in the blue pastures of the sky is supposed to be that fire all congregates there in its flight from the centre. Similarly, the topmost branches of trees could not break into leaf unless their food had this same upward urge. ⟨But,[61] if you allow matter to escape from the world in this way,⟩ you are leaving the ramparts of the world at liberty to crumble of a sudden and take flight with the speed of flame into the boundless void. The rest will follow. The thunder-breeding quarters of the sky will rush down from aloft. The ground will fall away from our feet, its particles dissolved amid the mingled wreckage of heaven and earth. The whole world will vanish into the abyss, and in the twinkling of an eye no remnant will be left but empty space and invisible atoms. At whatever point you first allow matter to fall short, this will be the gateway to perdition. Through this gate the whole concourse of matter will come streaming out.[62]

1085

1100

If you take a little trouble, you will attain to a thorough 1114
understanding of these truths. For one thing will be illumined
by another, and eyeless night will not rob you of your road till
you have looked into the heart of nature's darkest mysteries. So
surely will facts throw light upon facts.

BOOK TWO

MOVEMENTS AND SHAPES OF ATOMS

What joy it is, when out at sea the stormwinds are lashing the waters, to gaze from the shore at the heavy stress some other man is enduring![1] Not that anyone's afflictions are in themselves a source of delight; but to realize from what troubles you yourself are free is joy indeed. What joy, again, to watch opposing hosts marshalled on the field of battle when you have yourself no part in their peril! But this is the greatest joy of all: to possess a quiet sanctuary, stoutly fortified by the teaching of the wise, and to gaze down from that elevation on others wandering aimlessly in search of a way of life, pitting their wits one against another, disputing for precedence, struggling night and day[2] with unstinted effort to scale the pinnacles of wealth and power. O joyless hearts of men! O minds without vision! How dark and dangerous the life in which this tiny span is lived away! Do you not see that nature is barking for two things only, a body free from pain, a mind released from worry and fear for the enjoyment of pleasurable sensations?

So we find that the requirements of our bodily nature are few indeed, no more than is necessary to banish pain, and also to spread out[3] many pleasures for ourselves. Nature does not periodically seek anything more gratifying than this, not complaining if there are no golden images of youths about the house, holding flaming torches in their right hands to illumine banquets prolonged into the night.[4] What matter if the hall does not sparkle with silver and gleam with gold, and no carved and gilded rafters ring to the music of the lute? Nature does not miss these luxuries when men recline in company on the soft grass by a running stream under the branches of a tall tree and refresh their bodies pleasurably at small expense. Better still if the weather smiles upon them, and the season of the year stipples the green herbage with flowers. Burning fevers flee no swifter from your body if you toss under figured counterpanes and coverlets of crimson than if you must lie in rude homespun.[5]

If our bodies are not profited by treasures or titles or the   37
majesty of kingship, we must go on to admit that neither are
our minds. Or tell me, Memmius, when you see your legions
thronging the Campus Martius[6] in the ardour of mimic warfare,
supported by ample auxiliaries and a force of cavalry, magnifi-
cently armed and fired by a common purpose, does that sight
scare the terrors of superstition from your mind? Does the fear
of death retire from your breast and leave it carefree? Or do we   47
not find such resources absurdly ineffective? The fears and
anxieties that dog the human breast do not shrink from the
clash of arms or the fierce rain of missiles. They stalk unabashed
among princes and potentates. They are not awestruck by the
gleam of gold or the bright sheen of purple robes.

Can you doubt then that this power rests with reason alone?
All life is a struggle in the dark.[7] As children in blank darkness
tremble and start at everything, so we in broad daylight are
oppressed at times by fears as baseless as those horrors which
children imagine coming upon them in the dark. This dread   59
and darkness of the mind cannot be dispelled by the sunbeams,
the shining shafts of day, but only by an understanding of the
outward form and inner workings of nature.

And now to business. I will explain *the motion by which the
generative bodies of matter give birth to various things*, and, after they
are born, dissolve them once more; the force that compels them
to do this; and the power of movement through the boundless
void with which they are endowed. It is for you to devote
yourself attentively to my words.   67

Be sure that matter does not stick together in a solid mass.
For we see that everything grows less and seems to melt away
with the lapse of time and withdraw its old age from our eyes.
And yet we see no diminution in the sum of things. This is
because the bodies that are shed lessen the thing they leave but
enlarge the thing they join; here they bring decay, there full
bloom, but they do not settle. So the sum of things is perpetually
renewed. Mortals live by mutual interchange.[8] One race increases
by another's decrease. The generations of living things pass in
swift succession and like runners hand on the torch of life.[9]

80   If you think that the atoms can stop and by their stopping generate new motions in things, you are wandering far from the path of truth. Since the atoms are moving freely through the void, they must all be kept in motion either by their own weight or on occasion by the impact of another atom.[10] For it must often happen that two of them in their course knock together and immediately bounce apart in opposite directions, a natural consequence of their hardness and solidity and the 88 absence of anything behind to stop them.[11]

    As a further indication that all particles of matter are on the move, remember that the universe is bottomless: there is no place where the atoms could come to rest. As I have already shown by various arguments and proved conclusively, space is without end or limit and spreads out immeasurably in all directions alike.[12]

    It clearly follows that no rest is given to the atoms in their course through the depths of space. Driven along in an incessant but variable movement, some of them bounce far apart after a 98 collision while others recoil only a short distance from the impact. From those that do not recoil far, being driven into a closer union and held there by the entanglement of their interlocking shapes, are composed firmly rooted rock, the stubborn strength of steel and the like. Those others that move freely through larger tracts of space – few and far between, springing far apart and carried far by the rebound – these provide for us thin air and blazing sunlight. Besides these, there are many other atoms at large in empty space that have been thrown out of compound bodies and have nowhere even been 111 granted admittance so as to bring their motions into harmony.

    This process, as I might point out, is illustrated by an image[13] of it that is continually taking place before our very eyes. Observe what happens when sunbeams are admitted into a building and shed light on its shadowy places. You will see a multitude of tiny particles mingling in a multitude of ways in the empty space within the actual light of the beam, as though contending in everlasting conflict, rushing into battle rank upon rank with never a moment's pause in a rapid sequence of unions and disunions. From this you may picture what it is for

the atoms to be perpetually tossed about in the illimitable void. 122
To some extent a small thing may afford an illustration and an
imperfect image of great things. Besides, there is a further
reason why you should give your mind to these particles that
are seen dancing in a sunbeam: their dancing is an actual
indication of underlying movements of matter that are hidden
from sight. There you will see many particles under the impact
of invisible blows changing their course and driven back upon
their tracks, this way and that, in all directions. You must   131
understand that they all derive this restlessness from the atoms.
It originates with the atoms, which move of themselves. Then
those small compound bodies that are least removed from the
impetus of the atoms are set in motion by the impact of their
invisible blows and in turn cannon against slightly larger blows.
So the movement mounts up from the atoms and gradually
emerges to the level of our senses, so that those bodies are in
motion that we see in sunbeams, moved by blows that remain in-
visible.[14]

And now, Memmius, as to the rate at which the atoms move,   142
you may gauge this readily from these few indications. First,
when dawn sprays the earth with new-born light and the birds,
flitting through pathless thickets, fill the neighbourhood accord-
ing to their kind with liquid notes that glide through the thin
air, it is plain and palpable for all to see how suddenly the sun
at the moment of his rising drenches and clothes the world
with his radiance. But the heat and the bright light that the sun
emits do not travel through empty space. Therefore they are
forced to move more slowly, cleaving their way as it were   152
through waves of air. And the atoms that compose this radiance
do not travel as isolated individuals but linked and massed
together. Thus their pace is retarded by one dragging back
another as well as by external obstacles. But, when separate
atoms are travelling in solitary solidity through empty space,[15]
they encounter no obstruction from without and move as
single units, being composed of their own parts,[16] on the
course on which they have embarked. Obviously therefore they
must far outstrip the sunlight in speed of movement and
traverse an extent of space many times as great in the time it

165 takes for the sun's rays to flash across the sky ... ⟨No wonder that men⟩ cannot follow the individual atoms, so as to discern the agency by which everything is brought about.

171 In the face of these truths,[17] some people who know nothing of matter believe that nature without the guidance of the gods could not bring round the changing seasons in such perfect conformity to human needs, creating the crops and those other blessings that mortals are led to enjoy by the guide of life, divine pleasure, which coaxes them through the arts of Venus to reproduce their kind, lest the human race should perish. Obviously, in imagining that the gods established everything for the sake of men, they have stumbled in all respects far from the path of truth. Even if I knew nothing of the atoms, I would venture to assert on the evidence of the celestial phenomena themselves, supported by many other arguments, that the universe was certainly not created for us by divine power: it is so

182 full of imperfections. All this, Memmius, I will elucidate for you at a later stage.[18] Now let me complete my account of atomic movements.

Now, I should judge, is the place to insert a demonstration that *no material thing can be uplifted or travel upwards by its own power.* Do not be misled by the particles that compose flame. The fact that all weights taken by themselves tend downwards does not prevent lusty crops and trees[19] from being born with an upward thrust and from growing and increasing upwards. Similarly, when fires leap up to the housetops and lick beams and rafters with rapid flame, it must not be supposed that they

193 do this of their own accord with no force to fling them up. Their behaviour is like that of blood released from our body when it spouts forth[20] and springs aloft in a gory fountain. Observe also with what force beams and rafters are heaved up by water. The more we have shoved them down into the depths, many of us struggling strenuously together to push them under, the more eagerly the water spews and ejects them back again, so that more than half their bulk shoots up above the surface. And yet, I should judge, we have no doubt that all these, taken by themselves, would move downwards through

empty space. It must be just the same with flames: under 203
pressure they can shoot up through the gusty air, although
their weight, taken by itself, strives to tug them down. Do you
observe how the nocturnal torches of the sky in their lofty
flight draw in their wake long trails of flame in whatever
direction nature has set their course? Do you see how stars and
meteors fall upon the earth? The sun from the summit of the
sky scatters heat in all directions and sows the fields with light. 212
The sun's radiance therefore tends also towards the earth. Note
again how the lightning flies through the rain-storms aslant.
The fires that break out of the clouds rush together, now this
way, now that; often enough the fiery force falls upon the
earth.[21]

In this connection there is another fact that I want you to
grasp. *When the atoms are travelling straight down through empty*
space by their own weight, at quite indeterminate times and places they
swerve[22] *ever so little from their course*, just so much that you can call 220
it a change of direction. If it were not for this swerve, every-
thing would fall downwards like raindrops through the abyss
of space. No collision would take place and no impact of atom
upon atom would be created. Thus nature would never have
created anything.

If anyone[23] supposes that heavier atoms on a straight course
through empty space could outstrip lighter ones and fall on
them from above, thus causing impacts that might give rise to
generative motions, he is going far astray from the path of
truth. The reason why objects falling through water or thin air 230
must accelerate their fall in proportion to their weight is simply
that the matter composing water or air cannot obstruct all
objects equally, but is forced to give way more speedily to
heavier ones. But empty space can offer no resistance to any
object in any quarter at any time, so as not to yield free passage
as its own nature demands. Therefore, through undisturbed
vacuum all bodies must travel at equal speed though impelled
by unequal weights.[24] The heavier will never be able to fall on
the lighter from above or generate of themselves impacts
leading to that variety of motions out of which nature can

242 produce things. We are thus forced back to the conclusion that
the atoms swerve a little – but only by a minimum,[25] or we
shall be caught imagining slantwise movements, and the facts
will prove us wrong. For we see plainly and indisputably that
weights, when they come tumbling down, have no power of
their own to move aslant, so far as meets the eye. But who can
possibly perceive that they do not diverge in the very least
from a vertical course?

251

Again, if all movement is always interconnected, the new
arising from the old in a determinate order – if the atoms never
swerve so as to originate some new movement that will snap
the bonds of fate,[26] the everlasting sequence of cause and effect
– what is the source of the free will possessed by living things
throughout the earth? What, I repeat, is the source of that will-
power snatched from the fates, whereby we follow the path
along which we are severally led by pleasure, swerving from
our course at no set time or place but at the bidding of our
own hearts?[27] There is no doubt that on these occasions the will
261 of the individual originates the movements that trickle through
his limbs. Observe, when the starting-barriers are flung back,
how the racehorses in the eagerness of their strength cannot
break away as suddenly as their hearts desire. For the whole
supply of matter must first be mobilized throughout every
member of the body: only then, when it is mustered in a
continuous array, can it respond to the prompting of the heart.
So you may see that the beginning of movement is generated
by the heart; starting from the voluntary action of the mind,[28] it
272 is then transmitted throughout the body and the limbs. Quite
different is our experience when we are shoved along by a blow
inflicted with compulsive force by someone else. In that case it
is obvious that all the matter of our body is set going and
pushed along against our will, till a check is imposed through
the limbs by the will. Do you see the difference? Although
many men are driven by an external force and often constrained
involuntarily to advance or to rush headlong, yet there is
within the human breast something that can fight against this
force and resist it. At its command the supply of matter is
forced at times to take a new course through our limbs and

44

joints or is checked in its course and brought once more to a   283
halt. So also in the atoms you must recognize the same possibil-
ity: besides weight and impact there must be a third cause of
movement, the source of this inborn power of ours, since we
see that nothing can come out of nothing. For the weight of an
atom prevents its movements from being completely determined
by the impact of other atoms. But the fact that the mind itself
has no internal necessity to determine its every act and compel   291
it to suffer in helpless passivity – this is due to the slight swerve
of the atoms at no determinate time or place.[29]

The supply of matter[30] *in the universe was never more tightly packed*
than it is now, or more widely spaced out. For nothing is ever added
to it or subtracted from it. It follows that the movement of
atoms today is no different from what it was in bygone ages
and always will be. So the things that have regularly come into
being will continue to come into being in the same manner;
they will be and grow and flourish so far as each is allowed by   302
the laws of nature. The sum of things cannot be changed by
any force. For there is no place into which any kind of matter
might escape out of the universe or out of which some newly
risen force could break into the universe and transform the
whole nature of things and reverse their movements.

   In this connection there is one fact that need occasion no
surprise. *Although all the atoms are in motion, their totality appears*
to stand totally motionless,[31] except for such movements as particu-
lar objects may make with their own bodies. This is because the
atoms all lie far below the range of our senses. Since they are   314
themselves invisible, their movements must also elude observa-
tion. Indeed, even visible objects, when set at a distance, often
disguise their movements. Often on a hillside fleecy sheep, as
they crop their lush pasture, creep slowly onward, lured this
way or that by grass that sparkles with fresh dew, while the
full-fed lambs gaily frisk and butt. And yet, when we gaze from
a distance, we see only a blur – a white patch stationary on the
green hillside. Take another example. Mighty legions, waging
mimic war, are thronging the plain with their manoeuvres.[32]
The dazzling sheen flashes to the sky and all around the earth is

326 ablaze with bronze. Down below there sounds the tramp of mighty marching men's feet. A noise of shouting strikes upon the hills and reverberates to the celestial vault. Wheeling horsemen gallop hotfoot across the midst of the plain, till it quakes under the fury of their charge. And yet there is a vantage-ground high among the hills from which all these appear immobile – a blaze of light stationary upon the plain.

333 And now let us turn to a new theme – *the characteristics of the atoms of all substances, the extent to which they differ in shape and the rich multiplicity of their forms.* Not that there are not many of the same shape, but they are by no means all identical with one another. And no wonder. When the multitude of them, as I have shown, is such that it is without limit or total, it is not to be expected that they should all be identical in build and configuration.[33]

Consider the race of men, the tribes of scaly fish that swim in silence, the lusty herds, the creatures of the wild and the
343 various feathered breeds, those that throng the vivifying watery places, by river-banks and springs and lakes, and those that flock and flutter through pathless woodlands. Take a representative of any of these diverse species and you will still find that it differs in form from others of its kind. Otherwise the young could not recognize their mother, nor the mother her young. But we see that this can happen, and that individuals of these species are mutually recognizable no less than human beings.

Here is a familiar instance.[34] Outside some stately shrine of the gods incense is smouldering on the altar. Beside it a
353 slaughtered calf falls to the ground. From its breast it breathes out a hot stream of blood. But the bereaved dam, roaming through green glades, scans the ground for the twin-pitted imprint of familiar feet. Her eyes rove this way and that in search of the missing young one. She pauses and fills the leafy thickets with her plaints. Time and again she returns to the byre, sore at heart with yearning for her calf. Succulent osiers and herbage fresh with dew and her favourite streams flowing level with their banks – all these are powerless to console her and banish her new burden of distress. The sight of other

calves in the lush pastures is powerless to distract her mind relieve it of distress. So obvious is it that she misses something distinctive and recognized.

In like manner, baby kids[35] hail their own long-horned dams with quavering voices. Frisky lambs pick out their own mothers from the bleating flock. So, at nature's bidding, each usually runs to its own milk-swollen udder.

Among ears of corn, whatever the kind, you will not find one just like another; but each will be marked by some distinct- ive feature. The same holds good of the various shells we see painting the bosom of the land where the sea with pliant ripples laps on the thirsty sands of its winding shore. Here, then, is proof upon proof that in the stream of atoms likewise, since they exist by nature and are not handmade to a fixed pattern, there are certain individual differences of shape flying about.

On this principle it is quite easy to explain why the fire of lightning is far more penetrative than our fire which springs from earthly torches. You can say that the heavenly fire of the lightning is of finer texture, being composed of smaller atoms, and can therefore pass through apertures impervious to this fire of ours, which springs from wood and is generated by a torch.[36] Again, light passes through horn,[37] but rain is dashed back. Why, if not because the particles of light are smaller than those that form the life-giving drops of water? We see that wine flows through a strainer as fast as it is poured in; but sluggish oil loiters. This, no doubt, is either because oil consists of larger atoms,[38] or because these are more hooked and intertangled and, therefore, cannot separate as rapidly, so as to trickle through the holes one by one.

Here is a further example. Honey and milk, when they are rolled in the mouth, cause an agreeable sensation to the tongue. But bitter wormwood and astringent centaury screw the mouth awry with their nauseating flavour.[39] You may readily infer that such substances as titillate the senses agreeably are composed of smooth round atoms. Those that seem bitter and harsh are more tightly compacted of hooked particles and accordingly tear their way into our senses and rend our bodies by their inroads.

372

384

397

408 The same conflict between two types of structure applies to everything that strikes the senses as good or bad. You cannot suppose that the rasping stridulation of a screeching saw is formed of elements as smooth as the notes a minstrel's nimble fingers wake from the lyre-strings and mould to melody. You cannot suppose that atoms of the same shape are entering our nostrils when stinking corpses[40] are roasting as when the stage is freshly sprinkled with saffron of Cilicia[41] and a nearby altar exhales the perfumes of the Orient. You cannot attribute the same composition to sights that feast the eye with colour and those that make it smart and weep or that appear loathsome and repulsive through sheer ugliness. Nothing that gratifies the senses is ever without a certain smoothness of the constituent atoms. Whatever, on the other hand, is painful and harsh is characterized by a certain roughness of matter. Besides these there are some things that are not properly regarded as smooth but yet are not jagged with barbed spikes. These are characterized instead by slightly jutting ridges such as tickle the senses rather than hurt them. They include such things as wine-lees and piquant endive. Hot fire, again, and cold frost stab the senses of our body with teeth of a different pattern, as we learn from the different way they affect our sense of touch. For touch and nothing but touch (by all that men call holy!) is the essence of all our bodily sensations,[42] whether we feel something slipping in from outside or are hurt by something born in the body or pleasurably excited by something going out in the generative act of Venus.[43] It is touch again that is felt when the atoms are jarred by a knock so that they are disordered and upset the senses: strike any part of your own body with your hand, and you will experience this for yourself. There must, therefore, be great differences in the shapes of the atoms to provoke these different sensations.

417

429

439

Again, things that seem to us hard and stiff must be composed of deeply indented and hooked atoms and held firm by their intertangling branches.[44] In the front rank of this class stand diamonds, with their steadfast indifference to blows. Next come stout flints and the strength of hard iron and bronze that stands firm with shrieking protest when the bolt is shot.

Liquids, on the other hand, must owe their fluid consistency to   451
component atoms that are small and round. For poppy-seed can
be drawn off as easily as if it were water; the globules do not
hold one another back, and when they are jolted they tend to
roll downhill as water does. A third class is constituted by
things that you may see dissipated instantaneously, such as
smoke, clouds and flames. If their atoms are not all smooth and
round, yet they cannot be jagged and intertangled. They must   460
be such as to prick the body and even to penetrate rocks but
not to stick together; so you can readily grasp that substances
prickly to the senses are made of atoms which are sharp-pointed
but not entangled.

Do not be surprised to find that some things are both bitter
and fluid as, for instance, sea water. This, being fluid, consists
of smooth round atoms. It causes pain because of the admixture
of many rough atoms. There is no need for these to be held
together by hooks. Evidently they are spherical as well as
rough, so that they can roll round and yet hurt the senses. It   471
can be shown that Neptune's bitter brine results from a mixture
of rougher atoms with smooth. There is a way of separating the
two ingredients and viewing them in isolation by filtering the
sweet fluid through many layers of earth so that it flows out
into a pit and loses its tang. It leaves behind the atoms of
unpalatable brine because owing to their roughness they are
more apt to stick fast in the earth.

To the foregoing demonstration I will link on another fact
which will gain credence from this context: *the number of different*   480
forms of atoms is finite. If this were not so, some of the atoms
would have to be of infinite magnitude.[45] Within the narrow
limits of any single particle, there can be only a limited range of
forms. Suppose that atoms consist of three minimum parts, or
enlarge them by a few more. When by placing parts at top or
bottom and transposing left and right you have exhausted all
the possible variations of the shape of the whole atom that can
be produced by rearranging its parts; then you are obviously
left with no means of varying its form further except by adding
other parts. Thence it will follow, if you wish to vary its form

491 still further, that the arrangement will demand still other parts in exactly the same way. Variation in shape goes with increase in size. You cannot believe, therefore, that the atoms are distinguished by an infinity of forms; or you will compel some of them to be of enormous magnitude, which I have already proved to be demonstrably impossible.

502 Were it not so, the richest robes of the Orient, resplendent with the Meliboean[46] purple of Thessalian murex, or the gilded breed of peacocks, bright with laughing lustre, would pale before some new colour in things. The fragrance of myrrh and the flavour of honey would fall into contempt. The death notes of the swan and the intricate melody of Phoebus' lyre would be silenced in like manner. For whatever might be would always be surpassed by something more excellent. And, as all good things might yield to better, so might bad to worse. One thing would always be surpassed by another more offensive to nose or ear or eye or palate. Since this is not so, but things are bound by a set limit at either extreme, you must acknowledge a 514 corresponding limit to the different forms of matter. Similarly there is a limited range, from fire to the icy frosts of winter and back again. There are extremes of heat and cold, and the intermediate temperatures complete the series. They have been created, therefore, a limited distance apart, since the extremes are marked at either end with two points, one made intolerable with flames, the other by stiff frosts.[47]

524 To the foregoing demonstration I will link on another fact, which will gain credence from this context: *the number of atoms of any one form is infinite.* Since the varieties of form are limited, the number of uniform atoms must be unlimited. Otherwise the totality of matter would be finite, which I have proved in my verses[48] is not so. I have shown that the universe is kept going by an infinite succession of atoms, so that the chain of impacts from all directions remains unbroken.

You may object that certain species of animals appear to be relatively rare, so that nature seems less fertile in their case. But some other zone or environment in lands remote may abound in these, so as to make good the deficiency.[49] As the outstanding instance among quadrupeds, we may note the snaky-handed elephants. Countless thousands of these must have gone to the making of that impenetrable ivory wall with which India is barricaded.[50] Such is the abundance of these beasts, of which we see only very few samples.

537

Let us suppose for argument's sake that one unique object exists, with a body formed by birth – an object unlike anything else in the whole world. Unless there is an infinite supply of matter from which, once conceived, it can be brought to birth, it will have no chance even of being created, no prospect of further growth or replenishment. Let us further assume that a finite number of atoms generative of one particular thing are at large in the universe. What then will be the source or scene, the agency or mode, of their encounter in this multitudinous ocean of matter, this welter of foreign bodies? I see no possible means by which they could come together. Consider, when some great flotilla has been wrecked, how the mighty deep scatters floating wreckage – thwarts and ribs, yard-arms and prow, masts and oars; how stern-posts are seen adrift off the shores of every land – a warning to mortals to shun the stealth and violence and cunning of the treacherous sea and put no faith at any season in the false alluring laughter of that smooth still surface.[51] Just so will your finite class of atoms, if once you posit such a thing, be scattered and tossed about through all eternity by conflicting tides of matter. They could never be swept together so as to enter into combination; nor could they remain combined or grow by increment. Yet experience plainly shows that both these things happen: objects can be born, and after birth they can grow. It is evident, therefore, that there are infinite atoms of every kind to keep up the supply of everything.

543

553

566

The destructive motions can never permanently get the upper hand and entomb vitality for evermore. Neither can the generative and augmentative motions permanently safeguard what they have created. So the war of the elements that has raged throughout eternity continues on equal terms.[52] Now here, now there, the forces of life are victorious and in turn

576 vanquished. With the voice of mourning mingles the cry that infants raise when their eyes open on the sunlit world. Never has day given place to night or night to dawn that has not heard, blent with these infant wailings, the lamentation that attends on death and sombre obsequies.[53]

584 In this connection there is one fact that you should keep signed and sealed and recorded in the archives of memory: *there is no visible object that consists of atoms of one kind only*. Everything is composed of a mixture of elements. The more qualities and powers a thing possesses, the greater variety it attests in the form of its component atoms.

In the first place the earth contains in itself the atoms with which the measureless ocean is perpetually renewed by streams that roll down coolness. It also contains matter from which fires can arise: in many places the soil is set alight and burns, and subterranean fires sustain the furious outrush of Etna.[54] It 594 contains in addition the stores out of which it can thrust up thriving crops and lusty orchard-trees for the races of men and provide rivers and foliage and lush pasture for the wild beasts of the mountain. That is why this one being has earned such titles as Great Mother of the Gods, Mother of Beasts and progenitress of the human frame.[55]

This is she who was hymned by learned Greek poets of old. They pictured her a goddess,[56] driving a chariot drawn by a yoke of lions. By this they signified that the whole mighty mass hangs in airy space: for earth cannot rest on earth. They 604 harnessed wild beasts, because the fiercest of children cannot but be softened and subdued by the duty owed to parents.[57] Upon her head they set a battlemented crown, because earth in select spots is fortified and bears the weight of cities. Decked with this emblem even now the image of the Holy Mother, Cybele, is borne about the world in solemn state. Various nations hail her with time-honoured ceremony as the Idaean mother.[58] To bear her company they appoint a Phrygian retinue, because they claim that crops were first created[59] within the bounds of Phrygia and spread from there throughout the earth. They give her eunuchs as attendant priests, to signify that those

who have defied their mother's will and shown ingratitude to   615
their parents must be counted unworthy to bring forth living
children into the sunlit world. A thunder of drums attends her,
tight-stretched and pounded by palms, and a clash of hollow
cymbals; hoarse-throated horns bray their deep warning, and
the hollow pipe thrills every heart with Phrygian strains.[60]
Weapons are carried before her, symbolic of rabid frenzy,[61] to
chasten the thankless and profane hearts of the rabble with   623
dread of her divinity. So, when first she is escorted into some
great city and mutely enriches mortals with some wordless
benediction, they strew her path all along the route with a
lavish largesse of copper and silver and shadow the mother and
her retinue with a snow of roses. Next an armed band, whom
the Greeks call Curetes, join in rhythmic dances, merry with
blood and nodding their heads to set their terrifying crests
aflutter, whenever they joust together among the Phrygian
bands. They call to mind those Curetes of Dicte, who once
upon a time in Crete, as the story goes, drowned the wailing of   634
the infant Jove by dancing with swift feet, an armed band of
boys around a boy, and rhythmically clashing bronze on bronze,
lest Saturn should seize and crush him in his jaws and deal his
mother's heart a wound that would not heal.[62] That perhaps is
why they attend in arms upon the Great Mother. Or else they
signify that the goddess bids men be ready to defend their
native earth staunchly by force of arms and resolve to shield
their parents and do them credit. It may be claimed that all this
is aptly and admirably devised. It is nevertheless far removed
from the truth. For it is essential to the very nature of deity   646
that it should enjoy immortal existence in utter tranquillity,
aloof and detached from our affairs. It is free from all pain
and peril, strong in its own resources, exempt from any need
of us, indifferent to our merits and immune from anger. In
fact, the earth is and always has been an insentient being. The
reason why it sends up countless products in countless ways
into the sunlight is simply that it contains atoms of countless
substances.

If anyone[63] elects to call the sea Neptune and the crops Ceres
and would rather take Bacchus' name in vain than denote grape

657 juice by its proper title, we may allow him to refer to the earth as the Mother of the Gods, provided that he genuinely refrains from polluting his mind with the foul taint of superstition.

It often happens that fleecy flocks and martial steeds and horned cattle crop the herbage of a single field under the same canopy of sky and quench their thirst with the water of a single stream; yet they live according to their own kind and severally
668 keep the nature of their parents[64] and copy their behaviour. So varied is the store of matter in every sort of herb and in every stream.

Furthermore every individual animal of any species is a whole composed of various parts – bones, blood, veins, heat, moisture, flesh, sinews: and these are all widely different, being formed of differently shaped atoms.[65] Again, whatever can be set on fire and burnt must conceal in its body, if nothing else, at least the matter needed for emitting fire and radiating light, for shooting out sparks and scattering ashes all around. If you
678 mentally examine anything else by a similar procedure, you will find that it hides in its body the seeds of many substances and combines atoms of various forms.

You see that many objects are possessed of colour and taste together with smell. Principal amongst them are those many offerings ⟨which when kindled make the altars of the gods to smoke.⟩ Their component matter must therefore be multiform. For scent penetrates the human frame where tint does not[66] go; tint creeps into the senses by a different route from taste. So you may infer that they differ in their atomic forms. Different shapes
687 therefore combine in a single mass, and objects are composed of a mixture of seeds. Consider how in my verses,[67] for instance, you see many letters common to many words; yet you must admit that different verses and words are composed of different letters. Not that there is any lack of letters common to several words, or that there are no two words composed of precisely the same letters; but they do not all alike consist of exactly the same components. So in other things, although many atoms are common to many substances, yet these substances may still differ in their composition. So it can rightly be said that the human race differs in its composition from crops or orchard trees.

It must not be supposed that atoms of every sort can be linked in every 700
variety of combination. If that were so, you would see monsters
coming into being everywhere. Hybrid growths of man and
beast[68] would arise. Lofty branches would spread here and
there from a living body. Limbs of land-beast and sea-beast[69]
would often be conjoined. Chimeras[70] breathing flame from
hideous jaws would be reared by nature throughout the all-
generating earth. But it is evident that nothing of this sort 707
happens. We see that everything is created from specific seeds
and born of a specific mother and grows up true to type. We
may infer that this is determined by some specific necessity. In
every individual the atoms of its own kind, derived from all its
food,[71] disperse through its limbs and link together so as to set
going the appropriate motions. But we see extraneous matter
cast back by nature into the earth; and much is expelled from
the body,[72] under the impact of blows, in the form of invisible
particles which could not link on anywhere or harmonize with
the vital motions within so as to copy them. 717

Do not imagine that these laws are binding on animals alone.
The same principle determines everything. As all created things
differ from one another by their entire natures, so each one
must necessarily consist of distinctive forms of atoms. Not that
there is any lack of atoms of the same forms; but objects do not
all alike consist of exactly the same components. Since the seeds
are not identical, they must differ in their intervals, paths,
attachments, weights, impacts, clashes and motions. These do
not merely distinguish one animal body from another but
separate land from sea and hold the whole sky apart from the 729
earth.[73]

Give ear now to arguments that I have searched out with an
effort that was also a delight. Do not imagine that white objects
derive the snowy aspect they present to your eyes from white
atoms,[74] or that black objects are composed of a black element.
And in general do not believe that anything owes the colour it
displays to the fact that its atoms are tinted correspondingly.
The primary particles of matter have no colour whatsoever, neither the
same colour as the objects they compose nor a different one. If

739 you think the mind cannot lay hold of such bodies, you are quite wrong. Men who are blind from birth and have never looked on the sunlight have knowledge by touch of bodies that have never from the beginning been associated with any colour. It follows that on our minds also an image can impinge of bodies not marked by any tint. Indeed the things that we ourselves touch in pitch darkness are not felt by us as possessing any colour.

748 Having proved that colourless bodies are not unthinkable, I will proceed to demonstrate ⟨that the atoms must be such bodies.⟩

First, then, all colours may change completely, and all ⟨things that change colour also change themselves.⟩ But the atoms cannot possibly ⟨change colour⟩. For something must remain changeless, or everything would be absolutely annihilated. For, if ever anything is so transformed as to overstep its own limits, this means the immediate death of what was before. So do not

756 stain the atoms with colour, or you will find everything slipping back into nothing.[75]

Let us suppose, then, that the atoms are naturally colourless and that it is through the variety of their shapes that they produce the whole range of colours, a great deal depending on their combinations and positions and their reciprocal motions. You will now find it easy to explain without more ado why things that were dark-coloured a moment since can suddenly become as white as marble – as the sea, for instance, when its surface is ruffled by great winds, is turned into white wave-crests of marble lustre. You could say that something we often

768 see as dark is promptly transformed through the churning up of its matter and a reshuffling of atoms, with some additions and subtractions, so that it is seen as bleached and white. If, on the other hand, the waters of the sea were composed of blue atoms, they could not possibly be whitened: for, however you may stir up blue matter, it can never change its colour to the pallor of marble.

It might be supposed that the uniform lustre of the sea is made up of particles of different colours, as for instance a single object of a square shape is often made up of other objects of

various shapes.[76] But in the square we discern the different   780
shapes. So in the surface of the sea or in any other uniform
lustre we ought, on this hypothesis, to discern a variety of
widely different colours. Besides, differences in the shapes of
the parts are no hindrance to the whole being square in outline.
But differences in colour completely prevent it from displaying
an unvariegated lustre.

The seductive argument that sometimes tempts us to attribute   788
colours to the atoms is demolished by the fact that white
objects are not created from white material nor black from
black, but both from various colours.[77] Obviously, white could
much more readily spring from no colour at all than from
black, or from any other colour that interferes and conflicts
with it.

Again, since there can be no colours without light and the
atoms do not emerge into the light, it can be inferred that they
are not clothed in any colour. For what colour can there be in
blank darkness? Indeed, colour is itself changed by a change of   800
light, according as the beams strike it vertically or aslant.[78]
Observe the appearance in sunlight of the plumage that rings
the neck of a dove and crowns its nape: sometimes it is tinted
with the brilliant red of a ruby: at others it is seen from a
certain point of view to mingle emerald greens with the blue of
the sky. In the same way a peacock's tail, profusely illuminated,
changes colour as it is turned this way or that. These colours,
then, are produced by a particular incidence of light. Hence, no
light, no colour.

When the pupil of the eye is said to perceive the colour   810
white, it experiences in fact a particular kind of impact. When it
perceives black, or some other colour, the impact is different.
But, when you touch things, it makes no odds what colour they
may be, but only what is their shape. The inference is that the
atoms have no need of colour, but cause various sensations of
touch according to their various shapes.

Since there is no natural connection between particular col-
ours and particular shapes, atoms might equally well be of any
colour irrespective of their form. Why then are not their
compounds tinted with every shade of colour irrespective of

822 their kind? We should expect on this hypothesis that ravens in flight would often emit a snowy sheen from snowy wings: and that some swans would be black, being composed of black atoms, or would display some other uniform or variegated colour.[79]

Again, the more anything is divided into tiny parts, the more you can see its colour gradually dimming and fading out. When 830 red cloth, for instance, is pulled to pieces thread by thread, its crimson or scarlet colour, than which there is none brighter, is all dissipated. From this you may gather that, before its particles are reduced right down to atoms, they would shed all their colour.

Finally, since you acknowledge that not all objects emit noise or smell, you accept that as a reason for not attributing sounds and scents to everything. On the same principle, since we cannot perceive everything by eye, we may infer that some things are colourless, just as some things are scentless and 840 soundless, and that these can be apprehended by the percipient mind as readily as things that are lacking in some other quality.[80]

Do not imagine that colour is the only quality that is denied to the atoms. *They are also wholly devoid of warmth and cold and scorching heat: they are barren of sound and starved of savour, and emit* [81] *no inherent odour from their bodies.* When you are setting out to prepare a pleasant perfume[82] of marjoram or myrrh or flower of spikenard, which breathes nectar into our nostrils, your first task is to select so far as possible an oil that is naturally 851 colourless and sends out no exhalation to our nostrils. This will be least likely to corrupt the scents blended and concocted with its substance by contamination with its own taint. For the same reason the atoms must not impart to things at their birth a scent or sound that is their own property, since they can send nothing out of themselves; nor must they contribute any flavour or cold or heat, whether scorching or mild, or anything else of the kind.

These qualities, again, are perishable things, made pliable by the softness of their substance, breakable by its crumbliness and penetrable by its looseness of texture. They must be kept far

apart from the atoms, if we wish to provide the universe with   862
imperishable foundations on which it may rest secure; or else
you will find everything slipping back into nothing.

At this stage you must admit that *whatever is seen to be sentient is
nevertheless composed of atoms that are insentient.*[83] The phenomena
open to our observation do not contradict this conclusion or
conflict with it. Rather they lead us by the hand and compel us to   870
believe that the animate is born, as I maintain, of the insentient.

As a particular instance, we can point to living worms,
emerging from foul dung[84] when the earth is soaked and rotted
by intemperate showers. Besides, we see every sort of substance
transformed in the same way. Rivers, foliage and lush pastures
are transformed into cattle; the substance of cattle is transformed
into our bodies: and often enough our bodies go to build up
the strength of predatory beasts or the bodies of the lords of
the air. So nature transforms all foods into living bodies and
generates from them all the senses of animate creatures, just as   880
it makes dry wood blossom[85] out in flame and transfigures it
wholly into fire. So now do you see that it makes a great
difference in what order the various atoms are arranged and
with what others they are combined so as to impart and take
over motions?

What is it, then, that jogs the mind itself and moves and com-
pels it to express certain sentiments, so that you do not believe
that the sentient is generated by the insentient? Obviously it is
the fact that a mixture of water and wood and earth cannot of
itself bring about vital sensibility. There is one relevant point   890
you should bear in mind: I am not maintaining that sensations
are generated automatically from all the elements out of which
sentient things are created. Everything depends on the size and
shape of the sense-producing atoms and on their appropriate
motions, arrangements and positions.[86] None of these is found
in wood or clods of earth. And yet these substances, when they
are fairly well rotted by showers, give birth to little worms,
because the particles of matter are jolted out of their old
arrangements by a new factor and combined in such a way that
animate objects must result.

902 Again, those[87] who would have it that sensation can be produced only by sensitive bodies, which originate in their turn from others similarly sentient — ⟨these theorists are making the foundations of our senses perishable⟩, because they are making them soft. For sensitivity is always associated with flesh, sinews, veins — all things that we see to be soft and composed of perishable stuff.

907 Let us suppose, for argument's sake, that particles of these substances could endure everlastingly. The sensation with which they are credited must be either that of a part or else similar to that of an animate being as a whole. But it is impossible for parts by themselves to experience sensation: all the sensations felt in our limbs are felt by us as a whole; a hand or any other member severed from the whole body is quite powerless to retain sensation on its own.[88] There remains the alternative that such particles have senses like those of an animate being as a whole. They must then feel precisely what we feel, so as to share in all our vital sensations. How then can they pass for 917 elements and escape the path of death, since they are animate beings, and animate and mortal are one and the same thing? Even supposing they could escape death, yet they will make nothing by their combination and conjunction but a mob or horde of living things, just as men and cattle and wild beasts obviously could not combine so as to give birth to a single thing. If we suppose that they shed their own sentience from their bodies and acquire another one, what is the point of giving them the one that is taken away? Besides, as we saw before, from the fact that we perceive birds' eggs turning into live fledgelings and worms swarming out when the earth has been rotted by intemperate showers, we may infer that sense may be generated from the insentient.

Suppose someone[89] asserts that sense can indeed emerge from the insentient, but only by some transformation or some creative process comparable to birth. He will be adequately answered by a clear demonstration that birth and transformation occur only as the result of union or combination. Admittedly sensation cannot arise in any body until an animate creature has been born. This of course is because the requisite matter is

dispersed through air and streams and earth and the products   940
of earth: it has not come together in the appropriate manner, so
as to set in mutual operation those vivifying motions that
kindle the all-watchful senses which keep watch over every
animate creature.

When any animate creature is suddenly assailed by a more
powerful blow[90] than its nature can withstand, all the senses of
body and mind are promptly thrown into confusion. For the   947
juxtapositions of the atoms are unknit, and the vital motions
are inwardly obstructed, until the matter, jarred and jolted
throughout every limb, loosens the vital knots of the spirit
from the body and expels the spirit in scattered particles through
every pore. What other effect can we attribute to the infliction
of a blow than this of shaking and shattering everything to
bits? Besides, it often happens, when the blow is less violently
inflicted, that such vital motions as survive emerge victorious:
they assuage the immense upheavals resulting from the shock,
recall every particle to its proper courses, break up the advance   958
of death when it is all but master of the body and rekindle the
well-nigh extinguished senses. How else could living creatures
on the very threshold of death rally their consciousness and
return to life rather than make good their departure by a route
on which they have already travelled most of the way?

Again, pain occurs when particles of matter have been unset-
tled by some force within the living flesh of the limbs and
stagger in their inmost stations. When they slip back into place,
that is blissful pleasure.[91] It follows that the atoms cannot be
afflicted by any pain or experience any pleasure in themselves,   969
since they are not composed of any primal particles, by some
reversal of whose movements they might suffer anguish or reap
some fruition of life-giving bliss. They cannot therefore be
endowed with any power of sensation.

Again, if we are to account for the power of sensation
possessed by animate creatures in general by attributing sen-
tience to their atoms, what of those atoms that specifically
compose the human race? Presumably they are not merely
sentient, but also shake their sides with uproarious guffaws
and besprinkle their cheeks with dewy teardrops[92] and even

979 discourse profoundly and at length about the composition of the universe and proceed to ask of what elements they are themselves composed. If they are to be likened to entire mortals, they must certainly consist of other elemental particles, and these again of others. There is no point at which you may call a halt, but I will follow you there with your argument that whatever speaks or laughs or thinks is composed of particles that do the same. Let us acknowledge that this is stark madness

985 and lunacy: one can laugh without being composed of laughing particles, can think and proffer learned arguments though sprung from seeds neither thoughtful nor eloquent. Why then cannot the things that we see gifted with sensation be compounded of seeds that are wholly senseless?

Lastly, we are all sprung from heavenly seed. All alike have the same father, from whom all-nourishing mother earth receives the showering drops of moisture.[93] Thus fertilized, she gives birth to smiling crops and lusty trees, to mankind and all

996 the breeds of beasts. She it is that yields the food on which they all feed their bodies, lead their joyous lives and renew their race. So she has well earned the name of mother. In like manner this matter returns: what came from earth goes back into the earth; what was sent down from the ethereal vault is readmitted to the precincts of heaven. Death does not put an end to things by annihilating the component particles but by breaking up their conjunction.[94] Then it links them in new combinations, making everything change in shape and colour and give up in an instant the gift of sensation it has just

1008 acquired. So you may realize what a difference it makes in what combinations and positions the same elements occur, and what motions they mutually pass on and take over. You will thus avoid the mistake of conceiving as permanent properties of the atoms the qualities that are seen floating on the surface of things, coming into being from time to time and as suddenly perishing. Obviously it makes a great difference in these verses of mine in what context and order the letters are arranged. For the letters which denote sky, sea, earth and rivers also denote crops, trees and animals. If not all, at least the greater part is alike. But differences in their position distinguish word from

word. Just so with actual objects: when there is a change in the 1019
combination, motion, order, position or shapes of the com-
ponent matter, there must be a corresponding change in the
object composed.

Give your mind now to the true reasoning I have to unfold. A
new fact is battling strenuously for access to your ears. A new
aspect of the universe is striving to reveal itself. But no fact is so 1026
simple that it is not harder to believe than to doubt at the first
presentation. Equally, there is nothing so mighty or so marvel-
lous that the wonder it evokes does not tend to diminish in
time. Take first the pure and undimmed lustre of the sky and all
that it enshrines: the stars that roam across its surface, the moon
and the surpassing splendour of the sunlight. If all these sights
were now displayed to mortal view for the first time by a swift
unforeseen revelation, what miracle could be recounted greater
than this? What would men before the revelation have been less
prone to conceive as possible? Nothing, surely. So marvellous 1037
would have been that sight – a sight which no one now, you
will admit, thinks worthy of an upward glance into the luminous
regions of the sky. So has satiety blunted the appetite of our
eyes.[95] Desist, therefore, from thrusting out reasoning from
your mind because of its disconcerting novelty. Weigh it,
rather, with discerning judgement. Then, if it seems to you true,
give in. If it is false, gird yourself to oppose it. For the mind
wants to discover by reasoning what exists in the infinity of
space that lies out there, beyond the ramparts of this world –
that region into which the intellect longs to peer and into which 1047
the free projection of the mind does actually extend its flight.

Here, then, is my first point. In all directions alike, on this
side or that, upward or downward through the universe, there
is no end. This I have shown,[96] and indeed the fact proclaims
itself aloud and the nature of space makes it crystal clear.
Granted, then, that empty space extends without limit in every
direction and that seeds innumerable in number are rush-
ing on countless courses through an unfathomable universe
under the impulse of perpetual motion, *it is in the highest
degree unlikely that this earth and sky is the only one to have been*

1057   *created*[97] and that all those particles of matter outside are accomplishing nothing. This follows from the fact that our world has been made by nature through the spontaneous and casual collision and the multifarious, accidental, random[98] and purposeless congregation and coalescence of atoms whose suddenly formed combinations could serve on each occasion as the starting-point of substantial fabrics – earth and sea and sky and the races of living creatures. On every ground, therefore, you

1064 must admit that there exist elsewhere other clusters of matter similar to this one which the ether clasps in ardent embrace.

When there is plenty of matter in readiness, when space is available and no cause or circumstance impedes, then surely things must be wrought and effected. You have a store of atoms that could not be counted out by the whole population of living creatures throughout history. You have the same natural force to congregate them in any place precisely as they have been congregated here. You are bound therefore to

1076 acknowledge that in other regions there are other earths and various tribes of men and breeds of beasts.

Add to this the fact that nothing in the universe is the only one of its kind, unique and solitary in its birth and growth; everything is a member of a species comprising many individuals. Turn your mind first to the animals. You will find the rule applies to the brutes that prowl the mountains, to the double-breed[99] of men, the voiceless scaly fish and all the forms of flying things. So you must admit that sky, earth, sun, moon, sea and the rest are not solitary, but rather numberless. For a

1088 firmly established limit is set to their lives also and their bodies also are a product of birth, no less than that of any creature that flourishes here according to its kind.

Bear this well in mind, and you will immediately perceive that *nature is free and uncontrolled by proud masters* and runs the universe by herself without the aid of gods.[100] For who – by the sacred hearts of the gods who pass their unruffled lives, their placid aeon, in calm and peace! – who can rule the sum total of the measureless? Who can hold in coercive hand the strong reins of the unfathomable? Who can spin all the firma-

ments alike and foment with the fires of ether all the fruitful
earths? Who can be in all places at all times, ready to darken the
clear sky with clouds and rock it with a thunderclap – to launch
bolts that may often wreck his own temples, or retire and spend
his fury letting fly at deserts with that missile which often
passes by the guilty and slays the innocent and blameless?[101]

After the natal[102] season of the world, the birthday of sea and
lands and the uprising of the sun, many atoms have been added
from without, many seeds contributed on every side by bom-
bardment from the universe at large. From these the sea and
land could gather increase: the dome of heaven could gain
more room and lift its rafters high above the earth, and the air
could climb upwards. From every corner of the universe atoms
are being chipped and circulated to each thing according to its
own kind: water goes to water, earth swells with earthy matter;
fire is forged by fires, ether by ether. At length everything is
brought to its utmost limit of growth by nature, the creatress
and perfectress. This is reached when what is poured into the
veins of life is no more than what flows and drains away. Here
the growing-time of everything must halt. Here nature checks
the increase of her own strength. The things you see growing
merrily in stature and climbing the stairs of maturity step by
step – these are gaining more atoms than they lose. The food is
easily introduced into all their veins; and they themselves are
not so widely expanded as to shed much matter and squander
more than their age absorbs as nourishment. It must, of course,
be conceded that many particles ebb and drain away from
things. But more particles must accrue, until they have touched
the topmost peak of growth. Thereafter the strength and vigour
of maturity is gradually broken, and age slides down the path
of decay. Obviously the bulkier anything is and the more
expanded when it begins to wane, the more particles it sheds
and gives off from every surface. The food is not easily
distributed through all its veins, or supplied in sufficient quanti-
ties to make good the copious effluences it exudes. It is natural,
therefore, that everything should perish when it is thinned out
by the ebbing out of matter and succumbs to blows from

1141 without. The food supply is no longer adequate for its aged frame, and the deadly bombardment of particles from without never pauses in the work of dissolution and subdual.

In this way the ramparts of the great world also will be breached and collapse in crumbling ruin about us. For everything must be restored and renewed by food,[103] and by food buttressed and sustained. And the process is doomed to failure, because the veins do not admit enough and nature does not 1149 supply all that is needed. Already the life-force is broken. The earth, which generated every living species and once brought forth from its womb the bodies of huge beasts, has now scarcely strength to generate tiny creatures.[104] For I assume that the races of mortal creatures were not let down into the fields from heaven by a golden cord,[105] nor generated from the sea or the rock-beating surf,[106] but born of the same earth that now provides their nurture. The same earth in her prime spontaneously generated for mortals smiling crops and lusty vines, 1160 sweet fruits and gladsome pastures, which now can scarcely be made to grow by our toil. We wear down the oxen and wear out the strength of farmers, we wear out the ploughshare and find ourselves scarcely supplied by the fields that grudge their fruits and multiply our toil. Already the ploughman of ripe years shakes his head with many a sigh that his heavy labours have gone for nothing: and, when he compares the present with the past,[107] he often applauds his father's luck. In the same despondent vein, the cultivator of old and wilted vines decries the trend of the times and rails at heaven. He grumbles that 1171 past generations, when men were old-fashioned and god-fearing, supported life easily enough on their small farms, though one man's holding was then far less than now. He does not realize that everything is gradually decaying and going aground onto the rocks,[108] worn out by old age.

BOOK THREE

LIFE AND MIND

You,[1] who out of such black darkness were first[2] to lift up so shining a light,[3] revealing the hidden blessings of life – you are my leader, O glory of the Grecian race. In your well-marked footprints now I plant my resolute steps. It is from love alone that I long to imitate you, not from emulous ambition. Shall the swallow contend in song with the swan, or the kid match its rickety legs in a race with the strong-limbed steed? You are our father, illustrious discoverer of truth, and give me a father's guidance. From your pages, as bees in flowery glades sip every blossom, so do I crop all your golden sayings – golden indeed, and for ever worthy of everlasting life.

As soon as your reasoning, sprung from that godlike mind, lifts up its voice to proclaim the nature of the universe, then the terrors of the mind take flight, the ramparts of the world roll apart, and I see the march of events throughout the whole of space. The majesty of the gods[4] is revealed and those quiet habitations, never shaken by storms or drenched by rain-clouds or defaced by white drifts of snow which a harsh frost congeals. A cloudless ether roofs them and laughs with radiance lavishly diffused. All their wants are supplied by nature, and nothing at any time cankers their peace of mind. But nowhere do I see the halls of Acheron,[5] though the earth is no barrier to my beholding all that passes underfoot in the space beneath. At this I am seized with a divine delight and a shuddering awe that by your power nature stands thus unveiled and made manifest in every part.

I have already shown what the component bodies of everything are like: how they vary in shape: how they fly spontaneously through space, impelled by a perpetual motion: and how from these all objects can be created.[6] The next step now is evidently to elucidate in my verses the nature of mind and of spirit. In so doing I must throw out the fear of Acheron head over heels –

38 that fear which blasts the life of man from its very foundations, sullying everything with the blackness of death and leaving no pleasure pure and unalloyed.[7] I know that men often speak of sickness or of shameful life as more to be dreaded than the lowest pit of death; they claim to know that the mind consists of blood, or maybe wind,[8] if that is how the whim takes them, and to stand in no need whatever of our reasoning. But all this talk is based more on a desire to show off than on actual proof,

47 as you may infer from their conduct. These same men, though they may be exiled from home, banished far from the sight of their fellows, soiled with the accusation of some filthy crime, a prey to every torment, still cling to life. Wherever they come in their tribulation, they make propitiatory sacrifices, slaughter black cattle and despatch offerings to the Departed Spirits. The heavier their afflictions, the more devoutly they turn their minds to superstition. Look at a man in the midst of trouble and danger, and you will learn in his hour of adversity what he

58 really is. It is then that true utterances are wrung from the depths of his heart. The mask is torn off; the reality remains.[9]

Consider too the greed[10] and blind lust of status that drive pathetic men to overstep the bounds of right and may even turn them into accomplices or instruments of crime, struggling night and day with unstinted effort to scale the pinnacles of wealth. These running sores of life are fed in no small measure by the fear of death. For abject ignominy and irksome poverty seem far indeed from the joy and assurance of life, loitering already in effect at the gateway of death. From such a fate men

70 revolt in groundless terror and long to escape far, far away. So in their greed of gain they amass a fortune out of civil bloodshed;[11] piling wealth on wealth, they heap carnage on carnage. With heartless glee they welcome a brother's tragic death. They hate and fear the hospitable board of their own kin. Often, in the same spirit and influenced by the same fear, they are consumed with envy at the sight of another's success: he walks in a blaze of glory, looked up to by all, while they curse the dingy squalor in which their own lives are bogged. Some sacrifice life itself for the sake of statues and a title. Often from fear of death mortals are gripped by such a hate of living and

looking on the light that with anguished hearts they do them- 81
selves to death. They forget that this fear is the very fountain-
head of their troubles: this it is that harasses conscience, snaps
the bonds of friendship and in a word utterly destroys all moral
responsibility.[12] For many a time before now men have betrayed
their country and their beloved parents in an effort to escape
the halls of Acheron. *a river in the underworld*

As children in blank darkness tremble and start at everything, 88
so we in broad daylight are oppressed at times by fears as
baseless as those horrors which children imagine coming upon
them in the dark. This dread and darkness of the mind cannot
be dispelled by the sunbeams, the shining shafts of day, but
only by an understanding of the outward form and inner
workings of nature.

Must gain understanding to have (1)

First, I maintain that *the mind*,[13] which we often call the intellect,
the seat of the guidance and control of life, *is part of a man*, no
less than hand or foot or eyes are parts of a whole living 97
creature. ⟨There are some who argue that⟩ the sentience of the
mind is not lodged in any particular part, but is a vital condition
of the body, what the Greeks call a *harmony*,[14] which makes us
live as sentient beings without having any locally determined
mind. Just as good health may be said to belong[15] to the
healthy body without being any specific part of it, so they do
not station the sentience of the mind in any specific part. In this
they seem to me very wide of the mark. Often enough the
visible body is obviously ill, while in some other unseen part
we are enjoying ourselves. No less often the reverse happens: 108
one who is sick at heart enjoys bodily well-being.[16] This is no
different from the experience of an invalid whose foot is
hurting while his head is in no pain.

Or consider what happens when we have surrendered our
limbs to soothing slumber and our body, replete and relaxed,
lies insensible.[17] At that very time there is something else in us
that is awake to all sorts of stimuli – something that gives free
admittance to all the motions of joy and to heartaches void of
substance.

117 Next, you must understand that *there is also a vital spirit*[18] *in our limbs* and the body does not derive its sentience from any 'harmony'. In the first place, life often lingers in our limbs after a large part of the body has been cut off. On the other hand, when a few particles of heat have dispersed and some air has been let out through the mouth, life forsakes the veins forthwith and abandons the bones. Hence you may infer that all the elements do not hold equal portions of vitality or support it 125 equally, but it is chiefly thanks to the atoms of wind and heat that life lingers in the limbs. There is therefore in the body itself a vital breath and heat which forsakes our limbs at death.

Now that we have discovered the nature of the mind and of the vital spirit as a part of the man, drop this name harmony which was passed down to the musicians[19] from the heights of Helicon – or else perhaps they fetched it themselves from some other source and applied it to the matter of their art, which had then no name of its own. Whatever it be, let them keep it. And 135 give your attention now to the rest of my discourse.

Next, I maintain that *mind and spirit are interconnected* and compose between them a single substance. But what I may call the head and the dominant force in the whole body is that guiding principle which we term mind or intellect. This is firmly lodged in the mid-region of the breast.[20] Here is the place where fear and alarm pulsate. Here is felt the caressing touch of joy. Here, then, is the seat of intellect and mind. The rest of the vital spirit, diffused throughout the body, obeys the mind and 145 moves under its direction and impulse. The mind by itself experiences thought and joy of its own at a time when nothing moves either the body or the spirit.

When our head or eye suffers from an attack of pain, our whole body does not share in its aching. Just so the mind sometimes suffers by itself or jumps for joy when the rest of the spirit, diffused through every limb and member, is not stirred by any new impulse. But, when the mind is upset by some more overwhelming fear, we see all the spirit in every limb upset in sympathy. Sweat[21] and pallor break out all over the body. Speech grows inarticulate; the voice fails; the eyes

grow dim; the ears buzz; the limbs totter. Often we see men   156
actually drop down because of the terror that has gripped their
minds. Hence you may readily infer a connection between the
mind and the spirit, which, when shaken by the impact of the
mind, immediately jostles and propels the body.

The same reasoning proves that *mind and spirit are both composed
of matter*. We see them propelling the limbs, rousing the body   163
from sleep, changing the expression of the face and guiding and
steering the whole man – activities that all clearly involve
touch, as touch in turn involves matter. How then can we deny
their material nature? You see the mind sharing in the body's
experiences and sympathizing with it. When the nerve-racking
impact of a spear lays bare bones and sinews, even if it does
not penetrate to the seat of life, there ensues faintness and
a pleasant falling towards the ground and on the ground a
turmoil in the mind and an intermittent faltering impulse to
stand up again. The substance of the mind must therefore be   176
material, since it suffers the impact of material weapons.

My next task will be to demonstrate to you what sort of matter
it is of which this mind is composed and how it was formed.
First I affirm that *it is of very fine texture and composed of exceptionally
minute particles*. If you will mark my words, you will be able to
infer this from the following facts. It is evident that nothing
happens as quickly as the mind represents and sketches the
happening to itself. Therefore the mind sets itself in motion
more swiftly than any of those things whose substance is visible   185
to our eyes. But what is so mobile must consist of exceptionally
spherical and minute atoms, so that it can be set going by a
slight push. The reason why water is set going and flowing by
such a slight push is of course the smallness of its atoms and
their readiness to roll. The stickier consistency of honey[22] – its
relatively sluggish flow and dilatory progress – is due to the
closer coherence of the component matter, consisting, as it
obviously does, of particles not so smooth or so fine or so
round. A high pile of poppy seed[23] can be disturbed by a light
puff of breeze, so that seed trickles down from the top, but the

198 breeze cannot do the same to a heap of stones or corn ears. In proportion as objects are smaller and smoother, so much the more do they enjoy mobility; the greater their weight and roughness, the more firmly are they anchored. Since, therefore, the substance of the mind has been found to be extraordinarily mobile, it must consist of particles exceptionally small and smooth and round. This discovery, my good friend, will prove a timely aid to you in many problems.[24]

207 Here is a further indication how flimsy is the texture of the vital spirit and in how small a space it could be contained if it could be massed together. At the instant when a man is mastered by the carefree calm of death and forsaken by mind and spirit, you cannot tell either by sight or by weight that any part of the whole has been filched away from his body. Death leaves everything there, except vital sentience and warmth. Therefore the vital spirit as a whole must consist of very tiny atoms, linked together throughout veins, flesh and sinews –

218 atoms so small that, when all the spirit has escaped from the whole body, the outermost contour of the limbs appears intact and there is no loss of weight. The same thing happens when the bouquet has evaporated from the juice of Bacchus,[25] or the sweet perfume of an ointment has escaped into the air, or some substance has lost its savour. The substance itself is not visibly diminished by the loss, and its weight is not lessened, obviously because savour and scent are caused by many minute atoms distributed throughout the mass. On every ground, therefore, it may be inferred that mind and spirit are composed of exceptionally diminutive atoms, since their departure is not

230 accompanied by any loss of weight.

It must not be supposed that the stuff of mind or spirit is a single element. The body at death is abandoned by a sort of rarefied wind mixed with warmth, while the warmth carries with it also air. Indeed, heat never occurs without air being mixed with it; because it is naturally sparse, it must have many atoms of air moving in its interstices.

The composition of mind is thus so far found to be *at least three-fold*.[26] But all these three components together are not enough to create sentience, since the mind does not admit that any of these can create the sensory motions that originate the meditations revolved in the mind. *We must* accordingly *add to these a fourth component*, which is quite nameless. Than this there is nothing more mobile or more tenuous – nothing whose component atoms are smaller or smoother. This it is that first sets the sensory motions coursing through the limbs. Owing to the minuteness of its atoms, it is first to be stirred. Then the motions are caught up by warmth and the unseen energy of wind, then by air. Then everything is roused to movement: the blood is quickened; the impulse spreads throughout the flesh; last of all, bones and marrow are thrilled with pleasure or the opposite excitement. To this extremity pain cannot lightly penetrate, or the pangs of anguish win through. If they do, then everything is so confounded that no room is left for life, and the components of the vital spirit escape through all the pores[27] of the body. But usually a stop is put to these movements as near as may be at the surface of the body; and that is how we contrive to cling on to life.

At this point I should like to demonstrate *how these combinations are intermixed* and from what mode of combination they derive their powers. Reluctantly, I am thwarted in my purpose by the poverty of our native tongue.[28] But, so far as I can touch upon the surface of this topic, I will tackle it.

The atoms rush in and out amongst one another on atomic trajectories, so that no one of them can be segregated[29] nor its distinctive power isolated by intervening space. They coexist like the many properties of a single body. In the flesh of any living thing there are regularly scent and colour and taste; and yet from all these there is formed only one corporeal bulk. Just so, warmth and air and the unseen energy of wind create in combination a single substance, together with that mobile force which imparts to them from itself the initial impetus from which the sensory motion takes its rise throughout the flesh. This basic substance lurks at our very core. There is nothing in our bodies more fundamental than this, the most vital element of the whole vital spirit. Just as in our limbs and body as a

277 whole mind and spirit with their interconnected powers are latent, because their component atoms are small and sparse, so this nameless element composed of minute atoms is latent in the vital spirit and is in turn its vital element and rules the whole body.[30]

285 In the same way, wind and air and warmth commingled through the limbs must interact, one being relatively latent, another prominent. In appearance a single stuff is formed by them all: warmth and wind and air do not display their powers separately so as to blot out sentience and dissolve it by their disunion. First,[31] there is at the mind's disposal that element of heat, which it brings into play when it boils with rage and passion blazes more fiercely from the eyes. There is likewise no lack of that chill wind, companion of fright, which sets the limbs atremble and impels them to flight. There is lastly that calm and steady air which prevails in a tranquil breast and unruffled countenance.

294 In those creatures whose passionate hearts and angry dispositions easily boil up in anger, there is a surplus of the hot element. An outstanding example is the truculent temper of lions, who often roar till they burst their chests with bellowing and cannot keep the torrents of their rage pent within their breasts. But the cold hearts of deer are of a windier blend: they are quicker to set chill breezes blowing through the flesh, provoking a shuddering movement in the limbs. Cattle, again, have in their vital composition a bigger portion of calm air. They are never too hotly fired by a touch of that smoky torch of anger which clouds the mind with its black and blinding shadow. They are never transfixed 305 and benumbed by the icy shaft of fear. Their nature is a mean between the timidity of the deer and the lion's ferocity.

So it is with men. Though education may apply a similar polish to various individuals, it still leaves fundamental traces of their several temperaments. It must not be supposed that innate vices can be completely eradicated: one man will still incline too readily to outbursts of rage; another will give way to fear rather too soon; a third will accept some contingencies too impassively. And in a host of other ways men must differ one from another in temperament and so also in the resultant

is beyond m...
city of atomic...
I am clear that...
lingering traces of...
ated by philosophy...
prevent men leading a li...

This *vital spirit*, then, is prese...
guardian and preserver. For the...
roots and cannot be torn apart...
easily could the scent be torn out o...
destroying their nature as mind and ... could be ...ed
from the whole body without total dis... their
earliest origin the two are charged with a ... life by the
intertangled atoms that compose them. It is ... that neither
body nor mind by itself without the other's aid possesses the
power of sensation: it is by the interacting motions of the two
combined that the flame of sentience is kindled in our flesh.

Again,[34] body by itself never experiences birth or growth,
and we see that it does not persist after death. Water, we know,
often gives up the heat imparted to it without being torn apart
in the process and survives intact. Not so can the derelict limbs
outlast the departure of the vital spirit: they are utterly demol-
ished by internal decomposition and decay. So from the very
beginning, even when they are at rest in the mother's womb,
body and spirit in mutual contact acquire the motions that
generate life. They cannot be wrenched apart without hurt and
havoc. So you may see, since their very existence depends upon
conjunction, that their nature must likewise be conjoint.

If anyone still denies that the body is sentient, and believes it
is the spirit interfused throughout the body that assumes this
motion which we term sensation, he is fighting against manifest
facts. Who can explain what bodily sensation really is, if it be not
such as it is palpably presented to us by experience?[35] Admit-
tedly, when the spirit is banished, the body is quite insensible.
That is because what it loses was never one of its permanent
properties, but one of many attributes which it loses at death.

...n[36] that the eyes can see
... out through them as though
... sense of sight itself leads us the other
... tugging us right to the eyeballs. Often, for
... cannot see bright objects, because our eyes are
... by light. This is an experience unknown to doors: the
doorways through which we gaze suffer no distress by being
flung open. Besides, if our eyes are equivalent to doors, then
when the eyes are removed the mind obviously ought to see
things better now that the doors are away, doorposts and all.

Another error to be avoided, and one that is sanctioned by the
revered authority of the great Democritus,[37] is the belief that
the limbs are knit together by atoms of body and mind arranged
alternately, first one and then the other. In fact, *the atoms of
spirit are not only much smaller*[38] *than those composing our body and
flesh; they are also correspondingly fewer*[39] *in number* and scattered
but sparsely through our limbs. At least you could safely say
this: observe what are the smallest objects whose impact serves
to excite sensory motions in our bodies – these will give you
the measure of the gaps between the atoms of spirit. Sometimes
we are unaware that dust is sticking to our bodies or a cloud of
chalk has settled on our limbs: we do not feel the night mist, or
the slight threads of gossamer in our path that enmesh us as we
walk, or the fall of a flimsy cobweb on our heads, or feathers of
birds or flying thistledown, which from their very lightness do
not lightly descend. We do not mark the path of every creeping
thing that crawls across our body or all the separate footfalls
planted by gnats and other creatures. So quite a considerable
commotion must be made in our bodies before the atomic
disturbance is felt by the atoms of spirit interspersed through
our limbs and before these can knock together across the
intervening gaps and clash and combine and again bounce
apart.[40]

Note also that *it is mind, far more than spirit, that keeps life under
lock and key* – mind that has the greater mastery over life.
Without mind and intellect no scrap of vital spirit can linger

one instant in our limbs.[41] Spirit follows smoothly in the wake   400
of mind and scatters into the air, leaving the limbs cold with
the chill of death. While mind remains, life remains. One whose
limbs are all lopped from the mangled trunk,[42] despite the loss
of vital spirit released from the limbs, yet lives and inhales the
life-giving gusts of air. Though robbed, if not of all, at least of
a large proportion of his spirit, he lingers still in life and clings
fast to it. Just so, though the eye[43] is lacerated all round, so   410
long as the pupil remains intact, the faculty of vision remains
alive, provided always that you do not hack away the whole
encircling orb and leave the eyeball detached and isolated; for
that cannot be done without total destruction. But once that
tiny bit in the middle of the eye is eaten away – then the light
goes out there and then and darkness falls, although the shining
orb is otherwise unscathed. It is on just such terms that spirit
and mind are everlastingly linked together.

My next point[44] is this: you must understand that the *minds of*   418
living things and the light fabric of their spirits are neither birthless[45]
nor deathless. To this end I have long been mustering and
inventing verses with a labour that is also a joy. Now I will
try to set them out in a style worthy of your calling and
character.[46]

Please note that both objects are to be embraced under one
name. When, for instance, I proceed to demonstrate that 'spirit'
is mortal, you must understand that this applies equally to
'mind', since the two are so conjoined as to constitute a single
substance.

First of all, then, I have shown[47] that spirit is flimsy stuff   425
composed of tiny particles. Its atoms are obviously far smaller
than those of swift-flowing water or mist or smoke, since it far
outstrips them in mobility and is moved by a far slighter
impetus. Indeed, it is actually moved by images[48] of smoke and
mist. So, for instance, when we are sunk in sleep, we may see
altars sending up clouds of steam and giving off smoke; and we
cannot doubt that we are here dealing with images. Now we
see that water flows out in all directions from broken vessels
and the fluid departs, and mist and smoke vanish into thin air.

437 Be assured, therefore, that spirit is similarly dispelled and vanishes far more speedily and is sooner dissolved into its component atoms once it has been let loose from the human frame. When the body, which served as a vessel[49] for it, is by some means broken and attenuated by loss of blood from the veins, so as to be no longer able to contain it, how can you suppose that it can be contained by any kind of air, which is a far less solid container than our bodily frame?

445 Again, we are conscious that mind and body are born together, grow up together and together grow old. With the weak and delicate frame of wavering childhood goes a like infirmity of judgement. The robust vigour of ripening years is accompanied by a steadier resolve and a maturer strength of mind. Later, when the body is palsied by the potent forces of age and the limbs have collapsed with blunted vigour, the understanding limps, the tongue rambles and the mind totters: everything weakens and gives way at the same time. It is thus natural that the vital spirit should all evaporate like smoke, soaring into the gusty air, since we have seen that it shares the body's birth and growth and simultaneously wears out with the weariness of age.[50]

456 Furthermore, as the body suffers the horrors of disease and the pangs of pain, so we see the mind stabbed with anguish, grief and fear. What more natural than that it should likewise have a share in death? Often enough in the body's illness the mind wanders. It raves and babbles distractedly. At times it drifts on a tide of drowsiness, with drooping eyelids and nodding head, into a deep and unbroken sleep, from which it

467 cannot hear the voices or recognize the faces of those who stand around with streaming eyes and tear-stained cheeks,[51] striving to recall it to life. Since the mind is thus invaded by the contagion of disease, you must acknowledge that it is destructible. For pain and sickness are the architects of death, as we have been taught by the fate of many men[52] before us.

Again, when the pervasive power of wine has entered into a man and its glow is dispersed through his veins, his limbs are overcome with heaviness; his legs stagger and stumble; his speech is slurred, his mind besotted; his eyes swim; there is a

crescendo of shouts, hiccups, quarrelling; and all the other   480
symptoms follow in due order. Why should this be, if not
because the wanton wildness of the wine has power to dislodge
the vital spirit within the body? And, since things can be
dislodged and arrested, this is an indication that the inroad of a
slightly more potent attack would make an end of them and
rob them of a future.

Or it may happen that a man is seized with a sudden spasm
of epilepsy[53] before our eyes. He falls as though struck by   487
lightning and foams at the mouth. He groans and trembles in
every joint. He raves. He contracts his muscles. He writhes. He
gasps convulsively. He tires his limbs with tossing. The cause
of the foaming is that the spirit, torn apart by the violence of
the disease throughout the limbs, riots and whips up spray, just
as the wild wind's fury froths the salt sea waves. The groans
are wrung from him because his limbs are racked with pain and
in general because atoms of vocal sound are expelled and
whirled out in a lump through the mouth – their customary
outlet, where the way is already paved for them. The raving   498
occurs because mind and spirit are dislodged and, as I have
explained, split up and scattered this way and that by the same
poison. Then, when the cause of the disease has passed its
climax and the morbid secretion[54] of the distempered body has
returned to its secret abode, then the man rises, swaying
unsteadily at first, and returns bit by bit to all his senses and
recovers his vital spirit. When mind[55] and spirit in the body
itself are a prey to such violent maladies and suffer such
distressing dispersal, how can you believe them capable of   508
surviving apart from the body in the open air with the wild
winds for company?

Conversely, we see that the mind, like a sick body, can be
healed and directed by medicine. This too is a premonition that
its life is mortal. When you embark on an attempt to alter the
mind or to direct any other natural object, it is fair to suppose
that you are adding certain parts or transposing them or
subtracting some trifle at any rate from their sum. But an
immortal object will not let its parts be rearranged or added to,
or the least bit drop off. For, if ever anything is so transformed

520   as to overstep its own limits, this means the immediate death of what was before.[56] By this susceptibility both to sickness (as I have shown) and to medicine, the mind displays the marks of mortality. So false reasoning is plainly confronted by true fact. Every loophole is barred to its exponent, and by the two horns of a dilemma he is convicted of falsehood.

528   Again, we often see a man pass away little by little, and lose all sensation of life limb by limb: first the toes and toenails lose their colour; then the feet and legs die; after that the imprint of icy death steals by slow degrees through the other members.[57] Since the vital spirit is thus dispersed and does not come out all at once in its entirety, it must be regarded as mortal. You may be tempted to suppose that it can shrink into itself through the body and draw its parts together and so withdraw sensibility from every limb. But, if that were so, the place in which such a mass of spirit was concentrated ought to display an exceptional degree of sensibility. Since there is no such place, it is evidently

539   scattered forth torn into pieces, as I said before – in other words, it perishes. Let us, however, concede this false hypothesis and suppose that the spirit concentrates within the body of those who leave the light of day through a creeping palsy. You must still acknowledge that spirit is mortal. It makes no odds whether it is scattered to the winds and disintegrated, or concentrated and deadened. In either case, the victim as a whole is more and more drained of sensibility in every part, and in every part less and less of life remains.[58]

550   The mind, again, is one part[59] of a man and stays fixed in a particular spot, no less than the ears and eyes and other senses by which life is guided. Now, our hand or eye or nostrils in isolation from us cannot experience sensation or even exist; in a very short time they rot away. So mind cannot exist apart from body and from the man himself who is, as it were,[60] a vessel for it – or if you choose you may picture it as something still more intimately linked, since body clings to mind by close ties.

   Again, mind and body as a living force derive their vigour and their vitality from their conjunction. Without body, the mind alone cannot perform the vital motions. Bereft of vital spirit, the body cannot persist and exercise its senses. As the eye

uprooted and separated from the body cannot see, so we   563
perceive that spirit and mind by themselves are powerless. It is
only because their atoms are held in by the whole body,
intermingled through veins and flesh, sinews and bones, and
are not free to bounce far apart, that they are kept together so
as to perform the motions that generate sentience. After death,
when they are expelled out of the body into the gusty air, they
cannot perform the sensory motions because they are no longer   572
held together in the same way. The air indeed will itself be a
body,[61] and an animate one at that, if it allows the vital spirit to
hang together and keep up those motions which it used to go
through before in the sinews and the body itself. Here then is
proof upon proof. You must perforce admit that, when the
whole bodily envelope crumbles after the expulsion of the vital
breath, the senses of the mind and the spirit likewise disin-
tegrate, since body and mind can only exist when joined
together.

Again, the body cannot suffer the withdrawal of the vital   580
spirit without rotting away in a foul stench. How can you
doubt, then, but that the spirit diffused in the depths of the
body has come to the surface and evaporated like smoke?[62]
That explains why the body is transformed and collapses so
utterly into decay: its inmost foundations are sapped by the
effusion of the spirit through the limbs and through all the
body's winding channels and chinks. So there are many indica-
tions[63] that the vital spirit escapes through the limbs torn into
pieces and is already split up within the body before it slips out
and glides into the gusty air.

Even while the vital spirit yet lingers within the boundaries   592
of life, it often seems, when something has violently upset it, as
though it were struggling to escape and be wholly released
from the body – as though the features were relaxing into a
deathbed immobility and every limb were ready to hang limp
upon the bloodless trunk. It is at such times that we say 'the
mind has failed' or 'he has lost consciousness'. There is general
alarm, and everyone is straining to hold fast onto life's last
mooring. Then the mind and all the vital spirit are all churned
up and both these, together with the body, are on the point of

602 collapse, so that a slightly intensified force might shatter them.
How can you doubt, then, that the fragile spirit once stripped
of its envelope and thrust out of the body into the open would
be powerless not only to survive throughout eternity but even
to persist for a single instant?

No one on the point of death seems to feel his spirit retiring
intact right out of his body or rising first to his gullet and up
610 through his throat. On the contrary, he feels that it is failing in
a particular region which it occupies, just as he is conscious
that his other senses are being extinguished each in its own
sphere. If our mind were indeed immortal, it would not com-
plain of extinction in the hour of death, but would rather feel
that it was escaping from confinement and sloughing off its
garment like a snake.

Again, why is mind or thought never born in head or feet or
hands? Why does it cling fast in every man to one spot or a
specified region? It can only be that a specific place is assigned
619 to each thing where it can be born and survive. So every
creature is created with a great diversity of members, whose
mutual position is never reversed. One thing duly follows
another: flame is not born in a flood, nor frost begotten in fire.

Moreover, if the spirit is by nature immortal and can remain
sentient when divorced from our body, we must credit it, I
presume, with the possession of five senses. In no other way
can we picture to ourselves departed spirits wandering through
the Infernal Regions. So it is that painters[64] and bygone genera-
tions of writers[65] have portrayed spirits in possession of their
631 senses. But eyes or nostrils or hand or tongue or ears cannot be
attached to a disembodied spirit. Such a spirit cannot therefore
be sentient or so much as exist.

We feel that the sensation of living resides in the body as a
whole and we see that the whole body is animate. Suppose,
then, that it is suddenly sliced through the middle by some
swiftly delivered slash, so as to fall into two quite separate
parts. Without doubt the vital spirit will also be severed and
split in two along with the body. But what is cleft and falls
apart obviously gives up all pretensions to be immortal. They
say[66] that in the heat and indiscriminate carnage of battle limbs

are often lopped off by scythe-armed chariots so suddenly that 643
the fallen member hewn from the body is seen to writhe on the
ground. Yet the mind and consciousness of the man cannot yet
feel the pain: so abrupt is the hurt, and so intent the mind upon
the business of battle. With what is left of his body he presses
on with battle and bloodshed and does not grasp, it may be,
that his left arm together with its shield has been lost, whirled
away among the chargers by the chariot wheels with their 651
predatory blades. Another does not notice that his right arm
has gone, while he keeps struggling to climb aboard the
chariot.[67] Another, who has lost a leg, does his best to stand
up, while on the ground at his side the dying foot twitches its
toes. A head hewn from the still warm and living trunk retains
on the ground its lively features and open eyes till it has yielded
up the last shred of spirit. Or take for example a snake with
flickering tongue, menacing tail and protracted body. Should
you choose to hack both ends of it in many pieces with a blade,
you will see, while the wound is still fresh, every several portion 661
separately squirming and spattering the ground with gore, and
the foremost part twisting back with its mouth to bite itself in
the fierce agony of the wound. Shall we say that in each of
these parts there is an entire spirit? But on that hypothesis it
would follow that one animate creature had in its body many
spirits. Actually, a spirit that was one has been split up along
with the body. So both alike must be reckoned mortal, since
both alike are split into many parts.[68]

Next, if the spirit is by nature immortal and is slipped into[69]
the body at birth, why do we retain no memory[70] of an earlier
existence, no traces left by antecedent events? If the mind's 672
operation is so greatly changed that all record of former actions
has been expunged, it is no long journey, in my judgement,
from this experience to annihilation. So you must admit that
the pre-existent spirit has died and the one that is now is a new
creation.[71]

Let us suppose, for argument's sake, that the vital force of
mind is introduced into us when the body is already fully
formed, at the moment when we are born and step across the
threshold of life. This theory does not square with the observed

683 fact that the mind grows with the bodily frame and in the very
blood. It would imply that the mind lived in solitary confine-
ment,[72] alone in its cell, and yet at the same time the whole
body was overflowing with sensation. Here then is proof upon
proof that spirits are not to be regarded as birthless, nor yet as
exempt from the law of death. If they were slipped into our
bodies from outside, it cannot be supposed that the two would
690 be so closely interlocked as they are shown to be by the clearest
evidence. For spirit so interpenetrates veins, flesh, sinews,
bones, that our very teeth share in sensation – witness toothache
and the twinge of icy water or biting into a jagged stone buried
in a loaf. Being thus interwoven, it does not seem possible that
it should escape intact and extricate itself undamaged from
every sinew, bone and joint. Or, if you suppose that, after
being slipped in from outside, the spirit oozes through our
limbs, then it is all the more bound to perish with the body
through which it is thus interfused. To ooze through something
702 is to be dissolved in it and therefore to perish. We know that
food, when it is rationed out amongst our limbs and members
by diffusion through all the channels of the body, is destroyed
and takes on a different nature. Just so, on the assumption that
spirit and mind enter into the newly formed body as complete
entities, they must be dissolved in oozing through it: our limbs
must be interpenetrated through every channel by the particles
composing this mind which lords it now in our body – this
new mind born of the old one that must have perished in its
diffusion through our limbs. It is thus evident that the human
712 spirit is neither deprived of a birthday nor immune from a
funeral.

The further question arises whether or not any atoms of vital
spirit are left in a lifeless body. If some are left and lodge there,
we are not justified in regarding the spirit as immortal, since it
has come away mutilated by the loss of some of its parts. If, on
the other hand, it withdraws with its members intact, so that no
scrap of it remains in the body, how is it that corpses, when
their flesh begins to rot, exhale maggots?[73] What is the source
of that boneless and bloodless horde of animate things that
swarms through the swollen limbs? You may argue that spirits

can slip into the maggots from outside and settle individually in   722
their bodies. I will not ask why in that case many thousands of
spirits should forgather in the place from which one has with-
drawn. But there is another question that calls for a decisive
answer.[74] Do these supposed spirits each hunt out atoms of
maggots and manufacture dwelling-places for themselves? Or
do they slip into ready-made bodies? No adequate reason can
be given why they should undertake the labour of manufacture.
In their bodiless state they presumably flit about untroubled by   731
sickness, cold or hunger. For the body is far more subject to
these afflictions, and communion with it is the source of many
of the mind's troubles. But suppose they had the best of
reasons for making a body to which they could subject them-
selves: there is no discernible way in which they could set about
it. So much for the suggestion that spirits make bodies and
limbs for themselves. We may equally rule out the alternative
theory that they slip into ready-made bodies. For this would
not account for the intimate communion between body and   740
spirit and their sensory interaction.

Again, why is grim ferocity an attribute of the lions' surly
breed, as craftiness of foxes? Why are deer endowed by their
fathers[75] with timidity and their limbs impelled to flight by
hereditary panic? Why are all other traits of this sort implanted
in physique and character from birth? It can only be because
the mind always shares in the specific growth of the body
according to its seed and breed. If it were immortal and passed
from body to body, there would be living things of confused
characters. Often the hound of Hyrcanian[76] breed would turn   750
tail before the onset of the antlered stag. The hawk would flee
trembling through the gusty air at the coming of the dove.
Man would be witless, and brute beasts rational. It is an
untenable theory that an immortal spirit is modified by a
change of body. For whatever changes is disintegrated and
therefore destroyed. The component parts of spirits are in any
case transposed and reshuffled. So the spirits as a whole might
just as well be diffused through the limbs and eventually
destroyed with the body. If, on the other hand, it is maintained
that the spirits of men enter none but human bodies, then I

761 would ask why a wise one should become foolish – why a child is never sensible, nor a mare's foal as accomplished as a sturdy steed. The one loophole left is the assumption that in a frail body the mind too grows frail. But in that case you must admit that the spirit is mortal, since in its adaptation to the bodily frame it loses so utterly its previous vitality and sensibility. How can the mind wax strong in unison with each particular body till it attains with it the coveted season of full bloom,
770 unless the two are co-heirs of a single birth? Why, when the limbs are weighted with age, should the mind wish to slip out and away? Is it afraid to stay locked up in a mouldering body? Afraid that its lodging may collapse from the wear and tear of age? Surely an immortal being need fear no danger.[77]

Again, it is surely ludicrous to suppose that spirits are standing by at the mating and birth of animals – a numberless number of immortals on the look-out for mortal frames, jostling and squabbling to get in first and establish themselves most
781 firmly. Or is there perhaps an established compact that first come shall be first served, without any trial of strength between spirit and spirit?

A tree cannot exist high in air, or clouds in the depths of the sea, as fish cannot live in the fields, or blood flow in wood or sap in stones.[78] There is a determined and allotted place for the growth and place of everything. So mind cannot arise alone without body or apart from sinews and blood. If it could do this, then surely it could much more readily function in head or shoulders or the tips of the heels and be born in any other part,
793 so long as it was held in the same container, that is to say in the same man. Since, however, even in the human body we see a determined and allotted place set aside for the growth and presence of spirit and mind, we have even stronger grounds for denying that they could survive or come to birth outside the body altogether. You must admit, therefore, that when the body has perished there is an end also of the spirit ripped to shreds throughout the body. It is surely crazy to couple a mortal object with an eternal and suppose that they can work in harmony and mutually interact. What can be imagined more incongruous, what more repugnant and discordant, than that a

mortal object and one that is immortal and everlasting should
unite to form a compound and jointly weather the storms that
rage about them?

Again,[79] there can be only three kinds of everlasting objects.
The first, owing to the absolute solidity of their substance, can
repel blows and let nothing penetrate them so as to unknit their
close texture from within. Such are the atoms of matter, whose
nature I have already demonstrated. The second kind can last
for ever because it is immune from blows. Such is empty space,
which remains untouched and unaffected by any impact. Last is
that which has no available place surrounding it into which its
matter can disperse and disintegrate. It is for this reason that
the sum totality of the universe is everlasting, having no space
outside it into which the matter can escape and no matter that
can enter and disintegrate it by the force of impact.

Equally vain is the suggestion that the spirit is immortal
because it is shielded by life-preserving powers: or because it is
unassailed by forces hostile to its survival; or because such
forces, if they threaten, are somehow repelled before we are
conscious of the threat. ⟨Common sense makes it obvious that
this cannot be the case:⟩ apart from the spirit's participation in
the ailments of the body, it has maladies enough of its own.[80]
The prospect of the future torments it with fear and wearies it
with worry, and past misdeeds leave the sting of remorse.
Lastly, it may fall a prey to the mind's own specific afflictions,
madness and amnesia, and plunge into the black waters of ob-
livion.

From all this it follows that *death is nothing to us*[81] and no
concern of ours, since the nature of the mind is now held to be
mortal. In days of old, we felt no disquiet when the hosts of
Carthage[82] poured in to battle on every side – when the whole
earth, dizzied by the convulsive shock of war, reeled sickeningly
under the high ethereal vault, and between realm and realm the
empire of mankind by land and sea trembled in the balance. So,
when we shall be no more – when the union of body and spirit
that engenders us[83] has been disrupted – to us, who shall then
be nothing, nothing by any hazard will happen any more at all.

804

811

822

830

does the spirit come fr. atoms?

841 Nothing will have power to stir our senses, not though earth be fused with sea and sea with sky.

If any feeling remains in mind or spirit after it has been torn from our body, that is nothing to us, who are brought into being by the wedlock of body and spirit, conjoined and coalesced. Or even if the matter that composes us should be reassembled by time after our death and brought back into its present state — if the light of life were given to us anew [84] — even 850 that contingency would still be no concern of ours once the chain of our identity had been snapped. We who are now are not concerned with ourselves in any previous existence: the sufferings of those selves do not touch us. When you look at the immeasurable extent of time gone by and the multiform movements of matter, you will readily credit that these same atoms that compose us now must many a time before have entered into the selfsame combinations as now.[85] But our mind cannot recall this to remembrance. For between then and now 861 is interposed a break in life, and all the atomic motions have been wandering far astray from sentience.

If the future holds misery and anguish in store, the self must be in existence, when that time comes, in order to be miserable. But from this fate we are redeemed by death, which denies existence to the self that might have suffered these tribulations. Rest assured, therefore, that we have nothing to fear in death. One who no longer is cannot suffer, or differ in any way from one who has never been born, when once this mortal life has been usurped by death the immortal.

870 When you find a man treating it as a grievance that after death he will either moulder in the grave or fall a prey to flames or to the jaws of predatory beasts,[86] be sure that his utterance does not ring true. Subconsciously his heart is stabbed by a secret dread, however loudly the man himself may disavow the belief that after death he will still experience sensation. I am convinced that he does not grant the admission he professes, nor the grounds of it; he does not oust and pluck himself root and branch out of life, but all unwittingly makes something of himself linger on. When a living man confronts the thought that after death his body will be mauled by birds and beasts

prey,[87] he is filled with self-pity. He does not banish himself from the scene nor distinguish sharply enough between himself and that abandoned carcass. He visualizes that object as himself and infects it with his own feelings as an onlooker. That is why he is aggrieved at having been created mortal. He does not see that in real death there will be no other self alive to mourn his own decease – no other self standing by to flinch at the agony he suffers lying there being mangled, or indeed being cremated. For if it is really a bad thing after death to be mauled and crunched by ravening jaws, I cannot see why it should not be disagreeable to roast in the scorching flames of a funeral pyre, or to lie embalmed in honey,[88] stifled and stiff with cold, on the surface of a chilly slab, or to be squashed under a crushing weight of earth.

'Now it is all over. Now[89] the happy home and the best of wives will welcome you no more, nor delightful children rush to snatch the first kiss at your coming and touch your heart with speechless joy. No chance now to further your fortune or safeguard your family. Unhappy man,' they cry, 'unhappily cheated by one treacherous day out of all these blessings of life!' But they do not go on to say: 'And now no repining for these lost joys will oppress you any more.' If they perceived this clearly with their minds and acted according to the words, they would free their breasts from a great load of grief and dread.

'Ah yes! *You* are at peace now in the sleep of death, and so you will stay till the end of time. Pain and sorrow will never touch you again. But to *us*, who stood weeping inconsolably while you were consumed to ashes on the dreadful pyre – to us no day will come that will lift the undying sorrow from our hearts.' Ask the speaker, then, what is so heart-rending about this. If something returns to sleep and peace, what reason is that for pining in inconsolable grief?

Here again, is the way men often talk from the bottom of their hearts when they recline at a banquet,[90] goblet in hand and brows decked with garlands: 'How all too short are these good times that come to us poor creatures! Soon they will be past and gone, and there will be no recalling them.' You would

916 think the crowning calamity in store for them after death was
to be parched and shrivelled by a tormenting thirst or oppressed
by some other vain desire. But even in sleep, when mind and
body alike are at rest, no one misses himself or sighs for life. If
such sleep were prolonged to eternity, no longing for ourselves
would trouble us. And yet the vital atoms in our limbs cannot
be far removed from their sensory motions at a time when a
926 mere jolt out of sleep enables a man to pull himself together.
Death, therefore, must be regarded, so far as we are concerned,
as having much less existence than sleep, if anything can have
less existence than what we perceive to be nothing. For death is
followed by a far greater dispersal of the seething mass of
matter: once that icy break in life has intervened, there is no
more waking.

Suppose that Nature[91] herself were suddenly to find a voice
and round upon one of us in these terms: 'What is your
grievance, mortal, that you give yourself up to this whining
and repining? Why do you weep and wail over death? If the life
935 you have lived till now has been a pleasant thing – if all its
blessings have not leaked away like water poured into a cracked
pot[92] and run to waste unrelished – why then, you stupid man,
do you not retire like a dinner guest who has eaten his fill of
life, and take your carefree rest with a quiet mind? Or, if all
your gains have been poured profitless away and life has grown
distasteful, why do you seek to swell the total? The new can
but turn out as badly as the old and perish as unprofitably.
Why not rather make an end of life and trouble?[93] Do you
expect me to invent some new contrivance for your pleasure? I
945 tell you, there is none. All things are always the same. If your
body is not yet withered with age, nor your limbs decrepit and
flagging,[94] even so there is nothing new to look forward to –
not though you should outlive all living creatures, or even
though you should never die at all.' What are we to answer,
except that Nature's rebuttal is justified and the plea she puts
forward is a true one?

But suppose it is some man of riper years who complains –
some dismal greybeard who laments over his approaching end
far more than he ought. Would she not have every right to

protest more vehemently and repulse him in stern tones: 'Away 954
with your tears, old reprobate! Have done with your grumbling!
You are withering now after tasting all the joys of life. But
because you are always pining for what is not and unapprecia-
tive of the things at hand, your life has slipped away unfulfilled
and unprized. Death has stolen upon you unawares, before you
are ready to retire from life's banquet filled and satisfied. Come
now, put away all that is unbecoming to your years and 962
compose your mind to make way for others. You have no
choice.' I cannot question but that she would have right on her
side; her censure and rebuke would be well merited. The old is
always thrust aside to make way for the new, and one thing
must be built out of the wreck of others. There is no murky pit
of Tartarus awaiting anyone. There is need of matter, so that
later generations may arise; when they have lived out their
span, they will all follow you. Bygone generations have taken
your road, and those to come will take it no less. So one thing
will never cease to spring from another. To none is life given 971
in freehold; to all on lease.[95] Look back at the eternity that
passed before we were born, and mark how utterly it counts to
us as nothing. This is a mirror that Nature holds up to us, in
which we may see the time that shall be after we are dead. Is
there anything terrifying in the sight – anything depressing –
anything that is not more restful than the soundest sleep?

*As for all those torments that are said to take place in the depths of
Acheron, they are actually present here and now, in our own lives.*

There is no wretched Tantalus,[96] as the myth relates, trans- 980
fixed with groundless terror at the huge boulder poised above
him in the air. But in this life there really are mortals oppressed
by unfounded fear of the gods and trembling at the impending
doom that may fall upon any of them at the whim of chance.

There is no Tityos[97] lying in Acheron for ever opened up by
birds of prey. Assuredly they cannot find food by groping
under those giant ribs to glut them throughout eternity. No
matter to what length that titanic frame may lie outstretched, so
that he covers not a paltry nine acres with his spread-eagled
limbs but the whole extent of earth, he will not be able to

991 suffer an eternity of pain nor furnish food from his body for evermore. But Tityos is here in our midst – that poor devil prostrated by love, torn indeed by birds of prey, devoured by gnawing anxiety or rent by the fangs of some other passion.

Sisyphus[98] too is alive for all to see, bent on winning the insignia of office, its rods and ruthless axes, by the people's vote, and is embittered by perpetual defeat. To strive for this profitless and never-granted prize, and in striving toil and moil incessantly, this truly is to push a boulder laboriously up a steep hill, only to see it, once the top is reached, rolling and bounding down again to the flat levels of the plain.

1000

By the same token, to be for ever feeding a malcontent mind, filling it with good things but never satisfying it – the fate we suffer when the circling seasons enrich us with their products and their ever-changing charms although we are never filled with the fruits of life – this surely exemplifies the story of those maidens[99] in the flower of life for ever pouring water into a leaking vessel that can never by any technique be filled.

1010

As for Cerberus[100] and the Furies[101] and the pitchy darkness and Tartarus[102] belching abominable fumes from its throat, these do not and cannot exist anywhere at all. But life is darkened by the fear of retribution for our misdeeds, a fear enormous in proportion to their enormity, and by the penalties imposed for crime – imprisonment and ghastly precipitation from Tarpeia's Crag,[103] the lash, the executioners, the condemned cell, the boiling pitch, the hot metal plates and the branding torches. Even though these horrors are not physically present, yet the conscience-ridden mind in terrified anticipation torments itself with its own goads and whips. It does not see what term there can be to its suffering nor where its punishment can have an end. It is afraid that death may serve merely to intensify all this pain. So at length the life of misguided mortals becomes a Hell on earth.

1019

Here is something that you might well say to yourself from time to time: 'Even good king Ancus[104] looked his last on the daylight – a better man than you, my presumptuous friend, by a long reckoning. Death has come to many another monarch

and potentate, who ruled over mighty nations. Even that King 1027
of Kings[105] who once built a highway across the great deep –
who gave his legions a path to tread among the waves and
taught them to march on foot over the briny gulfs and with his
chargers trampled scornfully upon the ocean's roar – even he
was robbed of the light and poured out the spirit from a dying
frame. Scipio,[106] that thunderbolt of war, the terror of Carthage,
gave his bones to the earth as if he had been the meanest of 1035
serfs. Add to this company the discoverers of truth and beauty.
Add the attendants of the Muses, among them Homer,[107] who
in solitary glory bore the sceptre but has sunk into the same
slumber as the rest. Democritus,[108] when ripe age warned him
that the mindful motions of his intellect were running down,
made his unbowed head a willing sacrifice to death. And the
master himself, when his daylit race was run, Epicurus[109] himself
died, whose genius outshone the race of men and dimmed them
all, as the stars are dimmed by the rising of the fiery sun. And
will *you* kick and protest against your sentence? You, whose life 1046
is next-door to death although you still live and look on the
light. You, who waste the major part of your time in sleep and,
when you are awake, are snoring still and dreaming. You, who
bear a mind hag-ridden by baseless fear and cannot find the
commonest cause of your distress, hounded as you are, pathetic
creature, by a pack of troubles and drifting in a drunken stupor
upon a wavering tide of fantasy.'

   Men feel plainly enough within their minds a heavy burden,
whose weight depresses them. If only they perceived with equal
clearness the causes of this depression, the origin of this lump
of evil within their breasts, they would not lead such a life as 1055
we now see all too commonly – no one knowing what he really
wants and everyone for ever trying to get away from where he
is, as though travel alone could throw off the load.[110] Often the
owner of some stately mansion,[111] bored stiff by staying at
home, takes his departure, only to return as speedily when he
feels himself no better off out of doors. Off he goes to his
country seat, driving his Gaulish ponies hotfoot, as though
rushing to save a house on fire. No sooner has he crossed its
doorstep than he starts yawning or retires moodily to sleep and

1067 courts oblivion, or else rushes back to revisit the city. In so doing the individual is really running away from himself.[112] Since he remains reluctantly wedded to the self whom he cannot of course escape, he grows to hate him, because he is a sick man ignorant of the cause of his malady. If he did but see this, he would cast other thoughts aside and devote himself first to studying the nature of the universe. It is not the fortune of an hour that is in question, but of all time – the lot in store
1075 for mortals throughout the eternity that awaits them after death.

What is this deplorable lust for life that holds us trembling in bondage to such uncertainties and dangers? A fixed term is set to the life of mortals, and there is no way of dodging death. In any case the setting of our lives remains the same throughout, and by going on living we do not mint any new coin of pleasure. So long as the object of our craving is unattained, it seems more precious than anything besides. Once it is ours, we
1084 crave for something else. So an unquenchable thirst for life keeps us always on the gasp. There is no telling what fortune the future may bring – what chance may throw in our way, or what upshot lies in waiting. By prolonging life, we cannot subtract or whittle away one jot from the duration of our death. The time after our taking off remains constant. However many generations you may add to your store by living, there waits for you none the less the same eternal death.[113] The period of not-being will be no less for him who made an end of life with today's daylight than for him who perished many a
1094 moon and many a year before.

BOOK FOUR

SENSATION AND SEX

I[1] am blazing a trail through pathless tracts of the Muses'
Pierian realm, where no foot has ever trod before. What joy it
is to light upon virgin springs and drink their waters. What joy
to pluck new flowers and gather for my brow a glorious
garland from fields whose blossoms were never yet wreathed
by the Muses round any head. This is my reward for teaching
on these lofty topics, for struggling to loose men's minds from
the tight knots of superstition and shedding on dark material
the bright beam of my song, which irradiates everything with
the sparkle of the Muses. My art is not without a purpose.   10
Physicians, when they wish to treat children with a nasty dose
of wormwood, first smear the rim of the cup with the sweet
yellow syrup of honey. The children, too young as yet for
foresight, are lured by the sweetness at their lips into swallowing
the bitter draught. So they are tricked but not trapped; for the
treatment restores them to health. In the same way our doctrine
often seems unpalatable to those who have not handled it, and
the masses shrink from it. That is why I have tried to administer
my philosophy to you in the dulcet strains of poesy, to touch it
with the sweet honey of the Muses. My object has been to   24
engage your mind with my verses while you gain insight into
the nature of the universe and learn to appreciate the profit you
are reaping.

I have already shown[2] what is the nature of the mind; by what
forces it is brought to its full strength in union with the body;
and how it is disintegrated and returns to its component atoms.

Now I will embark on an explanation of a highly relevant
fact, *the existence of what we call 'images' of things*, a sort of outer
skin perpetually peeled off the surface of objects and flying
about this way and that through the air. It is these[3] whose
impact scares our minds, whether waking or sleeping, on those
occasions when we catch a glimpse of strange shapes and

36 phantoms of the dead. Often, when we are sunk in slumber, they startle us with the notion that spirits may get loose from the Underworld and ghosts hover about among the living, and that some part of us may survive after death when body and mind alike have been disintegrated and dissolved into their component atoms.[4]

44 I maintain therefore that replicas or insubstantial shapes of things are thrown off from the surface of objects. This you may infer, however dull your wit, from the following facts.

[I have already shown what the component bodies of everything are like; how they vary in shape; how they fly spontaneously through space, impelled by a perpetual motion; and how from these all objects can be created. Now I shall begin to broach a subject of great relevance to this, namely the existence of what we call 'images' of things, which we should perhaps term 'skins' or 'bark', since the image wears an appearance and form similar to the object – whatever it is – that discharged it on its travels.]

53 In the first place, within the range of vision, many objects give off particles. Some of these are rarefied and diffused, such as the smoke emitted by logs or the heat by fire. Others are denser and more closely-knit: cicadas, for instance, in summer periodically shed their tubular jackets; calves at birth cast off cauls from the surface of their bodies; or again the slippery green snake divests itself of its clothing on thorns – for we often see briars enriched by these fluttering scalps. Since these things happen, objects must also give off a much flimsier film from the surface of their bodies. For, since those more solid

63 emanations fall off, no reason can be given why such flimsy ones should not.[5] Besides, we know that on the surface of objects there are lots of tiny particles, which could be thrown off without altering the order of their arrangement or the outline of their shape, and all the faster because, being relatively few and marshalled on the front line, they are less liable to obstruction.

We certainly see that many objects throw off matter in abundance, not only from their inmost depths, as we have said before,[6] but from their surfaces in the form of colour. This is done conspicuously by the awnings, yellow, scarlet and maroon, stretched flapping and billowing on poles and rafters over spacious theatres.[7] The crowded pit below and the stage with all its scenery and the magnificence of the masked actors are made to glow and flow with the colours of the canopy. The more completely the theatre is hemmed in by surrounding walls, the more its interior, sheltered from the daylight, laughs in this flood of colour. Since canvasses thus give off colour from their surface, all objects must give off filmy images as a result of spraying particles from their surfaces this way and that. Here then, already definitely established, we have indications of images, flying about everywhere, extremely fine in texture and individually invisible.

Again, the reason why smell, smoke, heat and the like come streaming out of objects in shapeless clouds is that they originate in the inmost depths; so they are split up in their circuitous journey, and there are no straight vents to their channels through which they may issue directly in close formation. When the thin film of surface colour, on the other hand, is thrown off, there is nothing to disrupt it, since it lies ready positioned on the front line.

Lastly, the reflections that we see in mirrors[8] or in water or any polished surface have the same appearance as actual objects. They must therefore be composed of films given off by those objects. There exist therefore flimsy but accurate replicas of objects, individually invisible but such that, when flung back in a rapid succession of recoils from the flat surface of mirrors they produce a visible image. That is the only conceivable way in which these films can be preserved so as to reproduce such a perfect likeness of each object.

Let me now explain *how flimsy is the texture of these films*. In the first place, the atoms themselves are vastly below the range of our senses – vastly smaller than the first objects, on a descending scale, that the eye can no longer discern. In confirmation of this, let me illustrate in a few words the minuteness of the atoms of which everything is composed. First, there are animals that are already so tiny that a third part of them would be quite

75

84

94

108

118 invisible. How are we to picture the internal organs of these – the tiny globule of the heart, or the eyes? Of what size are its limbs or their joints? What must be the component atoms of its spirit and its mind? You cannot help seeing how slight and diminutive these must be. Or again, consider those substances that emit a pungent odour – all-healing opopanax, bitter worm- wood, oppressive southernwood, the astringent tang of cen-

126 taury. If you lightly crush one of these herbs between two ⟨fingers, the scent will cling to your hand, but its particles will be quite invisible⟩. This will convey some notion of the number of surface-films from objects that must be flying about in a variety of ways without producing any effect on the senses. You must not suppose that the only films moving about are those that emanate from objects. *There are also films spontaneously generated* and composed in this lower region of the sky that we call the air. These assume a diversity of shapes and travel at a great height. So at times we see clouds smoothly condensing up

136 aloft, defacing the bright aspect of the firmament and caressing the air by their motion. Often giant faces appear to be sailing by, trailing large patches of shadow. Sometimes it seems that great mountains, or crags uprooted from mountains, are drifting by and passing over the sun. Then other clouds, black with storm, appear to be towed along in the wake of some passing monster.[9] In their fluidity they never cease to change their form, assuming the outline now of one shape, now of another.

⟨Let us now consider⟩ *with what facility and speed the films are*
generated and ceaselessly stream out of objects and slide off their
144 surfaces. For the outermost skin of all objects is always in readiness for them to shed. When this comes in contact with other objects, it may pass through, as it does in particular through glass. When it encounters rough rocks or solid wood, then it is promptly chopped up, so that it cannot reproduce an image. But when it is confronted by something both polished and solid, in particular a mirror, then neither of these things happens. The films cannot penetrate, as they do through glass; nor are they chopped up, because the smoothness guarantees their safety. That is why such surfaces reflect images that are

visible to us. No matter how suddenly or at what time you set   155
any object in front of a mirror, an image appears. From this
you may infer that the surfaces of objects emit a ceaseless
stream of flimsy tissues and filmy shapes. Therefore a great
many films are generated in a brief space of time, so that their
origin can rightly be described as instantaneous. Just as a great
many particles of light must be emitted in a brief space of time
by the sun to keep the world continually filled with it, so   163
objects in general must correspondingly send off a great many
images in a great many ways from every surface and in all
directions instantaneously. Turn the mirror which way we will,
all objects[10] are reproduced in it with corresponding shape and
colour.

Again, when the weather has been most brilliant, it becomes
gloomy and overcast with amazing suddenness. You would
fancy that all the nether darkness from every quarter had
abandoned the Underworld and crowded the spacious vaults of
heaven: so grim a night of storm gathers aloft, from which   173
lours down the face of black fear.[11] In comparison with such a
mass of matter, no one can express how minute a surface-film
is, or convey any idea of the proportion in words.

Let me now explain in my verses *how speedily the films move* and
what power they possess of swimming swiftly through the air,
so that a brief hour is spent on a long journey, whatever course
each one may pursue in response to its particular impulse. My
account will be persuasive rather than exhaustive. Better the
fleeting melody of the swan[12] than the long-drawn clangour of   182
cranes high up among the northward-racing clouds.

First, then, it is a common observation that light objects and
those composed of small particles are swift-moving. A notable
example is the light and heat of the sun: these are composed of
minute atoms which are as it were beaten and lose no time in
shooting right across the interspace of air driven on by the
force following them. The supply of light is promptly renewed
by fresh light, and one flash is goaded on by another as in a
team of yoked animals. Similarly the films must be able to
traverse an incalculable space in an instant of time, and that for

194 two reasons. First, a very slight[13] initial impetus far away to
their rear sufficed to launch them and they continue on their
course with such bird-swift lightness. Secondly, they are thrown
off with such a loose-knit texture that they can readily penetrate
any object and filter through the interspace of air.

Again, certain particles thrown up to the surface from the
inmost depths of objects, namely those that form the light and
heat of the sun, are seen at the very instant of daybreak to drop
201 and spray out across the whole space of the sky and fly over sea
and lands and flood the sky. What then of particles that are
already stationed on the front line when they are thrown off
and whose egress is not hampered by any obstacle? Surely they
must go all the faster[14] and the farther and traverse an extent of
space many times as great in the time it takes for the sunlight to
flash across the sky?

A further and especially convincing indication of the velocity
of surface-films is this. Expose a smooth surface of water to the
open sky when it is bright with stars: immediately the sparkling
212 constellations of the firmament in all their unclouded splendour
twinkle back reproduced in the water. Does not this indicate
how instantaneous is the descent of the image from the border-
land of ether to the borders of earth? Here then is proof upon
proof that objects emit particles that strike upon the eyes and
provoke sight.

From certain objects there also flows a perpetual stream of
odour, as coolness flows from rivers, heat from the sun, and
from the ocean waves as spray that eats away walls round the
seashore.[15] Sounds of every sort are surging incessantly through
221 the air. When we walk by the seaside, a salty tang of brine
often enters our mouth; when we watch a draught of worm-
wood being mixed in our presence, a bitter effluence touches
us. So from every object flows a stream of matter, spreading
out in all directions. The stream must flow without rest or
intermission, since our senses are perpetually alert and every-
thing is always liable to be seen or smelt or to provoke
sensation by sound.

Again, when some shape or other is handled in the dark, it is recognized as the same shape that in a clear and shining light is plain to see. It follows that *touch and sight are provoked by the same stimulus.*[16] Suppose we touch a square object and it stimulates our sense in the dark. What can it be that, given light, will strike upon our vision as square, if it is not the film emanating from the object? This shows that the cause of seeing lies in these films and that without these nothing can be seen.

It is established, then, that these films, as I call them, are moving about everywhere, sprayed and scattered in all directions. Since we can see only with our eyes, it is only when we direct our vision towards any particular quarter that all the objects there strike it with their shapes and colours. Our power of perceiving and distinguishing the distance from us of each particular object is also due to the film. For, as soon as it is thrown off, it shoves and drives before it all the air that intervenes between itself and the eyes. All this air flows through our eyeballs and brushes through our pupils in passing.[17] That is how we perceive the distance of each object: the more air is driven in front of the film and the longer the draught that brushes through our eyes, the more remote the object is seen to be. Of course this all happens so quickly that we perceive the nature of the object and its distance simultaneously.

It need occasion no surprise that, while the individual films that strike upon the eye are invisible, the objects from which they emanate are perceived.[18] Wind too buffets us bit by bit, and cold strikes us in a piercing stream; yet we do not feel each particular unit of the wind or the cold, but simply the total effect. And we see that blows are then being delivered on our body with an effect as though some external object were buffeting it and making its presence felt. When we hit a stone with our toe, what we actually touch is only the outer surface of the rock, the overlying film of colour; but what we feel ourselves touching is not that but the hard inner core of the rock.[19]

Let us now consider *why the image is seen beyond the mirror* – for it certainly does appear to be some distance behind the surface. It is just as though we were really looking out through a doorway, when the door offers a free prospect through itself

273 and affords a glimpse of many objects outside the house. In this case also the vision is accompanied by a double dose of air. First we perceive the air within the door posts; then follow the posts themselves to right and left; then the light outside and a second stretch of air brushes through the eyes, followed by the objects that are really seen out of doors. A similar thing happens when a mirrored image projects itself upon our sight.

280 On its way to us the film shoves and drives before it all the air that intervenes between itself and the eyes, so that we feel all this before perceiving the mirror. When we have perceived the mirror itself, then the film that travels from us to it and is reflected comes back to our eyes, pushing another lot of air in front of it, so that we perceive this air before we see the image, which thus appears to lie at some distance from the mirror. Here then is ample reason why we should not be surprised ⟨that the same happens both in the case of things seen through doors, and also⟩ at this appearance of objects reflected in the

291 surface of a mirror, since they both involve a double journey with two lots of air.

Now for the question *why our right side appears in mirrors on the left*. The reason is that, when the film on its outward journey strikes the flat surface of a mirror, it is not slewed round intact, but flung straight back in reverse. It is just as if someone were to take a plaster mask before it had set and hurl it against a pillar or beam, so that it bounced straight back, preserving the features imprinted on its front but displaying them now in reverse. In this case what had been the right eye would now be

300 the left and the left correspondingly would have become the right.

It may also happen that a film is passed on from one mirror to another, so that as many as five or six images are produced. Objects tucked away in the inner part of a house, however long and winding the approach to their hiding place, can thus be brought into sight along devious routes by a series of mirrors. So clearly is the image flashed from mirror to mirror. And on each occasion what is transmitted as the left becomes the right and is then again reversed and returns to its original relative position.

Again, mirrors with projecting sides whose curvature 311
matches our own give back to us unreversed images.[20] This
may be because the film is thrown from one surface of the
mirror to the other and reaches us only after a double rebound.
Alternatively, it may be that on reaching the mirror the film is
slewed round, because the curved surface teaches it to twist
round towards us.

You would fancy that images walk along with us, keeping 318
step and copying our gestures. This is because, as soon as you
withdraw from a bit of the mirror, no films can be reflected
from that part. Nature ordains that every particle shall rebound
from the reflecting surface at equal angles.[21]

Now[22] for the fact that *the eyes avoid bright objects* and refuse to
gaze at them. The sun, indeed, actually blinds them if you
persist in directing them towards it. The reason is that its force
is immense and the films it gives off travel with great momen-
tum through a great depth of pure air and hit the eyes hard, so 328
as to disrupt their atomic structure. Besides, any bright light
that is painful can often scorch the eyes, because it contains
many particles of fire whose infiltration sets them smarting.

Sufferers from jaundice[23] again, *see everything they look at as yellow.*
This is because many particles of yellowness from their own
bodies are streaming out in the path of the approaching films.
There are also many such particles blended in the structure of
their own eyes, and by contamination with these everything is
painted with their sallowness.
336

When we are in the dark we see objects that are in the light for the
following reason. The black murky air that lies nearer to us
enters first into our open eyes and takes possession of them. It
is then closely followed by bright and shining air, which
cleanses them and dispels the shadows of the earlier air. For the
bright air is many degrees more mobile and many degrees finer-
grained and more potent. As soon as this has filled the passages
of the eyes with light and opened those that had previously
been blockaded by dark air, they are immediately followed by

347 films thrown off from the illuminated objects, and these stimulate our sense of sight. On the other hand, when we look out of light into darkness, we can see nothing: the murky air, of muddier consistency, arrives last and chokes all the inlets of the eyes and blockades their passages, so that they cannot be stirred by the impact of films from any object.

353 *When we see the square towers of a city in the distance, they often appear round.*[24] This is because every angle seen at a distance is blunted or even is not seen as an angle at all. Its impact is nullified and does not penetrate as far as the eyes, because films that travel through a great deal of air lose their sharp outlines through frequent collisions with it. When every angle has thus eluded our sense, the result is that the square ashlars look as if rounded off on the lathe – not that they resemble really round stones seen close up, but in a sketchy sort of way they counterfeit them.

364 Again, *our shadow in the sunlight seems to us to move* and keep step with us and imitate our gestures, incredible though it is that unillumined air should walk about in conformity with a man's movements and gestures. For what we commonly call a shadow can be nothing but air deprived of light. Actually the earth is robbed of sunlight in a definite succession of places wherever it is obstructed by us in our progression, and the part we have left is correspondingly replenished with it. That is why the successive shadows of our body seem to be the same shadow 375 following us along steadily step by step.[25] New particles of radiance are always streaming down and their predecessors are consumed, as the saying goes, like wool being spun into the fire. So the earth is easily robbed of light and is correspondingly replenished and washes off the black stains of shadow.

Here, as always, *we do not admit that the eyes are in any way deluded*. It is their function to see where light is, and where shadow. But whether one light is the same as another, and whether the shadow that was here is moving over there, or whether on the other hand what really happens is what I have just described – that is something to be discerned by the reasoning power of the mind.[26] The nature of phenomena cannot be understood by the eyes. You must not hold them responsible for this fault of the mind.

A ship[27] in which we are sailing is on the move, though it seems to stand still. Another that rides at anchor gives the impression of sailing by. Hills and plains appear to be drifting astern when our ship soars past them with sails for wings.

The stars[28] all seem motionless, embedded in the ethereal vault; yet they must all be in constant motion, since they rise and traverse the heavens with their luminous bodies till they return to the far-off scene of their setting. So too the sun and moon appear to remain at their posts, though the facts prove them travellers.

Mountains rising from the midst of the sea in the far distance, though there may be ample space between them for the free passage of a fleet, look as if linked together in a single island.

When children have come to a standstill after spinning round, they seem to see halls and pillars whirling round them — and so vividly that they can scarcely believe that the whole building is not threatening to tumble on top of them.

When nature is just beginning to fling up the light of day, ruddy with flickering fires, and lift it high above the hilltops, the glowing sun seems to perch upon the hills and kindle them by direct contact with its own fire. Yet these same hills are distant from us a bare two thousand bowshots — often indeed no more than five hundred javelin casts. But between hills and sun lie enormous tracts of ocean, overarched by vast ethereal vaults, and many thousands of intervening lands, peopled by all the various races of men and species of beasts.

A puddle no deeper than a finger's breadth, formed in a hollow between the cobble-stones of the highway, offers to the eye a downward view, below the ground, of as wide a scope as the towering immensity of sky that yawns above. You would fancy you saw clouds far down below you and a sky and heavenly bodies deep-buried in a miraculous heaven beneath the earth.

When the mettlesome steed we are riding stands stock-still in midstream and we glance down at the swift-flowing torrent,

385

391

402

413

422 our stationary mount seems to be breasting the flood and forcing its way rapidly upstream; and, wherever we cast our eyes, everything seems to be surging and forging ahead with the same movement as ourselves.

When we gaze from one end down the whole length of a colonnade,[29] though its structure is perfectly symmetrical and it is propped throughout on pillars of equal height, yet it contracts 430 by slow degrees in a narrowing cone that draws roof to floor and left to right till it unites them in the imperceptible apex of the cone.

To sailors at sea, the sun appears to rise out of the waves and to set in the waves and there hide its light. This is because they do in fact see only water and sky – another warning not to jump to the conclusion that the senses are shaky guides on all points.

To landsmen ignorant of the sea, ships in harbour seem to be riding crippled on the waves, with their poops broken. So much of the oars[30] as projects above the dew of the brine is 439 straight, and so is the upper part of the rudder. But all the submerged parts appear refracted and wrenched round in an upward direction and almost as though bent right back so as to float on the surface.

At a time when scattered clouds are scudding before the wind across the night sky, the sparkling constellations look as though they were gliding along in the teeth of the clouds and passing overhead in a direction quite different from their actual course.

447 If we press our hand against one eye[31] from below, a new sort of perception results. Whatever we look at, we see double: the lamplight, aflower with flame, becomes twin lights; the furniture throughout the house is doubled; men wear double faces and two bodies apiece.

When sleep has fettered all our limbs in the pleasant chains of slumber, and the whole body has sunk in utter tranquillity, we still seem to ourselves to be wide awake and moving our limbs. In the blind blackness of night we fancy ourselves gazing on the sun and the broad light of day. In a confined space, we seem to traverse sea and sky, rivers and mountains,

and tramp on foot over open plains. With the solemn hush of 460
night all around, we listen to sounds; we speak aloud without a
word uttered.[32]

We have many other paradoxical experiences of the same
kind, all of which seem bent on shaking our faith in the senses.
But all to no purpose. Most of this illusion is due to the mental
assumptions[33] that we ourselves superimpose, so that things
not perceived by the senses pass for perceptions. There is 467
nothing harder than to separate the plain facts from the question-
able interpretations promptly imposed on them by the mind.

If anyone thinks that nothing is ever known, he does not know whether
even this can be known, since he admits that he knows nothing.[34]
Against such an adversary, therefore, who deliberately stands
on his head,[35] I will not trouble to argue my case. And yet, if I
were to grant that he possessed this knowledge, I might ask
several pertinent questions. Since he has had no experience of
truth, how does he know what either knowledge or ignorance 475
are?[36] What has originated the concept of truth and falsehood?
Where is his proof that doubt is not the same as certainty?

You will find, in fact, that the concept of truth was originated
by the senses and that the senses cannot be rebutted. The
testimony that we must accept as more trustworthy is that
which can spontaneously overcome falsehood with truth. What
then are we to pronounce more trustworthy than the senses?
Can reason derived from the deceitful senses be invoked to
contradict them, when it is itself wholly derived from the
senses? If they are not true, then reason in its entirety is equally 485
false. Or can the ears upbraid the eyes, or touch judge the ears?
Can touch in turn be refuted by taste or silenced by the nostrils
or rebutted by the eyes? This, in my view, is out of the
question. Each sense has its own distinctive faculty, its specific
function. It is thus necessary to perceive softness, icy cold and
burning heat with sensation quite distinct from that with which
we feel the various colours of things and whatever goes with
the colours; taste in the mouth has its very own distinctive
power, and scents are generated in quite a different way from
sounds. This rules out the possibility of one sense confuting

497 another.[37] It will be equally out of the question for the senses to convict one another, since they will always be entitled to the same degree of credence. Whatever the senses may perceive at any time is all alike true. Suppose that reason cannot disentangle the cause why things that were square when close at hand are seen as round in the distance. Even so, it is better, in default of reason, to assign fictitious causes to the two shapes than to let
505 things clearly apprehended slip from our grasp. This is to attack belief at its very roots – to tear up the entire foundation on which life and safety depend. It is not only reason that would collapse completely. If you did not dare trust your senses so as to keep clear of precipices and other such things to be avoided and make for their opposites, there would be a speedy end to life itself.

So all this armament that you have marshalled against the senses is nothing but a futile array of words. If you set out to construct a building with a crooked ruler, a faulty square that is
516 set a little out of the straight and a level ever so slightly askew, there can be only one outcome – a crazy, crooked, higgledy-piggledy huddle, sagging here and bulging there, with bits that look like falling at any moment and are all in fact destined to fall, doomed by the initial miscalculations on which the structure is based. Just as crooked and just as defective must be the structure of your reasoning, if the senses on which it rests are themselves deceptive.

After this the problem that next confronts us – to determine
523 *how each of the remaining senses perceives its own objects* – is not a particularly thorny one.

In the first place, all forms of *sound and vocal utterance* become audible when they have slipped into the ear and provoked sensation by the impact of their own bodies. The fact that voices and other sounds can impinge on the senses is itself a proof of their corporeal nature. Besides, the voice often scrapes the throat and a shout roughens the windpipe on its outward path. What happens is that, when atoms of voice in greater numbers than usual have begun to squeeze out through the narrow outlet, the doorway of the mouth gets scraped as the

throat is congested. Undoubtedly, if voices and words have this   533
power of causing pain, they must consist of corporeal particles.
Again, you must have noticed how much it takes out of a man,
and what wear and tear it causes to his sinews and strength, to
keep on talking from the first glow of dawn till the evening
shadows darken,[38] especially if his words are poured forth at
full volume. Since much talking actually takes something out of
the body, it follows that voice is composed of bodily stuff.   542
Finally, the harshness of a sound is due to the harshness of its
component atoms, and its smoothness to their smoothness.
There is a marked difference in the shape of the atoms that
enter our ears when a low-toned trumpet booms its *basso
profondo* and the boxwood pipe, that virtuoso foreign instru-
ment, re-echoes its hoarse roar, and when the swans' plaintive
dirge floats up in doleful melody from the shrubbery of the
gardens.

When we force out[39] these utterances from the depths of our
body and launch them through the direct outlet of the mouth,   551
they are cut up into lengths by the flexible tongue, the craftsman
of words, and moulded in turn by the configuration of the lips.
At a point reached by each particular utterance after travelling
no great distance from its source, it naturally happens that the
individual words are also clearly audible and distinguishable
syllable by syllable. For the utterance preserves its shape and
configuration. But if the intervening space is unduly wide, the
words must inevitably be jumbled and the utterance disjointed
by its flight through a long stretch of gusty air. So it happens
that, while you are aware of a sound, you cannot discern the
sense of the words: the utterance comes to you so muddled and   561
entangled.

It often happens that a single word, uttered from the mouth
of a crier, penetrates the ears of a whole crowd. Evidently a
single utterance must split up immediately into a multitude of
utterances, since it is parcelled out amongst a number of
separate ears, imprinting upon each the shape of a word and its
distinctive sound. Such of these utterances as do not strike
upon the ears float by and are scattered to the winds and lost
without effect. Some of them, however, bump against solid

571 objects and bounce[40] back, so as to carry back a sound and sometimes mislead with the replica of a word. Once you have grasped this, you can explain to yourself and to others how it is that in desert places, when we are searching for comrades who have scattered and strayed among overshadowed glens and hail them at the top of our voices, the cliffs fling back the forms of our words in due sequence. I have observed places tossing back six or seven utterances when you have launched a single one: 578 being trained to rebound, the words were reverberated and reiterated from hill to hill. According to local legend,[41] these places are haunted by goat-footed Satyrs[42] and by Nymphs. Tales are told of Fauns,[43] whose noisy night-time revels and merry pranks shatter the mute hush of night for miles around; of twanging lyre-strings and plaintive melodies poured out by pipes at the touch of the players' fingers; of music far-heard by the country folk when Pan,[44] tossing the pine-branches that wreathe his brutish head, runs his arched lips again and again 589 along the wide-mouthed reeds, so that the pipe's wildwood rhapsody flows on unbroken. Many such fantasies and fairy tales are related by the rustics. Perhaps, in boasting of these marvels, they hope to dispel the notion that they live in backwoods abandoned even by the gods. Perhaps they have some other motive, since mankind everywhere has greedy ears for such romancing.

There remains the problem, not a very puzzling one, of how sounds can penetrate and strike on the ear through places through which objects cannot be clearly perceived by the eye. 598 The obvious reason why we often see a conversation going on through closed doors is that an utterance can make its way intact through the labyrinthine passages in objects impervious to visual films. For these are broken up, unless they are passing through straight fissures such as those in glass, which is penetrable by any sort of image. Again, sounds are disseminated in all directions because each one, after its initial splintering into a great many parts, gives birth to others, just as a spark of fire often propagates itself by starting fires of its own. So places out of the direct path are filled with voices, and all around they boil and thrill with sound. But visual films all continue in straight

lines along their initial paths, so that no one can see over a 609
wall, though he can hear voices from inside it. Even a voice,
however, is blunted in its passage through barriers and is
blurred when it pierces our ears, so that we seem to hear a mere
noise rather than words.

As for the organs of *taste*, the tongue and the palate, they do
not call for lengthier explanation or more expenditure of labour. 617
In the first place, we perceive taste in the mouth when we
squeeze it out by chewing food, just as if someone were to
grasp a sponge full of water in his hand and begin to squeeze it
dry. Next, all that we squeeze out is diffused through the pores
of the palate and the winding channels of the spongy tongue.
When the particles of trickling savour are smooth, they touch
the palate pleasantly and pleasurably tickle all the moist regions
of the tongue in their circuitous flow. Others, in proportion as
their shape is rougher, tend more to prick and tear the organs
of sense by their entry.

The pleasure derived from taste does not extend beyond the 627
palate. When the tasty morsel has all been gulped down the
gullet and is being distributed through the limbs, it gives no
more pleasure. It does not matter what food you take to
nourish your body so long as you can digest it and distribute it
through your limbs and preserve the sturdy condition of the
stomach.

Let me now explain why one man's meat is not another's,[45]
and what is bitter and unpalatable to one may strike another as
delicious. The difference in reaction is indeed so great that
what is food to one may be literally poison to others. There is 637
even, for instance, a snake that is so affected by human saliva
that it bites itself to death.[46] To us hellebore is rank poison; but
goats and quails grow fat on it.[47] In order to understand how
this happens, the first point to remember is one that I have
already mentioned,[48] the diversity of atoms that are commingled
in objects. With the outward differences between the various
types of animal that take food – the specific distinctions revealed
by the external contour of their limbs – there go corresponding
differences in the shapes of their component atoms. These in

649 their turn entail differences in the chinks and channels – the pores as we call them – in all parts of the body, including the mouth and palate itself. In some species these are naturally smaller, in others larger; in some triangular, in others square; while many are round, others are of various polygonal shapes. In short, the shapes and motions of the atoms rigidly determine the shapes of the pores: the atomic structure defines the inter-
658 atomic channels. When something sweet to one is bitter to another, it must be because its smoothest particles caressingly penetrate the palate of the former, whereas the latter's gullet is evidently invaded by particles that are rough and jagged. On this basis the whole problem becomes easily soluble. Thus, when some person is afflicted with fever through superfluity of bile, or sickness is provoked in him by some other factor, his entire body is simultaneously upset and all the positions of the component atoms are changed. It follows that particles which used to be conformable to the channels of sensation are so no
670 longer, whereas an easier ingress is afforded to those other particles whose entry can provoke a disagreeable sensation. For, as I have already demonstrated many times, the flavour of honey[49] actually consists of a mixture of both kinds, pleasant and unpleasant.

Let me now tackle the question *how the nostrils are touched by the impact of smell.*

First, then, there must be a multitude of objects giving off a multifarious effluence of smells, which is to be conceived as emitted in a stream and widely diffused. But particular smells,
677 owing to their distinctive shapes, are better adapted to particular species of animals. Bees are attracted for unlimited distances through the air by the smell of honey, vultures by carcasses. Where the cloven hoof of wild game has planted its spoor, the hunter is guided by his vanguard of hounds. The scent of man is detected far in advance by that lily-white guardian of the citadel of the sons of Romulus,[50] the goose. So each by its own particular gift of smell is attracted to its proper food or repelled from noxious poison: and thus the various species are preserved.

As for the smells that assail our nostrils, it is clear that some of them have a longer range than others. None of them, however, travels as far as voices or other sounds, not to speak of the films that strike the eyeballs and provoke sight. For smell is a straggling and tardy traveller and fades away before arriving, by the gradual dissipation of its flimsy body into the gusty air. One reason for this is that smell originates in the depths of objects and is thus given off haltingly: an indication that odours thus seep out and escape from the inner core of objects is the fact that everything smells more strongly when broken or crushed or dissolved by fire. A further reason is that smell is evidently composed of larger atoms than sound, since it does not pass through stone walls, which are readily permeable by voices and other sounds. That is why you will not find it so easy to locate the source of a smell as of a sound. The effluence grows cold by dawdling through the air and does not rush with its tidings to the senses hotfoot from its source. So it is that hounds are often at fault and have to cast round for the scent.

This is not confined to smells and tastes. The visible forms and colours of things are not all equally conformable to the sense organs of all species, but in some cases particular sights act as irritants. The sight of a cock, that herald of the dawn who banishes the night with clapping wings and lusty crowing, is intolerable to ravening lions.[51] At the first glimpse they think only of flight. The reason is, of course, that the cock's body contains certain atoms which, when they get into the lion's eyes, drill into the eyeballs and cause acute pain, so that even their bold spirits cannot long endure it. But these atoms have no power to hurt our eyes, either because they never get in at all or because, once in, they have a clear way out, so that they do not hurt the eyeball in any part by lingering there.

Let me now explain briefly *what it is that stimulates the imagination and where those images come from that enter the mind.*[52]

My first point is thus. There are a great many flimsy films from the surface of objects flying about in a great many ways in all directions. When these encounter one another in the air, they easily amalgamate, like spider's web or gold-leaf. In comparison

687

695

706

718

728   with those films that take possession of the eye and provoke sight, these are certainly of a much flimsier texture, since they penetrate through the chinks of the body and set in motion the delicate substance of the mind within and there provoke sensation. So it is that we see the composite shapes of Centaurs,[53] the limbs of Scyllas,[54] dogs with as many heads as Cerberus,[55] and phantoms of the dead whose bones lie in the embrace of earth.

735   The fact is that the films flying about everywhere are of all sorts: some are produced spontaneously in the air itself; others are derived from various objects and composed by the amalgamation of their shapes. The image of a Centaur, for instance, is certainly not formed from life, since no living creature of this sort has ever existed. But, as I have just explained, where surface films from a horse and a man accidentally come into contact, they may easily stick together on the spot, because of the delicacy and flimsiness of their texture. So also with other such chimerical creatures. Since, as I have shown above, these delicate films move with the utmost nimbleness and mobility,

747   any one of them may easily set our mind in motion with a single touch; for the mind itself is delicate and marvellously mobile.

  The truth of this explanation may be easily inferred from the following facts. First, in so far as a vision beheld by the mind closely resembles one beheld by the eyes, the two must have been created in a similar fashion. Now, I have shown that I see a lion, for example, through the impact of films on the eyes. It follows that something similar accounts for the motion of the

755   mind, which also, no less than the eyes, beholds a lion or whatever it may be by means of films. The only difference is that the objects of its vision are flimsier.

  Again, when our limbs are relaxed in slumber, our mind is as wakeful as ever.[56] The same sort of films impinge upon it then as when we are awake, but now with such vividness that in sleep we may even be convinced that we are seeing someone who has passed from life into the clutches of death and earth. This results quite naturally from the stoppage and quiescence of all the bodily senses throughout the frame, so that they cannot refute false impressions by true ones. The memory also is put

out of action by sleep and does not protest that the person   765
whom the mind fancies it sees alive has long since fallen into
the power of death and dissolution. It is not surprising that
dream images should move about with measured gestures of
their arms and other limbs. When this happens, it means that
one film has perished and is succeeded by another formed in a
different posture, so that it seems as though the earlier image
had changed its stance.[57] We must picture this succession as
taking place at high speed: the films fly so quickly and are   773
drawn from so many sources, and at any perceptible instant of
time there are so many atoms to keep up the supply.

This subject raises various questions that we must elucidate
if we wish to give a clear account of it.

The first question is this: Why is it that, as soon as the mind
takes a fancy to think about some particular object, it promptly
does so? Are we to suppose that images are waiting on our
will, so that we have only to wish and the appropriate film
immediately runs into our mind, whether it be the sea that we   783
fancy or the earth or the sky? Assemblages of men, processions,
banquets, battles – does nature create all these at a word and
make them ready for us? And we must remember that, at the
same time and in the same place, the minds of others are
contemplating utterly different objects.

Again, when in our dreams we see images walking with
measured step and moving their supple limbs, why do they
swing their supple arms in time with alternate legs and perform
repeated movements before our eyes in a suitable rhythm? Are
we to suppose the stray films are imbued with art and trained   793
to spend their nights putting on dancing shows?

Another answer can be given to both questions that is surely
nearer the truth. In one perceptible moment of time, that is, the
time required to utter a single syllable, there are many unper-
ceived units of time whose existence is recognized by reason.[58]
That explains why, at any given time, every sort of film is
ready to hand in every place: they fly so quickly and are drawn
from so many sources. When this happens, it means that one
film has perished and is succeeded by another formed in a differ-
ent posture, so that it seems as though the earlier image had

801 changed its stance. And, because they are so flimsy, the mind cannot distinctly perceive any but those it makes an effort to perceive. All the rest pass without effect, leaving only those for which the mind has prepared itself. And the mind prepares itself in the expectation of seeing each appearance followed by its natural sequel. So this, in fact, is what it does see. You must have noticed how even our eyes, when they set out to look at inconspicuous objects, make an effort and prepare themselves;

809 otherwise it is not possible for us to perceive detail distinctly. And, even when you are dealing with visible objects, you will find that, unless you direct your mind towards them, they have about them all the time an air of detachment and remoteness. What wonder, then, if the mind misses every impression except those to which it surrenders itself? The result is that we draw sweeping conclusions from trifling indications and lead ourselves into pitfalls of delusion.[59]

Sometimes it happens that an image is not forthcoming to match our expectation: what was a woman seems to be suddenly

819 transformed into a man before our eyes, or we are suddenly confronted by some swift change of feature or age. Any surprise we might feel at this is checked by drowsy forgetfulness.

In this context, there is one illusion that you must do your level best to escape – an error to guard against with all due caution. You must not imagine that the bright orbs of our eyes were created purposely,[60] so that we might be able to look before us; that our need to stride ahead determined our equipment with

828 the pliant props of thigh and ankle, set in the firm foundations of our feet; that our lower arms were fitted to stout upper arms, and helpful hands attached at either side, in order that we might do what is needful to sustain life. To interpret these or any other phenomena on these lines is perversely to turn the truth upside down. In fact, *nothing in our bodies was born in order that we might be able to use it, but whatever thing is born creates its own use.*[61] There was no seeing before eyes were born, no verbal pleading before the tongue was created. The origin of the tongue was far anterior to speech. The ears were created long before a sound was heard. All the limbs, I am well assured,

existed before their use. They cannot therefore have grown for   842
the sake of being used.

Battles were fought hand to hand, limbs were mangled and
bodies fouled with blood long before flashing spears were
hurled. Wounds were parried at the bidding of nature before
the left arm interposed a shield using skill. Yes, and laying the
weary frame to rest is an earlier institution than spreading
comfortable beds, and thirst was quenched before ever cups
were thought of.[62] We can believe, therefore, that these instru-   850
ments, whose invention sprang from experience and life, have
been designed to serve a purpose. Quite different are those
organs that were first born themselves and afterwards provided
a mental picture of their own functioning. And prominent in
this latter class we find our sense-organs and bodily members.
Here, then, is proof upon proof that you must banish the belief
that they could have been created for the purpose of performing
particular functions.

Another fact that need occasion no surprise is that *the body of*   858
every living creature by its own nature seeks after food. I have already
shown that vast numbers of particles in countless ways are
passing off things in a stream. But the greatest number of all
must be emitted by living things. Since animals are always on
the move, they lose a great many atoms, some squeezed out
from the inner depths by the process of perspiration, some
breathed out through the mouth when they gasp and pant. By
these processes the body's density is diminished and its sub-
stance sapped. This results in pain. Hence food is taken so that,   867
when duly distributed through limbs and veins, it may underpin
the frame and rebuild its strength and sate its open-mouthed
lust for eating. Moisture is similarly diffused into all the mem-
bers that demand moisture: and the many accumulated particles
of heat that inflame our stomach are dispelled by the advent of
the fluid and quenched like a fire, so that the frame is no longer
parched by burning drought. So it is that the thirst that sets
you gasping is swilled out of the body and the famished
craving is stuffed.

877 Let me now explain *how it comes about that we can stride forwards at will*[63] and are empowered to move our limbs in various ways, and what it is that has learnt to lift along this heavy load of our body. I count on you to mark my words. I will begin by repeating my previous statement that images of walking come to our mind and impinge upon it. Hence comes the will. For no one ever initiates any action without the mind first foreseeing what it wills.[64] What it foresees is the substance of the image. So

885 the mind, when the motions it experiences are such that it wishes to step forward, immediately jogs the vital spirit diffused through every limb and organ of the body. This is easily done, since mind and spirit are interconnected. The spirit in turn then jogs the body. And so bit by bit the whole bulk is pushed forward and set in motion.

A further effect is that the body grows less dense. The opened pores admit air, as is natural, since this is always highly mobile. The air rushes in in a stream and is thus diffused into every part

896 of the body, however small. From the combination of these two factors it results that the body is pushed along, just as a ship is propelled by the combined action of wind and sails.[65]

There is no need to be surprised that bodies so minute can twist round a body of such bulk and divert the course of our whole weight. The wind is tenuous enough, and its particles are diminutive; but it shoves along the mighty mass of a mighty ship, and, however fast it is travelling, a single hand steers it – a single tiller twists it this way or that. And many a heavy load is shifted and hoisted with an easy swing by a derrick, with the aid of pulleys and winches.

907

And now for *the problem of sleep*:[66] by what contrivance does it flood our limbs with peace and unravel from our breasts the mind's disquietude? My answer will be persuasive rather than exhaustive: better the fleeting melody of the swan than the long-drawn clangour of cranes high up among the northward-racing clouds.[67] It rests with you to lend an unresisting ear and an inquiring mind. Otherwise you may refuse to accept my explanation as possible and walk away with a mind that flings back the truth, though the blame lies with your own blindness.

In the first place, sleep occurs when the vital spirit through-   916
out the body is pulled to pieces: when part of it has been forced
out and lost, part compressed and driven into the inner depths.
At such times the limbs are unknit and grow limp. For undoubt-
edly the sensibility that is in us is caused by the spirit. When
sensation is deadened by sleep, we must suppose that this is due
to the derangement of the spirit or its expulsion. But it is not
all expelled, or else the body would be steeped in the everlasting   925
chill of death. If there were really no lurking particle of spirit
left in the limbs, as smothered fire lurks in a heap of ashes,
from what source could sentience be suddenly rekindled in the
limbs, as flame leaps up from hidden fire? I will explain how
this change is brought about and how the spirit can be disturbed
and the body grow limp. You must see to it that I do not waste
my words on the wind.

First, then, a body on its outer surface borders on the gusty
air and is touched by it. It must therefore be pelted by it with a
continual rain of blows. That is why almost all bodies are   935
covered with hide of shell, rind or bark. In bodies that breathe,
the interior also is battered by air as it is inhaled and exhaled.
Since our body is thus bombarded outside and in and the blows
penetrate through little pores to its primary parts and primal
elements, our limbs are subject in a sense to a gradual demoli-
tion. The relative positions of the atoms of body and mind are
mixed up. The result is that part of the spirit is forced out; part
becomes hidden away in the interior; part is loosely scattered
throughout the limbs, so that it cannot unite or engage in
interacting motions, because nature interposes obstacles to com-
bination and movement. This deep-seated change in motion   948
means the withdrawal of sentience.[68] At the same time, since
there is some lack of matter to support the frame, the body
grows weak; all the limbs slacken; arms and eyelids droop;
often, when a man is seeking rest, his knees lose their strength
and give way under him.[69]

Food, again, induces sleepiness, because its action, when it is
being distributed through all the veins, is the same as that of
air. The heaviest kind of sleep is that which ensues on satiety or
exhaustion, since it is then that the atoms are thrown into the

958 greatest confusion under stress of their heavy labour. The same cause makes the partial congestion of spirit more deep-seated and the evacuation more extensive, and aggravates the internal separation and dislocation.

Whatever employment has the strongest hold on our interest or has last filled our waking hours, so as to engage the mind's attention, that is what seems most often to keep us occupied in
966 dreams. Lawyers think that they are arguing cases and collating laws. Generals lead their troops into action. Sailors continue their pitched battle with the winds. And as for me,[70] I go on with my task, for ever exploring the nature of the universe and setting down my discoveries in my native tongue. The same principle generally applies when other crafts and occupations are observed to delude men's minds in dreams.

Similarly when men have devoted themselves wholeheartedly for days on end to the games,[71] we usually find that the objects that have ceased to engage the senses have left wide open
978 channels in the mind for the entry of their own images. So for many days the same sights hover before their eyes: even when awake, they seem to see figures dancing and swaying supple limbs; to fill their ears with the liquid melody and speaking strings of the lyre, and to watch the same crowded theatre, its stage ablaze with many-tinted splendour.

Such is the striking effect of interest and pleasure and customary employment, and not on men only but on all living creatures.[72] You will see mettlesome steeds, when their limbs are at rest, still continuing in sleep to sweat and pant as if straining all
990 their strength to win the palm, or as if racing out of the lifted barriers of the starting-post. And the huntsman's hounds, while wrapped in gentle slumber, often toss their legs with a quick jerk, bark suddenly and keep sniffing air into their nostrils as if they were hot on a newly found scent. Even when awake, they often chase after shadowy images of stags, as though they saw them in full flight, till they shake off the illusion and return to themselves. A friendly breed of domestic dogs are all agog to wriggle their bodies and lift them quickly from off the ground, just as if they were seeing the forms and faces of strangers. The fiercer the breed, the more savage must

be their behaviour in dreams. The various races of birds take to flight and startle the groves of the gods at dead of night with a sudden whirr of wings. Doubtless[73] their restless slumber is disturbed by visions of hawks swooping to the fray in fierce pursuit.

Very similar as a rule is the behaviour in sleep of human minds, whose mighty machinations produce massive feats. Kings[74] take cities by storm, are themselves taken captive, join in battle and cry aloud as though their throats were being slit – and all without stirring from the spot. There are many who fight for their lives, giving vent to their agony in groans or filling the night with piercing screams as though they were writhing in the jaws of a panther or a ravening lion.[75] Many talk in their sleep about matters of great moment and have often betrayed their own guilt.[76] Many die. Many, who feel themselves hurled bodily down to earth from towering crags,[77] are terrified out of sleep; like men who have lost their wits, they are slow in returning to themselves, so shaken are they by the tumult of their body. The thirsty man finds himself seated beside a river or a delectable spring and is near to gulping down the whole stream. Little boys often fancy when fast asleep that they are standing at a lavatory or a chamber pot and lifting up their clothes. Then they discharge all the filtered fluid of their body, and even the costly splendour of oriental coverlets does not escape a soaking.[78] Those boys in whom the seed is for the first time working its way into the choppy waters of their youth are invaded from without by images emanating from some body or other with tidings of an alluring face and a delightful complexion. This stimulates the organs swollen with an accumulation of seed. Often, as though their function were actually fulfilled, they discharge a flood of fluid and stain their clothes.[79]

In this last case, as I have explained, the thing in us that responds to the stimulus is the seed that comes with ripening years and stiffening limbs. For different things respond to different stimuli or provocations. *The one stimulus that evokes human seed from the human body is a human form.*[80] As soon as this

1041 seed is evicted from its abodes,[81] it travels through every member of the body, concentrating at certain reservoirs in the loins, and promptly awakens the generative organs. These organs are stimulated and swollen by the seed. Hence follows the will to eject it in the direction in which tyrannical lust is tugging. The body makes for the source from which the mind is pierced by love. For the wounded[82] normally fall in the direction of their wound: the blood spurts out towards the

1050 source of the blow; and the enemy who delivered it, if he is fighting at close quarters, is bespattered by the crimson stream. So, when a man is pierced by the shafts of Venus, whether they are launched by a lad[83] with womanish limbs or a woman radiating love from her whole body, he strives towards the source of the wound and craves to be united with it and to ejaculate the fluid drawn from out of his body into that body. His speechless[84] yearning foretells his pleasure.

This, then, is what we term Venus. This is the origin of the

1060 thing called love – that drop of Venus' honey that first drips into our heart, to be followed by icy heartache. Though the object of your love may be absent, images[85] of it still haunt you and the beloved name rings sweetly in your ears. If you find yourself thus passionately enamoured of an individual, you should keep well away from such images. Thrust from you anything that might feed your passion, and turn your mind elsewhere. Ejaculate the build-up of seed promiscuously and do not hold on to it – by clinging[86] to it you assure yourself the certainty of heartsickness and pain. With nourishment the fester-

1069 ing sore[87] quickens and strengthens. Day by day the madness[88] heightens and the grief deepens. Your only remedy is to lance the first wound with new incisions; to salve it, while it is still fresh, with promiscuous attachments or to guide the motions of your mind into a different direction.

Do not think that by avoiding romantic love you are missing the delights of sex. Rather, you are reaping the sort of profits that carry with them no penalty. Rest assured that this pleasure is enjoyed in a purer form by the sane than by the lovesick. Lovers' passion is storm-tossed, even in the moment of posses-sion, by waves of delusion and incertitude. They cannot make

up their mind what to enjoy first with eye or hand. They clasp   1078
the object of their longing so tightly that the embrace is
painful. They kiss so fiercely that teeth are driven into lips. All
this because their pleasure is not pure, but they are goaded by
an underlying impulse to hurt the thing, whatever it may be,
that gives rise to these budding shoots of madness.

In the actual presence of love Venus gives a slight break in
the penalties she imposes, and her sting is assuaged by an
admixture of alluring pleasure. For in love there is the hope   1085
that the flame of passion may be quenched by the same body
that kindled it. But this runs clean counter to the course of
nature. This is the one thing of which the more we have, the
more our breast burns with the evil lust of having. Food and
fluid are taken into our body; since they can fill their allotted
places, the desire for meat and drink is thus easily appeased.[89]
But a pretty face or a pleasing complexion gives the body
nothing to enjoy but insubstantial images, which all too often
pathetic hope scatters to the winds.

When a thirsty man tries to drink in his dreams but is given   1097
no drop to quench the fire in his limbs, he clutches at images of
water with fruitless effort and in the middle of a rushing stream
he remains thirsty as he drinks. Just so in the midst of love
Venus teases lovers with images. They cannot glut their eyes by
gazing on the beloved form, however closely. Their hands can
rub nothing from off those dainty limbs in their aimless roving
over all the body. Then comes the moment when with limbs
entwined they pluck the flower of youth. Their bodies thrill
with the joy to come, and Venus is just about to sow the seed   1107
in the female fields.[90] Body clings greedily to body; they mingle
the saliva of their mouths and breathe hard down each other's
mouths pressing them with their teeth. But all to no purpose.
One can remove nothing from the other by rubbing, nor enter
right in and be wholly absorbed, body in body; for sometimes
it seems that that is what they are craving and striving to do, so
hungrily do they cling together in Venus' fetters, while their
limbs are unnerved and liquefied by the intensity of pleasure.
At length, when the build-up of lust has burst out of their
groin, there comes a slight intermission in the raging fever. But

1117 not for long. Soon the same frenzy returns. The madness is
upon them once more. They ask themselves what it is they are
craving for, but find no device that will master their malady. In
aimless bewilderment they rot away, stricken by a secret[91] sore.

Add to this that they waste their strength and work them-
selves to death. Their days are passed at the mercy of another's
whim.[92] Their wealth slips from them, transmuted to Baby-
1124 lonian brocades. Their duties are neglected. Their reputation
totters and goes into a decline. Perfumes and lovely slippers
from Sicyon[93] laugh on her dainty feet; settings of gold enclasp
huge emeralds aglow with green fire, and sea-tinted garments
are worn thin with constant use and drink the sweat of Venus
in their exertions. A hard-won patrimony is metamorphosed
into coronets and tiaras or, it may be, into robes from the
looms of Malta[94] or Cos.[95] No matter how lavish the décor and
the cuisine – drinking parties (with no lack of drinks), entertain-
ments, perfumes, garlands, festoons[96] and all – they are still a
1134 waste of time. From the very heart of the fountain[97] of delight
there rises a jet of bitterness that poisons the fragrance of the
flowers. Perhaps the guilty conscience frets itself remorsefully
with the thought of life's best years squandered slothfully in
brothels. Perhaps the beloved has let fly some two-edged word,
which lodges in the impassioned heart and glows there like a
living flame. Perhaps he thinks she is rolling her eyes too freely
and turning them upon another, or he catches in her face a hint
of mockery.

And these are the evils inherent in love that prospers and
fulfils its hopes. In starved and unrequited love the evils you
1143 can see plainly without even opening your eyes are past all
counting. How much better to be on your guard beforehand, as
I have advised, and take care that you are not enmeshed!

To avoid enticement into the snares of love is not so difficult
as, once entrapped, to escape out of the toils and snap the
tenacious knots of Venus. And yet, be you never so tightly
entangled and embrangled, you can still free yourself from the
danger unless you stand in the way of your own freedom. First,
you should concentrate on all the faults of mind or body of her
whom you pursue and lust after. For men often behave as

though blinded by love and credit the beloved with charms to 1154
which she has no valid title. This is why we see foul and
disgusting women basking in a lover's adoration! One man
scoffs at another and urges him to propitiate Venus because he
is the victim of such a degrading infatuation; yet as like as not
the poor devil is in the same pathetic plight himself, but does
not realize it. A black girl[98] is acclaimed as 'honey-coloured'. A
filthy stinking slut is admired for her 'beauty unadorned'. Her 1161
eyes are never green, but grey as Athene's. If she is stringy and
woody, she is lithe as a gazelle. A stunted runt is 'one of the
Graces', a 'sheer delight from top to toe'. A massive dragon is
'a knockout – a fine figure of a woman'. She cannot speak for
stammering – a charming lisp, of course. She's as mute as a
stockfish – what modesty! A hateful blazing gossip is a
'livewire'; she's 'slender', 'a little love' when she is almost too
skinny to live; she is 'delicate' when she is half-dead with
coughing. The fat girl with enormous breasts is 'Ceres suckling
Bacchus'. The girl with the stumpy little nose is 'a Faun', then, 1169
or 'a lady Satyr'. The one with balloon lips is 'all one big kiss'.
It would be a wearisome task to run through the whole
catalogue of euphemisms. But suppose her face in fact is all that
could be desired and the charm of Venus radiates from her
whole body. Even so, there are still others. Even so, we lived
without her before. Even so, in her physical nature she is no
different, as we well know, from the ugly slut.[99] She too has to
fumigate her pathetic body with its disgusting smells. Her
maids keep well away from her and snigger behind her back.
The tearful lover, locked out[100] from her presence, heaps the
threshold with flowers and garlands, anoints the disdainful 1177
doorposts with marjoram, and plants rueful kisses on the door.
Often enough, were he admitted, one whiff would promptly
make him cast round for some decent pretext to clear off. His
fond elegy, long-pondered and drawn from the bottom of his
heart, would fall dismally flat. He would curse himself for a
fool to have endowed her with qualities above human im-
perfection.

To the daughters of Venus themselves all this is no secret.
Hence they are at pains to hide all the backstage activities of

1187 life from those whom they wish to keep fast bound in the bonds of love. But their pains are wasted, since your mind has power to drag all these mysteries into the daylight and get at the truth behind all the giggling. Then,[101] if the woman is good-hearted and void of malice, it is up to you in your turn to accept unpleasant facts and make allowance for human imperfection.

1192 Do not imagine that a woman is always sighing with feigned love when she clings to a man in a close embrace, body to body, and prolongs his kisses by the tension of moist lips. Often she is acting from the heart and is longing for a shared delight when she stimulates him to run love's race to the end. So, too, with birds and beasts, both tame and wild. Cows[102] and mares would never submit to the males, were it not that their female nature in its superabundance is all aglow thrusting in delight against the penis of the leaping male. Have you never

1202 noticed, again, how couples linked by mutual rapture are often tormented in their common bondage? How often dogs at a street corner, wishing to separate, tug lustily with all their might in opposite directions and yet remain united by the constraining fetters of Venus? This they would never do unless they knew the mutual joys which could entice them into the trap and hold them enchained. Here then is proof upon proof for my contention that the pleasure of sex is shared.

In the intermingling of seed[103] it may happen that the woman by a sudden effort overmasters the power of the man and takes

1211 control of it. Then children are conceived of the maternal seed and take after their mother. Correspondingly children may be conceived of the paternal seed and take after their father. The children in whom you see a two-sided likeness, combining features of both parents, are products alike of their father's body and their mother's blood. At their making the seeds that course through the limbs under the impulse of Venus were dashed together by the collision of mutual passion in which neither party was master or mastered.

It may also happen at times that children take after their grandparents, or recall the features of great-grandparents. This

is because the parents' bodies often preserve a quantity of latent   1221
seeds, grouped in many combinations, which derive from an
ancestral stock handed down from generation to generation.
From these Venus evokes a random[104] assortment of characters,
reproducing ancestral traits of expression, voice or hair; for
these characters are determined by specific seeds no less than
our faces and bodily members.

It may seem strange that female offspring is engendered from   1227
the father's seed, and the mother's body gives birth to males.
The fact is that the embryo is always composed of atoms from
both sources, only it derives more than half from the parent
which it more closely resembles. This is noticeable in either
case, whether the child's origin is predominantly male or
female.

Do not imagine that the sowing of fruitful seed is denied to any
man by the will of the gods,[105] so that he may never be called
father by delightful children but must live through a sexual life   1235
that yields no fruit. There are many who are moved by this
belief to spatter the sacrificial altars with rivers of blood and set
them alight with the smoke of burnt offerings in the pathetic
hope that their wives may be made big with floods of seed.[106] It
is all in vain that they importune gods or fates. For the
barrenness of the males is due in some cases to the thickness of
the seed, in others to its excessively watery fluidity. The watery
seed, because it cannot stick fast in its place, slips quickly away
and returns abortive. The thick type, because it is emitted in
too solid a form, either does not travel with enough momentum,   1245
or fails to penetrate where it is required or else, having got
there, fails to mix properly with the female seed. For the affairs
of Venus clearly involve wide variations in harmony. Men
differ in their power to impregnate different women, and
women similarly in the power to receive from different men
and grow big by them. Many women have proved barren in
earlier unions[107] yet have eventually found husbands by whom
they could conceive little ones and be enriched with the bless-
ings of childbirth. And men in whose homes fruitful women
have previously failed to bear have at length found a compatible

1256 character so that they too could fortify[108] their declining years
with sons.

The vital thing is to ensure the right mixture of seeds for
procreation, thick harmonizing with watery and watery with
thick. Another important factor is diet: some foods thicken the
seeds in the body, others in turn thin and diminish them. A
third factor of great importance is the manner in which the
1265 pleasures of intercourse are enjoyed. It is thought that women
conceive more readily in the manner of four-footed beasts with
breasts lowered and hips uplifted so as to give access to the
seed. Nor do our wives have any need of lascivious move-
ments;[109] for a woman can resist and hamper conception if in
her pleasure she thrusts away from the man's penis with her
buttocks, making her whole body floppy with sinuous wave-
movements. She diverts the furrow from the straight course of
the ploughshare and makes the seed fall wide of the plot.[110]
These tricks are employed by prostitutes for their own ends, so
1275 that they may not conceive too frequently and be laid up by
pregnancy and at the same time may make intercourse more
attractive to men. But obviously our wives do not need any of
them.

Lastly, it is by no divine intervention, no prick of Cupid's
darts, that a woman deficient in beauty sometimes becomes the
object of love. Often the woman herself, by her actions, by
humouring a man's fancies and keeping herself fresh and smart,
makes it easy for him to share his life with her. Over and above
this, love is built up bit by bit by mere usage.[111]

1285 Nothing can resist the continually repeated impact of a blow,
however light, as you see drops of water falling on one spot at
long last drill through a stone.

BOOK FIVE

COSMOLOGY AND SOCIOLOGY

Who[1] has such power within his breast that he could build up a song worthy of the majesty of nature and these discoveries? Who has such mastery of words that he could praise as he deserves the man who produced such treasures from his breast and bequeathed them to us? No one, I believe, whose body is of mortal growth. If I am to suit my language to the majesty of nature as revealed by him, he was a god[2] – a god indeed, my noble Memmius – who first discovered that rule of life that now is called *philosophy*, who by his art rescued life from such a stormy sea, so black a night, and steered it into such a calm and sun-lit haven.[3] Only compare with his achievement those ancient discoveries of other mortals that rank as the work of gods. Ceres, it is said, taught men to use cereals, and Bacchus the imbibing of the vine-grown liquid; yet without these things we could go on living, as we are told that some tribes live even now. But life could not be well lived till our breasts were swept clean. Therefore that man has a better claim to be called a god whose gospel, broadcast through the length and breadth of empires, is even now bringing soothing solace to the minds of men.

As for Hercules,[4] if you think his deeds will challenge comparison, you will stray farther still from the path of truth. The gaping jaws of that Nemean lion, or the bristly Arcadian boar – what harm could they do us now? Or the Cretan bull and the Hydra with its palisade of venomous snakes, the pest of Lerna? Or Geryon, with the triple strength of his three bodies? ⟨. . .⟩ Or the ⟨foul birds⟩ that haunted the Stymphalian lake, or Thracian Diomede's horses that breathed fire from their nostrils on the Thracian slopes of Ismara? Or if the scaly, fierce-eyed serpent guarded still the lustrous golden apples of the Hesperides, hugging the tree-trunk with huge coils, there by the forbidding Atlantic shore where none of us ever goes nor even

36 the natives venture? And the other monsters of this sort that met their death – if they had not been mastered, what harm would they do alive? None at all, that I can see. Even now the world swarms with wild beasts, enough and to spare – a thrill of terror lurking in thickets on the mountainside or in the depths of forests. But we usually have the power to avoid these places. However, if our breasts are not swept clean, then indeed
44 what battles and perils we must get mixed up in, whether we like it or not! And, when a man harbours these, what sharp stabs of desire with their answering fears tear him to pieces! Pride, lust, aggressive behaviour, self-indulgence, indolence – what calamities they inflict! The man who has defeated all these enemies and banished them from his mind, by words not by weapons, is surely entitled to a place among the gods. Remember, too, what inspired words he himself has uttered about the immortal gods,[5] and how by his teaching he has laid bare the nature of the universe.

55 Treading in his footsteps, I have been running arguments to earth and explaining in my verses the necessity that compels everything to abide by the compact under which it was created. For nothing has power to break the binding laws of eternity. As an instance of this, I have shown that the mind in particular is a natural growth: it is composed of a body that had first to be born, and it cannot remain intact for all time; but we are misled by images in sleep, when we fancy we see someone whose life has left him.[6]

64 The next stage in the argument is this. I must first demonstrate that the world also was born and is composed of a mortal body. Then I must deal with the concourse of matter that laid the foundation of land, sea and sky, stars and sun and the globe of the moon. I must show what living things have existed on earth, and which have never been born: how the human race began to employ various utterances among themselves for denoting various things; and how there crept into their minds that fear of the gods which, all the world over, sanctifies temples and lakes, groves and altars and images of the gods.

After that, I will explain by what forces nature steers the   76
courses of the sun and the journeyings of the moon, so that we
shall not suppose that they run their yearly races between
heaven and earth of their own free will with the amiable
intention[7] of promoting the growth of crops and animals, or
that they are rolled round in furtherance of some divine plan.
For it may happen that men who have learnt the truth about
the carefree existence of the gods fall to wondering by what   84
power the universe is kept going, especially those movements
that are seen overhead in the borderland of ether. Then the
.poor creatures[8] are plunged back into their old superstitions
and saddle themselves with cruel masters whom they believe to
be all-powerful. All this because they do not know what can be
and what cannot: how the power of each thing is limited, and
its boundary-stone sticks buried deep.

And now, Memmius,[9] I will not hold you off any longer with
promises. First of all, then, cast your eyes on sea, lands and sky.
These three bodies so different in nature, three distinct forms,   92
three fabrics such as you behold – all these a single day will
blot out. The whole substance and structure of the world,
upheld through many years, will crash.[10] I am well aware how
novel and strange in its impact on the mind is this impending
demolition of heaven and earth, and how hard it is for my
words to carry conviction. This is always so when you bring to
men's ears something outside their experience – something you
cannot set before their eyes or lay hold of by hand, which is the
shortest highway for belief to enter the human breast and the   103
compartments of the mind. But, for all that, I will proclaim it.
It may be that force will be given to my arguments by the
event itself; that your own eyes will see those violent earth-
quakes in a brief space dash the whole world to fragments.
From such a fate may guiding fortune[11] steer us clear! May
reason rather than the event itself convince you that the whole
world can collapse with one ear-splitting crack!

Before I attempt to utter oracles on this theme, with more
sanctity and far surer reason than those the Delphic prophetess
pronounces, drugged by the laurel fumes from Apollo's

113   tripod,[12] I will first set your mind at rest with words of wisdom. Do not imagine, bridled with the reins of superstition, that lands and sun and sky, sea, stars and moon, must endure for ever because they are endowed with a divine body. Do not for that reason think it right that punishment appropriate to a monstrous crime should be imposed, as on the rebellious giants,[13] on all those who by their reasoning breach the ramparts of the world and seek to snuff out heaven's brightest luminary, the sun,[14]

121   staining immortal beings with mortal speech. In fact these objects are so far from divinity, so unworthy of a place among the gods, that they may rather serve to impress upon us the type of the lifeless and the insensible. Obviously, it is only with certain bodies that mind and intelligence can coexist. A tree cannot exist in the ether, or clouds in the salt sea, as fishes cannot live in the fields or blood flow in wood or sap in stones.[15] There is a determined and allotted place for the growth and presence of everything. So mind cannot arise alone without body or apart from sinews and blood. If it could do this, then surely it could

134   much more readily function in head or shoulders or the tips of the heels or be born in any other part, so long as it was held in the same container, that is to say, in the same man. Since, however, even in the human body we see a determined and allotted place set aside for the growth and presence of spirit and mind, we have even stronger grounds for denying that they can survive apart from all body or animal form in the crumbling clods of earth or the fire of the sun or in water or the high borderland of ether. These objects, therefore, are not endowed with divine conscious-

146   ness, since they cannot possess even living spirit.[16]

Furthermore, you must not suppose that the holy dwelling-places of the gods are anywhere within the limits of the world. For the flimsy nature of the gods, far removed from our senses, is scarcely visible even to the perception of the mind. Since it eludes the touch and pressure of our hands, it can have no contact with anything that is tangible to us.[17] For what cannot be touched cannot touch. Therefore their dwelling-places also must be unlike ours, of the same flimsy texture as their bodies, as I will prove to you at length later on.[18]

Next, the theory that they deliberately created the world in all   156
its splendour for the sake of man, so that we ought to praise
this eminently praiseworthy piece of divine workmanship and
believe it eternal and immortal and think it a sin to unsettle by
violence the everlasting abode established for mankind by the
ancient purpose of the gods and to worry it with words and
turn it upside-down – this theory, Memmius, with all its
attendant fictions is sheer nonsense. For what benefit could   166
immortal and blessed beings reap from our gratitude, that they
should undertake any task on our behalf? Or what could tempt
those who had been at peace so long to change their old life for
a new? The revolutionary is one who is dissatisfied with the old
order. But one who has known no trouble in the past, but
spent his days joyfully – what could spark a desire for novelty
in such a being?[19] Or again, what harm would it have done us
to have remained uncreated? Are we to suppose that our life
was sunk in gloom and grief till the light of creation blazed
forth? True that, once a man is born, he must will to remain   178
alive so long as beguiling pleasure holds him. But one who has
never tasted the love of life, or been enrolled among the living,
what odds is it to him if he has never been created?[20]

Here is a further point. On what pattern did the gods model
their creation? From what source did a mental image[21] of
human beings first strike upon them, so that they might know
and see with their minds what they wished to make? How was
the power of the atoms made known to them, and the potential
effect of their various combinations, unless nature itself pro-   186
vided a model of the creation? So many atoms, clashing together
in so many ways as they are swept along through infinite time
by their own weight, have come together in every possible way
and realized everything that could be formed by their combina-
tions. No wonder, then, if they have actually fallen into those
groupings and movements by which the present world through
all its changes is kept in being.

Even if I knew nothing of the atoms, I would venture to
assert on the evidence of the celestial phenomena themselves,
supported by many other arguments, that the universe was

198 certainly not created for us by divine power: it is so full of imperfections. In the first place, of all that is covered by the wide sweep of the sky, part has been greedily seized by mountains and the woodland haunts of wild beasts. Part is usurped by crags and desolate bogs and the sea that holds far asunder the shores of the lands. Almost two-thirds is withheld from mankind by torrid heat and perennial deposits of frost. The
206 little that is left of cultivable soil, if the force of nature had its way, would be choked with briars, did not the force of man oppose it. It is man's way, for the sake of life, to groan over the stout mattock and cleave the earth with down-pressed plough.[22] Unless we turn the fruitful clods with the coulter and break up the soil to stimulate the growth of the crops, they cannot emerge of their own accord into the open air. Even so, when by dint of hard work all the fields at last burst forth into leaf and flower, then either the fiery sun withers them with intemperate heat, or sudden showers and icy frosts destroy them and
218 gales of wind batter them with hurricane force. Again, why does nature feed and breed the fearsome brood of wild beasts, a menace to the human race by land and sea? Why do the changing seasons bring pestilence in their train? Why does untimely death roam abroad? The human infant, like a shipwrecked sailor[23] cast ashore by the cruel waves, lies naked on the ground, speechless,[24] lacking all aids to life, when nature has first tossed him with pangs of labour from his mother's womb upon the shores of the sunlit world. He fills the air with his piteous wailing, and quite rightly, considering what evils life
228 holds in store for him. But beasts of every kind, both tame and wild, have no need of rattles or a nurse to lull them with babbling baby-talk. They do not want to change their clothes at every change in the weather. They need no weapons or fortifications to guard their possessions, since every need is lavishly supplied by mother earth herself and nature, the clever inventor.[25]

In the first place, *since the elements* of which we see this universe composed – solid earth and moisture, the light breaths of air and torrid fire[26] – *all consist of matter that is neither birthless nor deathless, we must believe the same of the world as a whole.*[27] It is a

matter of observation that objects whose component parts   239
consist of configurations of matter subject to birth and death
are certainly not exempt themselves. So, when we see the main
component members of the world disintegrated and reborn, it
is a fair inference that sky and earth too had their birthday and
will have their day of doom.

You need not tax me with begging the question when I
assume that earth and fire are mortal and entertain no doubt   248
about the death of wind and water or the rebirth and growth of
all these elements.

Take the earth first. Part of it, parched by incessant sun and
trampled by the tread of many feet, exhales a vapour and flying
clouds of dust which strong winds scatter throughout the
whole sky. Part of the soil is reconverted to flood-water by the
rains, and gnawing rivers nibble at their banks. And whatever
earth contributes to feed the growth of others is restored to it.
It is an observed fact that the universal mother is also the
common grave.[28] Earth, therefore, is whittled away and renewed   259
with fresh increment.

As for water, it needs no words to show that sea and river
and springs are perennially replenished and the flow of fluid is
unending. The evidence confronts us everywhere in the mighty
downrush of water. But the vanguard of the flood is perpetually
skimmed away, and on balance the surface-level does not rise.
The sea is reduced in volume partly by the strong winds that
scour its surface, partly by the fiery sun's unravelling ray,[29]
partly because it seeps away in all directions under the ground.
The brine[30] is filtered out, and the main bulk of the water flows   269
back and reassembles in full at the fountain-head. Hence it
flows overground, a steady column of sweet fluid marching
down the highway already hewn with liquid foot for the
guidance of its waves.

Now a word about air, whose whole mass undergoes innumer-
able transformations hour by hour. All the effluences that
objects are for ever shedding are swept into the vast ocean of
air.[31] Unless this in turn gave back matter to objects and rebuilt
their ever-flowing shapes, they would all by now have been
dissolved and turned to air. Accordingly it must be continuously

278 generated from other things and retransformed into them, since it is an established fact that everything is in perpetual flux.[32]

The fiery sun, too, the lavish fount of liquid light, drenches the sky unwearyingly with fresh brilliance, never tardy to replace old light with new. For each successive flash of radiance, whatever may come of it, means a loss to the fountain-head, as you may learn from the following indication. No sooner do

286 clouds begin to climb the sky and cut off the rays of sunlight than all the lower part of the rays immediately vanishes: wherever the clouds pass, the earth is overshadowed. So[33] you may gather that objects are always in need of new illumination; that every burst of radiance is short-lived; and that objects could never be seen in sunlight if a perpetual supply were not maintained by the fount of light itself.

So it is with those earthly lights that illumine the night – swinging lamps and flaring torches, their bright flames thick with sooty smoke. Fed by their burning, they race to supply

296 new light, pressing onward, onward, with ever-flickering flames, leaving no gap in the unbroken stream of brilliance: so hastily is its extinction hidden by the swift new birth of flame from every fire. That is how you should picture sun and moon and stars – as showering their splendour in successive outbursts and for ever losing flash after flash of flame, not as enduring essences untouched by time.

Look about you and you will see the very stones mastered by age; tall towers in ruin and their masonry crumbling; temples and images of the gods defaced, their destined span not length-

309 ened by any sanctity that avails against the laws of nature. Do we not see that the collapsed monuments of men ask whether you believe that they in their turn grow old?[34] The uprooted boulders rolling down a mountainside proclaim their weakness in the face of a lapse of time by no means infinite; for no sudden shock could dislodge them and set them falling if they had endured from everlasting, unbruised by all the assault and battery of time.

Last of all, consider this outer envelope that lies above and about the earth and holds it in its embrace. If it is this, as some assert, that generates all things from itself and reclaims them

when their days are ended, then it too must consist wholly of   320
matter that is neither birthless nor deathless; for everything that
gives of itself to feed the growth of others must thereby be
diminished, and be born anew when it reclaims its own.

Here is another line of reasoning. If earth and sky had no
starting-point in time but have always existed, why have no
poets sung of feats before the Theban war and the tragedy of
Troy?[35] Why have so many heroic deeds recurrently dropped   326
out of mind and not been grafted onto everlasting monuments
of fame to flower there? The answer, I believe, is that *this world
is newly made*:[36] its origin is a recent event, not one of remote
antiquity. That is why even now some arts are being perfected:
the process of development is still going on. Many improve-
ments have just been introduced in ships. It is no time since
musicians gave birth to their tuneful harmonies. Yes, and it is
not long since the truth about nature was first discovered, and I
myself am even now the first[37] who has been found to render   336
this revelation into my native speech.

Alternatively, you may believe that all these things existed
before, but that the human race was wiped out by a burst of
fiery heat or its cities were laid low by some great upheaval of
the world or engulfed by greedy rivers which persistent rains
had driven to overflow their banks.[38] All the more reason,
then, to concede my point and admit that an end is coming to
earth and sky. If the world was indeed shaken by such plagues
and perils, then it needs only a more violent shock to make it
collapse in universal ruin. There is no clearer proof of our own   347
mortality than the fact that we are subject to the same ailments
as those whom nature has already recalled from life.

Again, there can be only three kinds of everlasting objects.
The first, owing to the absolute solidity of their substance, can
repel blows and let nothing penetrate them so as to unknit their
close texture from within. Such are the atoms of matter whose
nature I have already demonstrated. The second kind can last
for ever because it is immune from blows. Such is empty space,
which remains untouched and unaffected by any impact. Last is
that which has no available place surrounding it into which its

359 matter can disperse and disintegrate. It is for this reason that
the sum totality of the universe is everlasting, having no space
outside it into which the matter can escape and no matter that
can enter and disintegrate it by the force of impact. But, as I
have shown, the world is not a solid mass of matter, since there
is an admixture of vacuity in things. It is not of the same nature
as vacuity. There is no lack of external bodies to rally out of
367 infinite space and blast it with a turbulent tornado or inflict
some other mortal disaster. And finally in the depths of space
there is no lack of room into which the walls of the world may
crumble away or collapse under the impact of some other
shock. It follows, then, that the doorway of death is not barred
to sky and sun and earth and the sea's unfathomed floods. It
lies tremendously open and confronts them with a yawning
chasm. So, for this reason, too, you must acknowledge them to
have been born. For nothing with a frame of mortal build
could have endured from everlasting until now, proof against
the stark strength of immeasurable age.

379 Consider another possibility. Since civil strife rages among
the world's warring elements on so vast a scale, it may[39] be that
their long battle will some day be decided. Perhaps the sun and
heat will overcome and drink all the waters dry. They are
struggling to do this now, but have not yet accomplished their
aim: the rivers maintain such ample resources and threaten on
their side to deluge everything from the deep reservoir of the
ocean. They, too, are thwarted: their ranks are thinned by the
ocean-scouring winds and the fiery sun's unravelling rays,
confident of their power to dry up every drop before the water
390 can achieve the goal of its enterprise. So these opposing forces
maintain their heated conflict, contending on equal terms for
gigantic issues. But legend[40] tells of one occasion when fire
got the upper hand and once when water was king over the
land.

For fire was victorious and went round scorching many parts
of the earth when the galloping steeds that draw the chariot of
the sun swept Phaethon from the true course, right out of the
zone of ether and far over all the lands. Then the Father
Almighty, in a fierce gust of anger, struck down the aspiring

Phaethon with a sudden stroke of his thunderbolt,[41] down out   400
of the chariot to the earth. But the sun intercepted his fall and
took up the everlasting torch of the firmament, and brought
the trembling steeds back to the yoke from their stampede and,
guiding them along their proper course, restored the universe
to order. Such is the story as recited by the ancient bards of
Greece,[42] a story utterly rejected by true doctrine. What may
really lead to the triumph of fire is an increase in the accumula-   408
tion of its particles out of infinite space. Then comes the crisis:
either its forces for some reason suffer a setback, or the world
shrivels in its parching blasts and comes to an end.

   Another legend[43] tells how water likewise once massed its
forces and began to prevail, till many men were drowned
beneath its waves. Then, when there came some diversion and
withdrawal of the reinforcements mustered out of the infinite,
the rains halted and the rivers checked their flow.

I will now set out in order *the stages by which the initial*
concentration[44] *of matter laid the foundation of earth and sky*, of the   417
ocean depths and the orbits of sun and moon. Certainly the
atoms did not post themselves purposefully in due order by an
act of intelligence, nor did they stipulate what movements each
should perform. But multitudinous atoms, swept along in multi-
tudinous courses through infinite time by mutual clashes and
their own weight, have come together in every possible way
and tested everything that could be formed by their combina-
tions. So it comes about that a voyage of immense[45] duration,
in which they have experienced every variety of movement and   428
conjunction, has at length brought together those whose sudden
encounter often forms the starting-point of substantial fabrics –
earth and sea and sky and the races of living creatures.

   At that[46] time the sun's bright disc was not to be seen here,
soaring aloft and lavishing its light, nor the stars that crowd the
far-flung firmament, nor sea nor sky nor earth nor air nor
anything in the likeness of the things we know – nothing but a
hurricane raging, a newly congregated mass of atoms of every
sort. From their disharmony sprang conflict, which provoked
wars in their interspaces, courses, unions, thrusts, impacts,

439 collisions and motions, because owing to their diversity of shape and pattern they could not all remain in the combinations in which they found themselves or mutually reconcile their motions. From this medley they started to sort themselves out, like combining with like,[47] and to divide out the world, setting out its separate limbs and laying out its main sections: they began, in fact, to separate the heights of heaven from the earth, to single out the sea as a receptacle for water detached from the mass and to set apart the fires of pure and isolated ether.

447

In the first place all the particles of earth, because they were heavy and intertangled, collected in the middle and took up the undermost stations. The more closely they cohered and clung together, the more they squeezed out the atoms that went to the making of sea and stars, sun and moon and the outer walls of this great world. For all these are composed of smooth round seeds, much smaller than the particles of earth. The first element to break out of the earth through the pores in its spongy crust and to shoot up aloft was ether, the generator of fire. Owing to its lightness, it carried off with it a quantity of fire. We may compare[48] a sight we often see when the sun's golden rays blush with the first flush of dawn among the dew-spangled herbage: the lakes and perennial watercourses exhale a vapour, while at times we see the earth itself steaming. It is these vapours, when they all coalesce and combine their substance in the upper air, that weave a cloudy curtain under the sky. Just so in those days the ethereal fire, buoyant and expansive, coalesced at the circumference and turned this way and that till it became generally diffused and enveloped the other elements in an ardent embrace.

458

470

On this ensued the birth of the sun and moon, whose globes revolve at middle height in the atmosphere. The earth did not claim them for itself, nor did the transcendent ether because they were neither heavy enough to sink and settle nor light enough to soar through the uppermost zones. Yet in their midway station they are so placed as to revolve actual bodies and to form parts of the world as a whole. Just so in our own bodies, while some members remain fixed at their posts, others are free to move.

When these elements had withdrawn, the earth suddenly   480
caved in, throughout the zone now covered by the blue extent
of sea, and flooded the cavity with surging brine. Day by day
the encircling ethereal fires and the sun's rays by continual
bombardment of the outer crust from every quarter compressed
the earth into an ever narrower compass, so that it shrank into
itself in its middle reaches and cohered more compactly. So
even ampler floods of salty fluid perspired from the body to   488
swell the billowy plain of ocean. Ever fresh contingents of
those particles of heat and air of which I have spoken slipped
out to reinforce the sparkling vault of heaven far up above the
earth. As the plains settled down, the mountain steeps grew
more prominent; for the crags could not sink in, and it was not
possible for every part to subside to the same extent.

So the earth by its weight and the coalescing of its substance
came to rest. All the sediment of the world, because it was
heavy, drifted downwards together and settled at the bottom
like dregs. Then sea and air and fiery ether itself were each in   498
turn left unalloyed in their elemental purity, one being lighter
than another. Ether, as the clearest and the lightest, floats upon
the gusty air and does not mingle its clear substance with the
air's tempestuous tumult. It leaves the lower regions to be spun
round by eddying whirlwinds, tossed to and fro by veering
squalls. It bears its own fires on a steady course as it glides
along. The possibility of such a regular and constant flow as
this of ether is demonstrated by the Black Sea,[49] which flows
with a uniform tide, maintaining perpetually the single tenor of
its current.

509

Let us now take as our theme *the cause of stellar movements*. First,
let us suppose that the great globe of sky itself rotates. We must
then say that the poles of the celestial sphere are held in place and
hemmed in at either extremity by the external pressure of air on
both of them. In addition, there must be another current of air,
either flowing above in the same direction in which the flashing
lights of the ageless firmament revolve, or else moving below in
the reverse direction, so that it rotates the sphere on the same
principle as we see rivers turning the scoops of water-wheels.

517   There remains the alternative possibility that the sky as a whole is stationary while the shining constellations are in motion. This may happen because swift currents of ether are shut up inside and in their search for an outlet whirl round and round and roll their fires at large across the night-thundering regions of the sky. Or an external current of air from some other quarter may whirl them along in its course. Or they may creep forward of their own accord, each responsive to the call

524 of its own food, and feed their fiery bodies in the broad pastures of the sky. Which of these possibilities is the truth, so far as this world is concerned, is not easy to establish.[50] But my argument shows what could and may happen throughout the universe in the various worlds formed on various patterns. So I have worked through the list of causes that may produce stellar motions throughout the universe. One of these causes must certainly operate in our world also to speed the march of the constellations. But to lay down which of them it is lies beyond

534 the range of our stumbling progress.

We have now to consider *how the earth remains fixed in the middle of the world*. The answer is that its mass gradually attenuates and dwindles away and that its lower parts are formed of another substance, and this ever since the beginning of time has been combined and united with the airy regions of the world on which it is grafted and lives.[51] That is why it is no burden to the air and does not press down upon it. We know that a man's own limbs, so far as he himself is concerned, have no weight;

542 his head is not a burden to his shoulders, and we do not feel the whole bulk of our bodies pressing down on our feet. But weights of external origin that are laid upon us are burdensome, though often they are much less. The decisive factor is the extent of the power possessed by each particular object. In the same way, the earth is not a foreign body suddenly introduced and plumped down upon unfamiliar air. It is a definite part of the world, conceived simultaneously with it at birth, as we know our own limbs are with us.

    Again, when the earth is suddenly shaken by a sizeable thunderclap, it involves all the atmosphere above it in the

shock. This it could not possibly do if it were not attached to   552
the airy regions of the world and to the sky. In fact, they have
been linked together and united from the beginning of their
existence and cling to each other by common roots.

Or consider[52] how all the bulk of our body is upheld by the
flimsy tissue of the spirit, because the two are so closely
interlinked and united. What is it that lifts the body up in a
vigorous jump if not the pervasive spirit that directs the limbs?
Here, then, is evidence of the strength a flimsy substance can   561
possess when it is united with a massive one, as the air is with
the earth or the human mind with the human body.

Next, as to *the size and heat of the sun's disc*: it cannot in fact be
either much larger or much smaller than it appears to our
senses.[53] So long as fires are near enough both to transmit their
light and to breathe a warm blast upon our bodies, the bulk of
their flames suffers no loss through distance: the fire is not
visibly diminished. Since, therefore, the heat of the sun and the   570
light it gives off travel all the way to our senses and cause the
world to shine, its shape and size also must appear as they
really are, with virtually no room for any lessening or enlarge-
ment.

The moon, too, whether it sheds a bastard light upon the
landscape in its progress or emits a native radiance from its
own body, is not in either case of bulkier dimensions than
those with which it appears to our eyes. For objects seen at a
distance through a thick screen of air appear blurred in outline
before they are diminished in bulk.[54] It follows that the moon,   582
which presents a sharp outline and a precise shape, must appear
to us up there just as it is, with its limits truly defined and in its
actual dimensions.

So too with every spark of ethereal fire that is visible from
the earth. The magnitude of fires that we see on earth is very
little changed in appearance, one way or the other, by distance
so long as their flickering is still distinct and their blaze
perceptible. This does not exclude the possibility that the stars
may be just a shade smaller than they look or the least little bit
bigger.

592   How then, if the sun is so small, can it give off such a flood
of light, enough to deluge lands and seas and sky and permeate
the world with a glow of warmth? There is nothing miraculous
about this. It is quite possible that from this one outlet the light
of all the world may break out and gush in an abounding
fountain, this being the centre at which all the atoms of heat
gather together from all the world. This universal confluence
601   then becomes the source from which the radiance is again
dispersed. See how widely a tiny spring may sometimes water
the meadows and inundate the plain. There is the further
possibility that heat issuing from the relatively small fire of the
sun may set the air ablaze, if it happens that there is air
available that is readily kindled by contact with small emana-
tions of heat. Just so we sometimes see a general conflagration
in corn or stubble started by a single spark. It may be, again,
that round the sun's ruddy torch, where it flares on high, there
extends a wide zone of fire, charged with invisible heat with no
613   distinguishing effulgence. Such a heat-bearing zone might add
its share to the impact of the rays.

There is no obvious way of accounting by a simple and
straightforward hypothesis for the *movements of the sun* from its
summer quarters to its midwinter turning-point of Capricorn
and back again upon its tracks to its midsummer tropic of
Cancer, or of explaining *how the moon is seen to cover in a month the
distance on which the sun in its travels spends a full year*. No simple
cause, I repeat, can be assigned to these phenomena.

621   The first possible explanation that suggests itself is that
advanced by the revered authority of the great Democritus.[55]
On this view, the nearer the heavenly bodies are to the earth,
the less are they caught up in the vortex of the heavens. The
rushing and impulsive energy of the vortex, it is supposed,
fades out and dwindles at lower levels. So the sun, whose path
lies far below the ardent constellations, gradually lags behind
and drops towards their rear. Much more the moon: the more
its lowlier course falls short of the sky and approaches the
earth, the less can it keep pace with the stars. The more
sluggish the vortex in which it is involved, down here below

the sun, the sooner it is overtaken and passed by in the cyclic 634
march by each successive constellation. That is why the moon
seems to return more rapidly than the sun to each constellation:
it is they in fact that catch up faster on the moon.

Another possibility[56] is that two crosscurrents of air blow
through the sky, alternating with the seasons: one drives the
sun down from the summer constellations towards the ice-
bound frigidity of its midwinter turning-point; the other tosses 641
it back out of the cold and dark into the heat-bearing region
and the torrid stars. So also with the moon and with the
planets, which complete great years in orbits as great: we may
picture them as blown before winds from alternating quarters.
See how the clouds at different levels move in different direc-
tions, impelled by conflicting winds. Why should not the
heavenly bodies, out in the wide zones of ether, be sped on
their several courses by conflicting currents?

The reason why night shrouds the earth in far-flung gloom
may be that the sun, exhausted by its long day's journey, has
reached the utmost limits of the sky and puffed out its travel- 652
spent fires,[57] enfeebled by excess of air. Alternatively, it may be
driven to double back under the earth by the same force that
guided its globe above the earth. Correspondingly, when
Matuta[58] at the determined hour diffuses its rose-red glow
through the ethereal regions and flings wide the light of day, it
may be that the same sun, which we have pictured as doubling
back under the earth, takes possession of the sky with precursive
rays and strives to set it ablaze. Or it may be that at the
determined hour there is a concentration of fires, a confluence 661
of many particles of heat, which regularly causes the solar
radiance to be born anew. So it is related that from the heights
of Mount Ida at daybreak scattered fires are seen in the East
coalescing as it were into a ball till they form a single sphere.
There would be nothing miraculous about such a confluence of
fiery particles at such a regularly determined time rebuilding the
sun in its splendour. In every department of nature we see a host
of phenomena recurring at a determined time. The trees have
a set time for blossoming and for shedding their blossoms. At a
set time age decrees the shedding of teeth, the growth of a soft

674 down on the downless skin and with it the sprouting of a soft
beard from either cheek. Even climatic phenomena – thunder-
storms, snow, rain, clouds, winds – do not occur at wholly
undetermined seasons of the year. In a world in which the
operative causes began in this particular way and phenomena at
the outset fell into this pattern, they continue even now to
recur consecutively in the same pattern.

680 As to the lengthening of the day coupled with the wasting
away of night, and the waning of daylight when night is
waxing, various views are again tenable. It may be that the
same sun traverses unequal arcs of the ethereal sphere below
the earth and above, dividing its daily orbit into a greater part
and a less. Thus, what it has subtracted from the one half it
adds to the opposite one in its revolution, till it comes round to
that constellation in which the equinox equates the shades of
night with the light of day. At the mid-point of the sun's flight
before the north[59] wind and again before the south wind, the
690 sky holds apart the tropics at an equal distance on either side of
the sun. This follows from the position of the whole zodiacal
belt through which the sun creeps to complete its annual cycle,
lighting heaven and earth with radiance cast aslant. Such is the
account given by those who have plotted all the regions of the
sky and marked the ordered sequence of constellations.

Or it may be that the air in certain regions is denser, so that
the flickering glow of fire loiters beneath the earth and cannot
easily win through and struggle out to its rising; and that this is
why the long winter nights drag on till the advent of day's
701 flashing banner.

Or again, for the same reason it may be that the fiery
particles flow together more slowly or more quickly at alternate
seasons of the year; these determine the place where the sun
rises. Therefore those people ⟨who say that no single cause can
be assigned to these things⟩ seem to be telling the truth.

What, then, of the moon? It may be that it shines only when
the sun's rays hit it. Then day by day, as it moves away from
the sun's orb, it turns more of its illumined surface towards our
view till in its rising it gazes down face to face upon the setting
sun and beams with lustre at the full. Thereafter, it is bound to

hide its light bit by bit behind it as it glides round heaven   712
towards the solar fire from the opposite point of the zodiac.
Such is the view of those who picture the moon as a spherical
body moving in an orbit below the sun.

It is equally possible that it rolls round with a lustre of its
own[60] and displays changing shapes of luminosity. For there
may be another body that glides along by its side, masking and
obstructing it in every way but remaining invisible because it   719
sheds no light.[61]

Or perhaps the moon is a rotating sphere of which one half
is gilded with resplendent light. Then in the course of its
rotation it displays changing shapes, until it turns towards our
wide-eyed gaze that half which is enriched with fire. Thereafter
by the reverse process it veers round and turns away the
luminous half of its rounded globe. Such is the contention by
which the Babylonian lore of the Chaldaeans[62] strives to confute
the skill of the astronomers – as though the theory for which
either party fights might not be true, and there were any reason   730
why you should be more reluctant to adopt the one than the
other.

Lastly, why should not a new moon be created periodically
with a definite sequence of determinate shapes? Why should
not each in turn dwindle day by day, and in its place another be
built up to play the same part? It is hard to formulate any
convincing argument that would rule this out when so many
things are created in a definite sequence. Spring comes, and
Venus, and Venus' winged courier Cupid runs in front. And all
along the path that they will tread mother Flora[63] carpets the   740
whole trail of Zephyr with a wealth of blossoms exquisite in
hue and fragrance. Next follows parching heat, hand in hand
with dusty Ceres[64] and the north wind's Etesian[65] blasts. Then
autumn steps on the scene, with Bacchus'[66] revel rout. Soon
other seasons follow and other winds, high thundering Vultur-
nus[67] and the south wind, ablaze with its lightning. To end the
pageant, midwinter brings back its snows and stiffening frost,
attended by that old tooth-chatterer, cold. What wonder, then,
if the moon is born at a set time and again at a set time effaced,
when so many things are created in a definite sequence?

751   In the same way you must understand that various causes may account for eclipses[68] of the sun and the moon's occultations. If the moon can cut off sunlight from the earth, uprearing its obstructive head between the two and planting a dark sphere in the path of the glowing rays, why should we not picture the same effect as produced by another body that glides round for ever lustreless? Or why should not the sun periodic-
759   ally fail and dim its own fires and afterwards rekindle its light when it has passed through a stretch of atmosphere uncongenial to its flames, which causes the quenching and quelling of its fire? And again, if the earth in turn can rob the moon of light by screening off the sun that shines below while the moon in its monthly round glides through the clear-cut cone[69] of shadow, why should not some other body equally well pass under the moon or glide over the solar orb so as to interrupt the radiant stream of light? And, supposing that the moon shines by its own lustre, why should it not grow faint in a
770   determinate quarter of the heavens while it is passing through a region uncongenial to its particular light?

I have explained the processes by which the various phenomena may be brought about in the blue expanses of the firmament. I have made intelligible the forces that may actuate the movements of the sun and the moon's wanderings. I have shown how both may suffer eclipse through the obscuration of their light and plunge the unsuspecting earth into gloom, as though they blinked and then with reopened eye surveyed the world, aglow with limpid radiance. I return now to the childhood of the
780   world, to consider what fruits the tender fields of earth in youthful parturition first ventured to fling up into the light of day and entrust to the fickle breezes.

First of all, the earth girdled its hills with a green glow of herbage,[70] and over every plain the flowery meadows gleamed with verdure. The trees of every sort were given free rein to join in an eager race for growth into the gusty air. As feathers, hair and bristles[71] are generated at the outset from the bodies of winged lords of the air and four-footed creatures, so then *the new-born earth first flung up herbs and shrubs. Next in order it*

engendered the various breeds of mortal creatures, different in their   791
many modes of origin as in form. The animals cannot have
fallen from the sky,[72] and those that live on land cannot have
emerged from the briny gulfs.[73] We are left with the conclusion
that the name of mother has rightly been bestowed on the
earth, since out of the earth everything is born.

Even now multitudes of animals are formed out of the
earth[74] with the aid of showers and the sun's genial warmth. So   800
it would not have been surprising if more and bigger ones had
taken shape and developed in those days, when earth and ether
were young. First, the various breeds of winged birds were
hatched out of eggs in the spring season, just as now the
cicadas in summer crawl out spontaneously from their tubular
integuments in quest of livelihood and life. Then it was that the
earth brought forth the first mammals. There was a great
superfluity of heat and moisture in the soil. So, wherever a
suitable spot occurred, there grew up wombs,[75] clinging to the
earth by roots. These, when the time was ripe, were burst open   810
by the maturation of the embryos, rejecting moisture now and
struggling for air. Then nature directed towards that spot the
pores of the earth, making it open its veins and exude a juice
resembling milk, just as nowadays every female when she has
given birth is filled with sweet milk because all the flow of
nourishment within her is directed into the breasts. The young
were fed by the earth, clothed by the warmth and bedded by
the herbage, which was then covered with abundance of soft
down. The childhood of the world provoked no sharp frosts or
excessive heats or winds of boisterous violence.[76] For all things   820
keep pace in their growth and the attainment of their full
strength. Here then is further proof that the name of mother
has rightly been bestowed on the earth, since it brought forth
the human race and gave birth at the appointed season to every
beast that runs wild among the high hills and at the same time
to the birds of the air in all their rich variety.

Then, because there must be an end to such parturition, the
earth ceased to bear, like a woman worn out with age.[77] For the
nature of the world as a whole is altered by age. Everything
must pass through successive phases. Nothing remains for ever

830 what it was. Everything is on the move. Everything is transformed by nature and forced into new paths. One thing, withered by time, decays and dwindles. Another grows strong and emerges from ignominy. So the nature of the world as a whole is altered by age. The earth passes through successive phases, so that the earth which used to be able to bear can do so no longer, while mammals which could never bear in the past can now produce.

836

In those days the earth attempted[78] also to produce a host of monsters, grotesque in build and aspect – hermaphrodites, halfway between the sexes yet cut off from either, creatures bereft of feet or dispossessed of hands, dumb, mouthless brutes, or eyeless and blind, or disabled by the adhesion of their limbs to the body, so that they could neither do anything nor go anywhere nor keep out of harm's way nor take what they needed. These and other such *monstrous and misshapen births were*
846 *created. But all in vain.* Nature debarred them from increase. They could not gain the coveted flower of maturity nor procure food nor be coupled by the arts of Venus. For it is evident that many contributory factors are essential to be able to forge the chain of a species in procreation. First, it must have a food-supply. Then it must have some channel by which the procreative seeds can travel outward through the body when the limbs are relaxed. Then, in order that male and female may couple, they must have some means of interchanging their mutual delight.

855

In those days, again, *many species must have died out altogether* and failed to forge the chain of offspring. Every species that you now see drawing the breath of life has been protected and preserved from the beginning of the world either by cunning or by courage or by speed. In addition, there are many that survive under human protection because their usefulness has commended them to our care. The surly breed of lions, for instance, in their native ferocity have been preserved by courage, the fox by cunning and the stag by flight.[79] The intelligent dog, loyal of heart and light of sleep, all beasts of burden of

whatever breed, fleecy sheep and horned cattle, over all these,   867
my Memmius, man has established his protectorate. They have
gladly escaped from predatory beasts and sought peace and the
lavish meals, procured by no effort of theirs, with which we
recompense their service. But those that were gifted with none
of these natural assets, unable either to live on their own
resources or to make any contribution to human welfare, in
return for which we might let their race feed in safety under   874
our guardianship – all these, trapped in the toils of their own
destiny, were fair game and an easy prey for others, till nature
brought their race to extinction.

But *there never were*, nor ever can be, centaurs[80] – *creatures with a
double nature*, combining organs of different origin in a single
body so that there may be a balance of power between attributes
drawn from two distinct sources. This can be inferred by the
dullest wit from these facts. First, a horse reaches its vigorous
prime in about three years, a boy far from it: for often even at   885
that age he will fumble in sleep for his mother's suckling
breasts. Then, when the horse's limbs are flagging and his
mettle is fading with the onset of age and the ebbing of life,
then is the very time when the boy is crowned with the flower
of youth and his cheeks are clothed with a soft down. You
need not suppose, therefore, that there can ever be a centaur,
compounded of man and draught-horse, or a Scylla,[81] half sea-
monster, with a girdle of mad dogs, or any other such mon-
strous hybrid between species whose bodies are obviously
incompatible. They do not correspond in their maturing, in   895
gaining strength or in losing it with advancing years. They
blaze differently with the flame of Venus. Their habits are
discordant. Their senses are not gratified by the same stimuli.
You may even see bearded goats fattening on hemlock, which
to man is deadly poison.[82] Since flame sears and burns the
tawny frames of lions no less than any other form of flesh and
blood that exists on earth, how could there be a chimera[83] with
three bodies rolled into one, in front a lion, at the rear a
serpent, in the middle the she-goat (that her name implies)
belching from her jaws a dire flame born of her body? If

907 anyone pretends that such monsters could have been begotten
when earth was young and the sky new, pinning his faith
merely on that empty word 'young', he is welcome to trot out a
string of fairy tales of the same stamp. Let him declare that
rivers of gold in those days flowed in profusion over the earth:
that the trees bore jewels for blossoms, or that a man was born
with such a stretch of limbs that he could bestride the high seas
and spin the whole sky around him with his hands.[84] The fact
916 that there were abundant seeds of things in the earth at the time
when it first gave birth to living creatures is no indication that
beasts could have been created of intermingled shapes with
limbs compounded from different species. The growths that
even now spring profusely from the soil – the varieties of herbs
and cereals and lusty trees – cannot be produced in this
composite fashion: each species develops according to its own
kind, and they all guard their specific characters in obedience to
the laws of nature.

925 The *human beings* that peopled these fields were far tougher than
the men of today,[85] as became the offspring of tough earth.
They were built on a framework of bigger and more solid
bones, fastened through their flesh to stout sinews. They were
relatively insensitive to heat and cold, to unaccustomed diet
and bodily ailments in general. Through many decades of the
sun's cyclic course they lived out their lives in the fashion of
wild beasts roaming at large. No one spent his strength in
guiding the curved plough. No one knew how to work the
earth with iron, or to plant young saplings in the soil or lop the
935 old branches from tall trees with pruning hooks. Their hearts
were well content to accept as a free gift what the sun and
showers had given and the earth had produced unsolicited.
Often they stayed their hunger among the acorn-laden oaks.
Arbutus berries, whose scarlet tint now betrays their winter
ripening, were then produced by the earth in plenty and of a
larger size. In addition the lusty childhood of the earth yielded
a great variety of tough foods, ample for poor mortals. Rivers
and springs called to them to slake their thirst, as nowadays a
clamorous cataract of water, tumbling out of the high hills,

summons from far away the thirsty creatures of the wild. They   947
lived in those woodland sanctuaries of the nymphs, familiar to
them in their wandering, from which they knew that trickling
streams of water issued to bathe the dripping rocks in a
bountiful shower, sprinkled over green moss, and gushed out
here and there over the open plain.

They did not know as yet how to enlist the aid of fire, or to
make use of skins, or to clothe their bodies with trophies of the
chase. They lived in thickets and hillside caves and forests and   954
stowed their rough limbs among bushes when driven to seek
shelter from the lash of wind and rain.

They could have no thought of the common good, no
notion of the mutual restraint of morals and laws.[86] The indi-
vidual, taught only to live and fend for himself, carried off on
his own account such prey as fortune brought him. Venus
coupled the bodies of lovers in the woods. Mutual desire
brought them together, or the male's mastering might and
profligate lust, or a bribe of acorns or arbutus berries or choice   965
pears. Thanks to their surpassing strength of hand and foot,
they hunted the woodland beasts by hurling stones and wielding
ponderous clubs. They were more than a match for many of
them: from a few they took refuge in hiding-places.

When night overtook them, they flung their jungle-bred
limbs naked on the earth like bristly boars, and wrapped
themselves round with a coverlet of leaves and branches. It is
not true[87] that they wandered panic-stricken over the countryside
through the darkness of night, searching with loud lamentations
for the daylight and the sun. In fact they waited, sunk in quiet
sleep, till the sun with his rose-red torch should bring back   975
radiance to the sky. Accustomed as they were from infancy to
seeing the alternate birth of darkness and light, they could never
have been struck with amazement or misgiving that the with-
drawal of the sunlight might plunge the earth in everlasting
night. They were more worried by the peril to which unlucky
sleepers were often exposed from predatory beasts. Turned out
of house and home by the intrusion of a slavering boar or a burly
lion, they would abandon their rocky roofs at dead of night and
yield up their leaf-strewn beds in terror to the savage visitors.

988   The proportion of mortal men that relinquished the dear light of life lamenting before it was all spent was not appreciably higher then than now.[88] Then it more often happened that an individual victim would furnish living food to a beast of prey: engulfed in its jaws, he would fill thicket and mountainside and forest with his shrieks, at the sight of his living flesh entombed in a living sepulchre.[89] Those who saved their mangled bodies

996 by flight would press trembling palms over ghastly sores, calling upon Orcus in heart-rending voices, till life was wrenched from them by savage torments. They had no source of help in their ignorance of the treatment that wounds demand. But it never happened then that many thousands of men following the standards were led to death on a single day. Never did the ocean levels, lashed into tumult, hurl ships and men together upon the reefs. Here, time after time, the sea would rise and vainly vent its fruitless ineffectual fury, then lightly lay aside its idle threats. The crafty blandishment of the unruffled deep could not tempt any man to his undoing with its

1005 rippling laughter.[90] Then, when the mariner's presumptuous art lay still unguessed, it was lack of food that brought failing limbs at last to death. Now it is superfluity that proves too much for them. The men of old often served poison to themselves out of ignorance. Now, with greater skill, they give it out to other people.[91]

As time went by, men began to build huts and to use skins and fire. Woman mated with man, moved into a single ⟨home and the laws of marriage⟩ were learnt as they watched over their

1013 joint progeny. Then it was that humanity first began to mellow. Thanks to fire, their chilly bodies could no longer so easily endure the cold under the canopy of heaven. Venus subdued brute strength. Children by their wheedling easily broke down their parents' stubborn temper. The neighbours began to form *mutual alliances*, wishing neither to do nor to suffer violence among themselves.[92] They appealed on behalf of their children and womenfolk, pointing out with gestures and inarticulate cries that it is right for everyone to pity the weak. It was not possible to achieve perfect unity of purpose. Yet a substantial

majority kept faith honestly. Otherwise the entire human race 1025
would have been wiped out there and then instead of being
propagated, generation after generation, down to the present
day.

As for the various sounds of *spoken language*,[93] it was nature that
drove men to utter these, and practical convenience that gave a
form to the names of objects. We see a similar process at work 1031
when babies are led by their speechless plight to employ
gestures, such as pointing with a finger at objects in view. For
every creature has a sense of the purposes for which he can use
his own powers. A bull-calf, before even his horns have grown
and sprouted from his forehead, butts and thrusts with them
aggressively when his temper is roused. Panther kittens and
lion cubs tussle with paws and jaws when their claws and teeth
are scarcely yet in existence. We see every species of winged
bird trust in its wings and seek unsteady help from flight. To
suppose that someone[94] on some particular occasion allotted 1041
names to objects, and that by this means men learnt their first
words, is stark madness. Why should we suppose that one man
had this power of indicating everything by vocal utterances and
emitting the various sounds of speech when others could not
do it? Besides, if others had not used such utterances among
themselves, from what source was the mental image[95] of its use
implanted in him? Whence did this one man derive the power
in the first instance of seeing with his mind what he wanted to
do? One man could not subdue a greater number and induce
them by force to learn his names for things. It is far from easy
to convince deaf listeners by any demonstration what needs to 1052
be done. They would not endure it or submit for long on any
terms to have unfamiliar noises senselessly dinned into their
ears.

And what, after all, is so surprising in the notion that the
human race, possessed of a vigorous voice and tongue, should
indicate objects by various vocal utterances expressive of vari-
ous feelings? Even dumb cattle and wild beasts utter distinct
and various sounds when they are gripped by fear or pain or
when joy wells up within them. Indeed we have direct evidence

1063 of such distinctions. Molossian[96] hounds, for instance, when
first their gaping flabby jowls are drawn back in a grim snarl
that bares their hard teeth, give vent to a gruff growl. Very
different is the sound when the growl has grown to a loud-
mouthed reverberating barking. Different again is the soft
crooning with which they fondle their pups when they fall to
licking them lovingly with their tongues or when they toss
1069 them with their paws, snapping with open jaws in a playful
pretence of gobbling them up with teeth that never close. And
different from all these are the howls when left alone in the
house, or the whimpering with which they shrink and cringe to
avoid the whip. In the same way, when a stallion in the prime
of his youth is let loose among the mares, smarting from the
prick of winged Cupid's darts, and snorts defiance to his rivals
through distended nostrils, his neigh is surely not the same that
shakes his limbs on other occasions. So also with the various
species of winged birds. The hawks and ospreys and gulls that
1081 seek a livelihood among the salt sea waves all have distinctive
cries that show when they are squabbling over their food and
their prey is fighting back. Some birds even vary their note
according to the weather. So the hoarse-throated cawing of
long-lived[97] ravens and gregarious rooks varies from time to
time according to whether they are clamouring for showers of
rain, as it is said, or summoning wind and breezes. If the
animals, dumb though they be, are impelled by different feelings
to utter different cries, how much the more reason to suppose
that men in those days had the power of distinguishing between
one thing and another by distinctive utterances!
1091

Here is the answer to another question that you may be putting
to yourself. *The agent by which fire was first brought down to earth*
and made available to mortal man *was lightning.*[98] It is from this
source that the blaze of fire has spread. Think how many things
we see ablaze with heaven-sent flame implanted in them, when
a stroke from heaven has endowed them with heat. There is
also, however, another possible source. When a branching tree,
struck by the winds, is swaying and surging to and fro and
stooping to touch the branches of another tree, the violent

friction squeezes out seeds of fire, till sometimes from the   1100
rubbing of bough against bough, trunk against trunk, there
flashes out a blazing burst of flame. Either of these occurrences
may have given fire to mortals. Later it was the sun that taught
them to cook food and soften it by heating on the flames, since
they noticed in roaming through the fields how many things
were subdued and mellowed by the impact of its ardent rays.

As time went by, men learnt to change their old way of life by   1105
means of fire and other new inventions, instructed by those of
outstanding ability and mental energy. *Kings began to found cities*
and establish citadels for their own safeguard and refuge. They
parcelled out cattle and lands, giving to each according to his
looks, his strength and his ability; for good looks were highly
prized and strength counted for much. Later came the invention
of property and the discovery of gold, which speedily robbed
the strong and the handsome of their status. The man of
greater riches finds no lack of strong frames and comely faces   1116
to follow in his train. And yet, if a man would guide his life by
true philosophy,[99] he will find ample riches in a modest liveli-
hood enjoyed with a tranquil mind. Of that little he need never
be beggared. Men craved for fame and power so that their
fortune might rest on a firm foundation and they might live out
a peaceful life in the enjoyment of plenty. An idle dream. In
struggling to gain the pinnacle of power they beset their own
road with perils.[100] And then from the very peak, as though by
a thunderbolt, they are cast down by envy into a foul Tartar-
ean[101] abyss of ignominy. For envy, like the thunderbolt, most   1127
often strikes the highest and all that stands out above the
common level. Far better to lead a quiet life[102] in subjection
than to long for sovereign authority and lordship over king-
doms. So leave them to sweat blood in their wearisome unprofit-
able struggle along the narrow pathway of ambition. Since
their wisdom is taken from the mouths of other people and
their objectives chosen by hearsay rather than by the evidence
of their own senses,[103] it avails them now, and will avail them,
no more than it has ever done.

So the kings[104] were killed. Down in the dust lay the ancient

1137 majesty of thrones, the haughty sceptres. The illustrious emblem
of the sovereign head, dabbled in gore and trampled under the
feet of the rabble, mourned its high estate. What once was
feared too much is now passionately downtrodden. So the con-
duct of affairs sank back into the filthy lower depths of mob rule,
with each man struggling to win dominance and supremacy
for himself. Then some men showed how to appoint state
officials, to establish civil rights and duties so that men would
1144 want to obey the laws. Mankind, worn out by a life of violence
and enfeebled by feuds,[105] was the more ready to submit of its
own free will to the bondage of laws and institutions. This
distaste for a life of violence came naturally to a society in
which every individual was ready to gratify his anger by a
harsher vengeance than is now tolerated by equitable laws.
Ever since then the enjoyment of life's prizes has been tempered
by the fear of punishment. A man is enmeshed by his own
violence and wrongdoing, which commonly recoil upon their
1154 author. It is not easy for one who breaks by his acts the mutual
compact of social peace to lead a peaceful and untroubled life.
Even if he hides his guilt from gods and men, he must feel a
secret misgiving that it will not rest hidden for ever.[106] He
cannot forget those oft-told tales of men betraying themselves
by words, spoken in dreams[107] or delirium, that drag out long-
buried crimes into the daylight.

Let us now consider why *reverence for the gods*[108] is widespread
among the nations. What has crowded their cities with altars
and inaugurated those solemn rites that are in vogue today in
1164 great and powerful states? What has implanted in mortal hearts
that chill of dread which even now rears new temples of the
gods the wide world over and packs them on holy days with
pious multitudes? The explanation is not far to seek. Already in
those early days men had visions when their minds were awake,
and more clearly in sleep,[109] of divine figures, outstanding in
beauty and impressive in stature. To these figures they attrib-
uted feeling, because they were seen to move their limbs[110] and
give voice to lordly utterances appropriate to their stately
features and their tremendous strength. They further credited

them with eternal life, because the substance of their shapes was ~~1175~~
perpetually renewed and their appearance unchanging and in
general because they thought that beings of such strength could
not lightly be subdued by any force. They pictured their lot as
far superior to that of mortals, because none of them were
tormented by the fear of death, and also because in dreams they
saw them perform all sorts of miracles without the slightest
effort.

Again, men noticed the orderly succession of celestial phen- ~~1183~~
omena and the round of the seasons and were at a loss to
account for them. So they took refuge in handing over every-
thing to the gods and making everything dependent on their
whim. They chose the sky to be the home and headquarters of
the gods because it is through the sky that the night and the
moon are seen to tread their cyclic course, moon, day and night
and night's ominous constellations and the night-flying torches
and soaring flames of the firmament, clouds and sun and rain,
snow and wind, lightning and hail, the sudden thunder-crash ~~1193~~
and the long-drawn-out intimidating rumble.

Poor humanity,[111] to saddle the gods with such responsibil-
ities and throw in a vindictive temper! What griefs they hatched
then for themselves, what festering sores for us, what tears for
our posterity! This is not piety,[112] this oft-repeated show of
bowing a veiled head before a stone;[113] this bustling to every
altar; this kowtowing and prostration on the ground with
palms outspread before the shrines of the gods; this deluging of
altars with the blood of beasts; this heaping of vow on vow.
True piety lies rather in the power to contemplate the universe ~~1203~~
with a quiet mind.

When we gaze up at the supernal regions of this mighty
world, at the ether poised above, studded with flashing stars,
and there comes into our minds the thought of the sun and
moon and their migrations, then in hearts already racked by
other woes a new anxiety begins to waken and rear up its head.
We fall to wondering whether we may not be subject to some
unfathomable divine power, which speeds the shining stars
along their various tracks. It comes as a shock to our faltering
minds to realize how little they know about the world. Had it a

1212 birth and a beginning? Is there some limit in time, beyond which its bastions will be unable to endure the strain of jarring motion? Or are they divinely gifted with everlasting surety, so that in their journey through the termless tract of time they can mock the stubborn strength of measureless time?

Again, who does not feel his mind quailing and his limbs creep with shuddering dread of the gods when the parched earth reels at the dire stroke of the thunderbolt and tumult rolls
1221 across the breadth of heaven? Do not multitudes quake and nations tremble? Do not proud monarchs flinch, stricken in every limb by terror of the gods and the thought that the time has come when some foul deed or arrogant word must pay its heavy price?

Or picture a storm at sea, the wind scouring the water with hurricane force and some high admiral of the fleet swept before the blast with all his mighty legions and battle elephants.[114] How he importunes the peace of the gods with vows! How fervently
1230 he prays in his terror that the winds, too, may be at peace and favouring breezes blow! But, for all his prayers, the tornado does not relax its grip, and all too often he is dashed upon the reefs of death. So irresistibly is human power ground to dust by some unseen force, which seems to mock at the majestic rods and ruthless axes[115] of authority and trample on them as a joke.

Lastly, when the whole earth quakes[116] beneath their feet, when shaken cities fall in ruins or hang hesitantly tottering, what wonder if mortal men despise themselves and find a place
1240 in nature for superhuman forces and miraculous divine powers with supreme control over the universe?

We come next to *the discovery of copper, gold and iron, weighty silver and useful lead*. This occurred when fire among the high hills had consumed huge forests in its blaze. The blaze may have been started by a stroke of lightning, or by men who had employed fire to scare their enemies in some woodland war, or were tempted by the fertility of the country to enrich their large ploughlands and turn the wilds into pasturage. Or they may have wished to kill the forest beasts and profit by their spoils;

for hunting by means of pitfall and fire developed earlier than   1250
fencing round a glade with nets and driving the game with
dogs. Let us take it, then, that for one reason or another, no
matter what, a fierce conflagration, roaring balefully, has de-
voured a forest down to the roots and roasted the earth with
penetrative fire. Out of the melted veins there would flow into
hollows on the earth's surface a convergent stream of silver and
gold, copper and lead. Afterwards, when men saw these lying   1258
solidified on the earth and flashing with resplendent colour,
they would be tempted by their attractive lustre and polish to
pick them up. They would notice that each lump was moulded
into a shape like that of the bed from which it had been lifted.
Then it would enter their minds that these substances, when
liquefied by heat, could run into any mould or the shape of any
object they might desire, and could also be drawn out by
hammering into pointed tips of any slenderness and sharpness.
Here was a means by which they could equip themselves with
weapons, chop down forests, rough-hew timber and plane it   1268
into smooth planks and pierce holes in it by boring, punching
or drilling. At the outset they would try to do this with silver
or gold no less than with tough and stubborn bronze.[117] But
this would not work. These metals would give under the strain,
lacking strength to stand up to such exacting tasks. So bronze
was more highly prized, and gold with its quickly blunted edge
was despised as useless. Now it is bronze that is despised, while
gold has succeeded to the highest honours. So the circling years
bring round reversals of fortune. What once was prized is
afterwards held cheap. In its place, something else emerges   1278
from ignominy, is daily more and more coveted and, as its
merits are detected, blossoms into glory and is acclaimed by
mankind with extravagant praises.

At this point, Memmius, you should find it easy to puzzle
out for yourself how men discovered the properties of iron.
The earliest weapons were hands, nails and teeth. Next came
stones and branches wrenched from trees, and fire and flame as
soon as these were discovered. Then men learnt to use tough
iron and bronze. Actually the use of bronze was discovered
before that of iron, because it is more easily handled and in

1288 more plentiful supply. With bronze they tilled the soil. With bronze they whipped up the clashing waves of war, scattered a withering seed[118] of wounds and made a spoil of flocks and fields. Before their armaments all else, naked and unarmed, fell an easy prey. Then by slow degrees the iron sword came to the fore, the bronze sickle fell into disrepute, the ploughman began to cleave the earth with iron and on the darkling field of battle

1296 the odds were made even.

The art of mounting armed on horseback, guiding the steed with reins and keeping the right hand free for action, came earlier than braving the hazards of war in a two-horsed chariot.[119] This again preceded the yoking of two pairs in one harness and the charge of armed warriors in chariots set with scythes.[120] Later the 'Lucanian oxen',[121] the snake-handed elephants, their bodies crowned by towers, were taught by the men of Carthage to endure the wounds of war and embroil the long-drawn ranks

1305 of Mars. So tragic discord gave birth to one invention after another for the intimidation of the nation's fighting men and added daily increments to the horrors of war.

Bulls,[122] too, were enlisted in the service of war and the experiment was made of launching savage boars against the enemy. Some even tried an advance guard of doughty lions with armed trainers and harsh masters to discipline them and keep them on the lead. But these experiments failed. The savage brutes, inflamed by promiscuous carnage, spread indiscriminate confusion among the squadrons, as they tossed the

1316 terrifying manes upon their heads this way and that. The riders failed to soothe the breast of their steeds, panic-stricken by uproar, and direct them with reins against the enemy. The lionesses hurled their frenzied bodies in a random spring, now leaping full in the face of oncomers, now snatching the unsuspecting victims from behind and dragging them to the ground, mortally wounded in the embrace and gripped fast by tenacious jaws and crooked claws. The bulls tossed men of their own side and trampled them underfoot and with their horns gored the flanks and bellies of horses from below and hacked up the very earth with minds determined on violence. The infuriated boars

with their stout tusks slashed their allies. They reddened with 1326
their own blood the weapons broken in their bodies. They
mowed down horse and foot pell-mell. The horses would shy
away, or rear up and paw the air in a vain attempt to escape the
savage onslaught of those tusks. But down you would see them
tumble hamstrung, and bury the earth beneath their fallen
mass. Even such beasts as their masters had once thought tame
enough at home were seen to boil over in the stir of action — 1335
wounds, yells, stampedes, panic and turmoil: and none of them
would obey the recall. Brutes of every breed were rushing
wildly about. The sight must have been such as is sometimes
seen in our own times when these 'Lucanian oxen', badly
wounded by the steel, run wild after turning savagely upon
their own associates. If, indeed, the experiment was ever tried.[123]
For my part, I find it hard to believe that men had no mental
apprehension and premonition of this mutual disaster and dis-
grace before it could happen. It would be safer to assert that
this has happened somewhere in the universe, somewhere in 1345
the multiplicity of diversely formed worlds, than in any one
specific globe. In any event it must have been undertaken more
to spite the enemy than with any hope of victory, by men
mistrustful of their own numbers and armaments but not afraid
to die.

As to *costume*, plaited clothes came before woven ones. Woven
fabrics came after iron, because iron is needed for making a
loom. Apart from it no material can be made smooth enough
for treadles and spindles and shuttles and clattering heddles.
Nature ordained that this should be men's work before it was 1354
women's. For the male sex as a whole is by far the more skilful
and gifted in the arts.[124] But eventually it was damned as
effeminate by a censorious peasantry, so that they chose rather
to leave it to women's hands while they joined in the endurance
of hard labour and by the hardness of their toil hardened hands
and limbs.

For the *sowing and grafting of plants* the first model was provided
by creative nature herself. Berries and acorns, lying below the

1364   trees from which they had fallen, were seen to put forth a swarm of shoots in due season. From the same source men learnt to engraft slips in branches and to plant young saplings in the soil of their fields. After that they tried one type of cultivation after another in their treasured plot. They saw the wild fruits grow mild in the ground with cosseting and humouring. Day by day they kept forcing the woodland to creep further up the hillside, surrendering the lower reaches to

1371   tillage. Over hill and plain they extended meadowland, reservoirs, watercourses, cornland and laughing vineyards, with the distinctive strip of grey-green olives running between, rippling over hump and hollow and along the level ground. So the countryside assumed its present aspect of varied beauty, interspersed with luscious orchards and marked out by encircling hedges of luxuriant trees.

    Men learnt to mimic with their mouths the trilling notes of birds

1381   long before they were able to enchant the ear by joining together in *tuneful song*. It was the whistling of the breeze through hollow reeds that first taught countryfolk to blow through hollow hemlock stalks.[125] After that, by slow degrees, they learnt those plaintive melodies that flow from the flute at the touch of the player's fingers, melodies that took shape far from the busy highways, amid groves and glades and thickets in the solitudes where the shepherd spends his sunlit leisure. These are the tunes that soothed and cheered their hearts after a full meal: for at such times everything is enjoyable. So they would often recline in

1392   company on the soft grass by a running stream under the branches of a tall tree and refresh their bodies pleasurably at small expense. Better still if the weather smiled upon them and the season of the year emblazoned the green herbage with flowers.[126] Then was the time for joking and talking and merry laughter. Then was the heyday of the rustic muse. Then light-hearted jollity prompted them to wreathe head and shoulders with garlands twisted of flowers and leaves and dance out of step, moving their limbs clumsily and with clumsy foot stamping on mother earth. This was matter enough for mirth and boisterous laughter. For these arts were still in their youth, with all the charm of novelty.

In the same occupation the wakeful found a means to while
away their sleepless hours, pitching their voices high or low
through the twisted intricacies of song and running over the
pipes with curving lips. This remains a recognized tradition
among watchmen to this day, and they have now learnt to keep
in tune. But this does not mean that they derive any greater
enjoyment from it than did the woodland race sprung from the
soil. For what we have here and now, unless we have known
something more pleasing in the past, gives the greatest satisfac-
tion and is reckoned the best of its kind. Afterwards the
discovery of something new and better blunts and vitiates our
enjoyment of the old. So it is that we have lost our taste for
acorns. So we have abandoned those couches littered with
herbage and heaped with leaves. So the wearing of wild beasts'
skins has gone out of fashion. And yet I daresay that the
invention of this costume provoked such envy that its first
wearer met his death in an ambush and the costume itself was
so daubed with blood and torn to shreds by rival claimants that
it could not be used by anyone. Skins yesterday, purple and
gold today – such are the baubles that embitter human life with
resentment and waste it with war. In this, I do not doubt, the
greater blame rests with us. To the earth-born generation in
their naked state the lack of skins meant real discomfort through
cold; but we suffer no distress by going without robes of
purple, brocaded with gold and extravagant figures, so long as
we have some plebeian wrap to throw around us. So mankind
is perpetually the victim of a pointless and futile martyrdom,
fretting life away in fruitless worries through failure to realize
what limit is set to acquisition and to the growth of genuine
pleasure.[127] It is this discontent that has driven life steadily
onward, out to the high seas, and has stirred up from the
depths the surging tumultuous tides of war.

It was the sun and moon, the watchmen of the world, encircling
with their light that vast rotating vault, who taught men that
the seasons of the year revolve and that there is a constant
pattern in things and a constant sequence.

By this time men were living their lives fenced by forti-

1405

1412

1422

1433

1440   fications and tilling an earth already parcelled out and allotted. The deep sea flowered with sail-flying ships. Societies were bound together by compacts and alliances. Poets were beginning to record history in song. But letters were still a recent invention. Therefore our age cannot look back to see what happened before this stage,[128] except in so far as its traces can be uncovered by reason.

1448   So we find that not only such arts as seafaring and agriculture, city walls and laws, weapons, roads and clothing, but also without exception the amenities and refinements of life, poetry, pictures and statues, artfully carved and polished, *all were taught gradually by usage* and the active mind's experiments as men groped their way forward step by step. So each particular development is brought gradually to the fore by the advance of time, and reason lifts it into the light of day. Men saw one notion after another take shape within their minds until by their arts they scaled the topmost peak.

BOOK SIX

METEOROLOGY AND GEOLOGY

In days of old it was from Athens[1] of high renown that the knowledge of cereal crops was first disseminated among suffering mankind. It was Athens that built life on a new plan and promulgated laws.[2] It was Athens no less that first gave to life a message of good cheer through the birth of that man,[3] gifted with no ordinary mind, whose unerring lips gave utterance to the whole of truth. Even now, when he is no more, the widespread and long-established fame of his divine discoveries is exalted to the very skies.[4]

He saw that, practically speaking, all that was wanted to 9
meet men's vital needs was already at their disposal, and, so far as could be managed, their livelihood was assured.[5] He saw some men in the full enjoyment of riches and reputation, dignity and authority, and happy in the fair fame of their children. Yet, for all that, he found aching hearts in every home, racked incessantly by pangs the mind was powerless to assuage, forced to vent themselves in recalcitrant repining. He concluded that the source of this illness was the container itself,[6] which infected with its own malady everything that was collected outside and brought into it, however beneficial. He 19
arrived at this conclusion partly because he perceived that the container was cracked and leaky, so that it could never by any possibility be filled: partly because he saw it taint whatever it took in with the taste of its own foulness. Therefore he purged men's breasts with words of truth. He set bounds to desire and fear. He demonstrated what is the highest good,[7] after which we all strive, and pointed the way by which we can achieve it, keeping straight ahead along a narrow track. He revealed the element of pain[8] inherent in the life of mortals generally, resulting whether casually or determinately from the operations of nature and prowling round in various forms. He showed by what gate it is best to sally out against each one of these evils. And he made it clear that, more often than not, it was quite

34 needlessly that mankind stirred up stormy waves of disquietude within their breasts.

As children[9] in blind darkness tremble and start at everything, so we in broad daylight are oppressed at times by fears as baseless as those horrors which children imagine coming upon them in the dark. This dread and darkness of the mind cannot be dispelled by the sunbeams, the shining shafts of day, but only by an understanding of the outward form and inner workings of nature. The more reason, then, why I should weave further the argument that I have started.

41

I have taught[10] that the sky in all its zones is mortal and its substance was formed by a process of birth, and I have also elucidated most of the phenomena that occur in the heavens and that must inevitably occur. Listen now to what still remains to tell.

48

Since I have ventured to climb into the lofty chariot[11] ⟨of the Muses, I will explain how the wrath⟩ of the winds is roused and how it is appeased and how all *disturbances of nature* are allayed when their fury is spent; also the other things on earth or in the heavens that frighten men, when the balance of their minds is upset by fear, and that abase their spirits with terror of the gods and crush them cringing on the ground,[12] because ignorance of the causes of phenomena drives them to commit everything to the rule of the gods and to acknowledge their sovereignty. [They are in no way able to see what causes these things and they believe them to be done by the power of the gods.] For it may happen that men who have learnt the truth about the carefree[13] existence of the gods fall to wondering by what power the universe is kept going, especially those movements that are seen overhead in the ethereal borderland. Then the poor creatures are plunged back into their old superstitions and saddle themselves with cruel masters whom they believe to be all-powerful. All this because they do not know what can be and what cannot – how the power of each thing is limited, and its boundary-stone sticks buried deep. Therefore they are the more prone to go astray, misled by blind reasoning. Unless you vomit such notions out of your mind and banish far away all

58

thoughts unworthy of the gods and foreign to their tranquillity, 69
then the holy beings whom you thus diminish will often do you
real harm. This is not because the supreme majesty of the gods
can in fact be wronged, so as to be tempted in a fit of anger to
wreak a savage revenge.[14] No, the fault will be in you. Because
you will picture the quiet ones in their untroubled peace as
tossed on turbulent waves of anger, you will not approach their
temples with a tranquil heart; you will not be able to admit into 77
a breast at peace those images emanating from a holy body that
bring to the minds of men their tidings of a form divine. From
this you can gather what sort of life must ensue. If this is to be
averted from us by true reason, there is still much to add in
finely polished verse to the much that I have already delivered.
I must grasp the system and phenomena of the heavens. I must
sing of storms and the vivid lightning flash, their effects and
the causes of their outbreak. Otherwise you may be so scared
out of your wits as to map out different quarters of the sky[15]
and speculate from which one the darting fire has come or into 88
which other it has passed: how it has entered a closed building,
and how after taking possession of it has emerged victorious.
[They are not in any way able to see the causes of these doings
and they believe them to be done by the power of the gods.]

For this task I invoke your aid, Calliope,[16] most gifted of the
Muses, repose of men and delight of gods. Point out my path
along the last lap to the predetermined winning-post, that by
your guidance I may earn with eminent acclaim the victor's
crown.

First, then, the reason why the blue expanses of heaven are 96
shaken by *thunder* is the clashing of clouds soaring high in the
ether, when conflicting winds cause them to collide. A thunder-
clap does not issue from a clear stretch of sky:[17] the normal
source of that terrific crash and roll is the point where the
advancing columns of cloud are most densely serried. Clouds
cannot be composed of such dense bodies as make up stones
and logs, nor of such flimsy ones as mist and drifting smoke. In
the one case, they would be forced to fall like stones by the
drag of their dead weight; in the other, they would be no better

106 able than smoke to cohere or to contain icy snow and showers of hail. The noise they make above the levels of the outspread world is comparable to the intermittent clap of the awning[18] stretched over a large theatre, when it flaps between poles and cross-beams; or to the loud crackling, reminiscent of rending paper, that it makes when riotous winds have ripped it. You can pick out the former sound in thunder, and you hear it
115 again when hanging clothes or flying scraps of paper are whipped and whirled by the wind and swished through the air. At other times it happens that the clouds cannot so much collide head-on as pass side by side on different courses, scraping their bodies together in a dragging movement. That is when our ears are rubbed by the dry crackling sound, long drawn out, until the clouds have drifted out of close quarters.

Here is another way in which it often seems that a violent burst of thunder has made the whole earth reel and has suddenly cracked and rent apart the ramparts of the all-embracing firmament. A swiftly gathered squall of stormy wind has thrust its
125 way into the clouds. There, being hemmed in, its eddying swirl scoops out an ever-growing hollow walled on every side by cloud with its substance more and more condensed. Finally, the concentrated energy of the wind splits the cloud and explodes it with a nerve-shattering crash.[19] And no wonder, considering that a little bladder of wind, when suddenly burst, often gives out this loud a sound.

Another cause of the noise emitted by clouds is the wind blowing through them. We often see clouds scudding by profusely branched and jagged; and we all know that when a gale
135 blows through a dense wood, the leaves rustle and the branches creak. It also happens sometimes that the impetuous power of a strong blast shears through a cloud, smashing it by a direct hit. What a gale can do up there is clearly shown by its behaviour down here, where it is relatively gentle: even here on earth it bowls over tall trees and hauls them out by the roots.[20]

There are also waves in the clouds – waves that make a booming sound when they break heavily, just as happens in deep rivers and in the wide sea when the surf is breaking.

Another cause of thunder is when a blaze of lightning leaps

from cloud to cloud. If the receiving cloud is full of water, this 145
promptly quenches the blaze with a loud hiss like the sizzling[21]
of red-hot iron fresh from the fiery furnace when we have
plunged it straight into cold water. If, on the other hand, the
receiving cloud is drier, it immediately catches fire and burns
with a fierce crackling, as when a flame is swept over laurel-
haired hills by a squall of wind, spreading conflagration in its
impetuous advance; for nothing can compare with Apollo's 155
Delphic[22] laurel in the baleful roar of crackling flames with
which it is consumed.

Lastly, a noise is produced aloft among the mighty clouds by
widespread crumbling of hoar-frost and crashing of hail. For
mountains of storm-clouds mingled with hail are packed to-
gether by the compression of the wind and pulverized.

As for *lightning*,[23] it is caused when many seeds of fire[24] have
been squeezed out of clouds by their collision. Just so, if stone
is struck by stone or steel, a light leaps out and scatters bright 163
sparks of fire. Thunder follows later, when our ears receive
what our eyes saw flashing; for impulses always travel more
slowly to the ears than to the eyes. You can test this by
watching from a distance a man felling a towering tree with a
two-bladed axe: it so happens that you see the blow fall before
the sound of the stroke reaches your ears. In the same way we
see the lightning before we are aware of the thunder, which is
in fact emitted simultaneously with the flash from the same
cause, being born of the same collision.

Here is another way in which the clouds paint the landscape in 173
fleeting brilliance and the lightning is launched on its quivering
flight. When wind has forced its way into a cloud and, as I
explained before,[25] has hollowed and condensed it by eddying
round, it becomes heated by its own movement. You see
everything grow fiery hot with motion: the speed of a long flight
even liquefies a leaden sling-bolt.[26] So then, when this blazing
wind has burst open a black cloud, it scatters seeds of fire pushed
out by the force of the sudden explosion. These cause the zig-zag
flashes of flame. Then follows the noise, which affects our ears
more tardily than the visual impulse strikes our eyeballs.

185   This happens, you must understand, when the clouds are dense and when they are piled high one above another in an amazing array. Do not be misled by the fact that to us, gazing from below, the width of the clouds is more conspicuous than the height to which they are built up. Take note when next you get an oblique view of clouds that mimic mountains wafted through the air by the wind, or on some day when all the

193   winds are becalmed you see along a mountain range a motionless mass of clouds heaped upon clouds and weighing them down. Then you will be able to form some notion of their colossal bulk. Then you will see caverns overarched, as it seems, by beetling crags. When squally winds have filled these caverns, they protest clamorously in their cloudy prison with the roar of caged beasts.[27] This way and that they hurl their menacing growls through the clouds. In search of an outlet they prowl round and round. They dislodge seeds of fire from the clouds and roll together a multitude of them. Soon they are

203   spinning a flame within a hollow furnace, till the cloud bursts and out they tumble in a dazzling flash.

    Here is yet another reason why that fleeting golden glow of liquid fire leaps down upon the earth. The clouds themselves must contain a great many seeds of fire; for, when they are devoid of water, their colour is mostly flame-like and sparkling. Since they must inevitably absorb many such seeds from the sunlight, it is natural that they should blush and emit a fiery glow. So, when a driving wind has concentrated and compressed them forcibly in a single spot, they release under

213   pressure those atoms that are the cause of flame-bright flashes.

    Lightning may occur also when the clouds in the sky are thinning out. When the wind gently dissipates and dissolves them in their flight, they must perforce let drop the particles that generate flashes. But at such times the flash is a quiet one, without that appalling accompaniment of crash and rumble.

    What, then, of *the nature and composition of thunderbolts?*[28] We may learn from the stricken spots, branded with the mark of heat and breathing out the thick breath of sulphur. These are signs of fire, not of wind or rain. Besides, they often set fire to

buildings and work their will with darting flame in the heart of   224
the house. You must know that this rarefied fire, more than all
other fires, is composed by nature of minute and mobile
particles to which absolutely nothing can bar the way. So
potent is a thunderbolt that it passes through shut rooms like
sounds and voices.[29] It passes through stone and metal, and in
an instant liquefies bronze and gold. It causes wine to vaporize
from unbroken jars,[30] because its heat on arrival easily unknits   232
and loosens all the earthenware fabric of the jar, slips nimbly in,
scatters the atoms of wine and sweeps them away. This, as we
see, is more than the sun's heat can accomplish in an age,
though never so intense in its radiance. So much more mobile
and more masterful is the force of a thunderbolt.

I will now without more ado fulfil my promise to explain to
you how thunderbolts originate and how they possess such
momentum that their stroke can split towers open, demolish
buildings, tear out beams and rafters, uproot and fling down
the monuments of the great, rob men of life, butcher cattle all   244
around and wreak all those other forms of mischief that lie
within their power.

It must be supposed that thunderbolts originate from thick
and high-piled clouds. They are never really hurled from the
blue, nor from clouds of slight density. This is unmistakably
shown by experience. Indeed, at such times the air is so
crammed with a solid mass of cloud that we fancy[31] all the
darkness has forsaken the Underworld and come trooping from
every side into the roomy vaults of Heaven. Such is the
ominous night of storm-clouds that gathers overhead, out of   254
whose gloom the visage of black dread lours down upon us,
when the storm is making ready to forge its bolts. Add to this
that very often out at sea a black tornado falls upon the waves,
like a river of pitch[32] poured out of the sky, stuffed with far-
shadowing gloom. With its heavy freight of fire and wind, it
trails in its wake a black tempest big with thunderbolts and
squalls. Even on shore men shudder at the sight and take cover
under their roofs. From this we may infer what a depth of
cloud is heaped above our heads. For surely the earth would
not be overcast by such intensity of gloom were it not that

264 clouds are piled on clouds up and up, till the sun is blotted out. And surely in their downfall they would not drench it in such a deluge of rain that rivers overflow and fields are drowned unless a great bulk of them were stacked up in the ether.

Here then everything is full of wind and fire, producing crashes and flashes everywhere. For I have already shown[33] that hollow clouds contain a great many particles of heat and necessarily acquire more from the solar rays and their calorific

273 energy. Therefore, when the same wind that happens to accumulate them in some one particular spot has squeezed out many seeds of heat and in so doing has itself become intermingled with that fire, the imprisoned eddy spins in a cramped space and there in a glowing furnace sharpens a thunderbolt.[34] Two causes combine to set the whirlwind ablaze, the heat generated by its own motion and contact with the fire. Then, when the wind is well aglow and the deadly momentum of the fire has heightened, the now mature thunderbolt suddenly splits the

284 cloud and out shoots the spurt of flame, darting its vivid blaze across the whole scene. There follows that shattering roar that sounds as though the celestial vault had burst apart and were crashing down upon our heads. A tremor lays violent hold upon the earth, and tumult rumbles through the depth of heaven; for then the whole mass of storm-cloud is rocked and shaken and crackles far and wide. After the shock follows a pelting sluicing shower. It seems as though the whole ether were transmuted into rain, and the cascade heralded a return of the universal Deluge[35] – such a cataract is loosed by the

294 bursting cloud and unpent whirlwind in the wake of the crashing, darting, devastating fire.

At other times a violent squall of wind impinges externally upon a cloud already pregnant with a full-grown thunderbolt. The wind rips open the cloud, and out drops that fiery whirlwind which is what we in our traditional language term a thunderbolt. This may happen in various directions according to the direction of the liberating force.

Sometimes again a gust of wind that is fireless at the outset grows fiery in the course of a long flight before it arrives. It loses on the way certain large atoms, which cannot keep pace in

piercing the air. At the same time it rakes together out of the   304
air itself and carries along other atoms of tiny size which
commingle in flight so as to form fire. It is in much the same
way that a leaden sling-bolt[36] often grows hot in its flight
through dropping many petrifactive particles and picking up
fire in the air.

Lastly, it may happen that fire is kindled by the sheer force
of the impact when an object is hit by a wind that is itself cold
and fireless. This, of course, is because the shock of the blow   310
causes a conflux of heat atoms both from the wind itself and
from the object that receives the blow. When we strike stone
with steel, out leaps fire: the coldness of the steel does not
prevent atoms of blazing heat from rushing together at the
point of impact. In the same way an object may be set ablaze by
a thunderbolt, provided that it is suitably inflammable. In any
case a strong wind cannot be absolutely cold, certainly not one
launched with such violence from above. If it is not already
ignited *en route*, it must arrive at any rate warmed up by having   322
heat mixed up in it.

As for the high speed of thunderbolts, the weight of their
impact and the rapidity with which they complete their hurtling
descent, these are due in the first instance to the accumulation
of pent-up energy within the clouds and the momentum thus
acquired. Then, when the cloud can no longer contain the
mounting impetus, the energy is released and let fly with
tremendous drive, like missiles discharged from powerful cata-
pults. Add to this that the thunderbolt is composed of small,
smooth atoms. Such a substance is not easily obstructed by   332
anything. It slips and slides through the chinks in things and
hence does not lose much way on account of the stoppages
caused by collisions. That accounts for the impetuous onrush
of its swooping flight.

Again, while all weights are always possessed of a natural
downward urge, the addition of a push doubles their speed and
enhances their momentum. So the thunderbolt, with its impetus
and velocity thus redoubled, dashes aside whatever may block
its advance and hurtles on its way.

Yet again, because it gathers momentum over a long course,[37]

341 it must acquire ever greater and greater velocity, which grows as it goes, reinforcing and intensifying the energy of the impact. It sweeps up all its eddying atoms into one main current and directs them along a straight course to a single target. Possibly in its flight it may extract from the air itself certain particles whose impact inflames its own speed.

350 It passes through many substances without damaging or disturbing them, because its fluid fire slips through the gaps. It forces its way through many, the atoms of the thunderbolt glancing against the opposing atoms at their points of interconnection. It readily dissolves bronze and boils gold in an instant, because its component atoms, being tiny and smooth, easily worm their way in and, once in, are quick to untie every knot and loosen all cohesion.

360 It is in autumn that the starlit dome of heaven throughout its breadth and the whole earth are most often rocked by thunderbolts, and again when the flowery season of spring shows itself.[38] In cold weather there is a scarcity of fire, and in hot weather of winds, and then, too, the clouds are not so thick. So it is in weather between these extremes that the various causes of the thunderbolt all conspire. Then the year's turning tide mingles cold and heat, which are both needed to forge a thunderbolt within a cloud. Then there may be a clash of opposites, and the air tormented by fire and wind may surge in tumultuous upheaval. The vanguard of hot weather is the rear of cold. That is springtime, when there must accordingly be tussle and turmoil of opposing forces. Similarly when the

371 retiring heat is embroiled with the advancing cold in the season we know as autumn, here again there is a conflict between summer and grim winter. These then are the year's crises. No wonder if these are the seasons of abundant thunderbolts; these are the times when seething tempests rock the sky, engaged as it is on either hand in the turmoil of a stalemate battle, on this side flames, on the other winds and water interfused.

Here then is a plain and intelligible account of the fiery thunderbolt and how it does what it does. It is a fruitless task to unroll the Etruscan[39] scrolls, seeking some revelation of the gods' hidden purpose. That is no way to study from which

quarter the darting fire has come or into which other it has   383
passed; how it has entered a closed building, and how after
working its will it has slipped out again. That is no way to find
out the damage that a thunderbolt from heaven can do. If it is
really Jupiter[40] and the other gods who rock the flashing frame
of heaven with this appalling din and hurl their fire wherever
they have a mind, why do they not see to it that those who
have perpetrated some abominable outrage are struck by light-   391
ning and exhale its flames from a breast transfixed, for a dire
warning to mortals?[41] Why, instead, is some man with a con-
science clear of any sin shrouded unmeriting in a sheet of flame,
trapped and tangled without warning in the fiery storm from
heaven? Why[42] do the throwers waste their strength on deserts?
Are they getting their hand in and strengthening their arms?
And why do they allow the Father's weapon to be blunted on
the ground? Why does Jupiter himself put up with this, instead
of saving it for his enemies? Why, again, does he never hurl his
bolt upon the earth and let loose his thunder out of a sky that is   401
wholly blue? Does he wait till clouds have gathered so that he
can slip down into them and aim his blows at close range? Why
does he launch them into the sea? What is his grudge against
the waves and the liquid masses of the ocean plains? If he wants
us to beware of the flying bolt, why is he loath to let us see it on
its path? If on the other hand he intends the fire to strike us
unawares, why does he thunder from the same quarter and so
put us on our guard? Why does he herald its coming with
darkness and roarings and rumblings? And how can you believe
that he hurls it in several directions at once? Or dare you assert   412
that it never happens that several strokes are let fly at the same
time? In fact it does and must happen very often; just as
downpours of rain occur simultaneously in many districts, so it
must happen that many thunderbolts fall simultaneously. Lastly,
why does he demolish the holy shrines of the gods and his own
splendid abodes[43] with an aggressive bolt? Why does he smash
masterly images of the gods and rob his own portraits of
reverence with a sacrilegious stroke? Why has he a special
fondness for high places, so that we see most traces of his fire
on mountain tops?

423 From what has been said, it is easy to understand what force flings down into the sea those waterspouts[44] which the Greeks aptly term *presteres* or 'scorchers'. It sometimes happens that a sort of pillar descends into the sea as though let down from the sky. Around it the waters boil, lashed by madly blowing blasts, and woe to any ship that is embroiled in this storm.

432 This is sometimes brought about when an imprisoned wind fails to burst the cloud it is trying to burst but forces it downwards. So it sags down like a pillar lowered into the sea out of the sky – gradually, like something pushed from above by a fist at the end of an outthrust arm and so protruding down into the waves. When the wind has burst this bulge, out it rushes into the sea and creates a bewildering boiling among the waves. In fact, the cloud, with its elastic structure, is forced down by a spiralling whirlwind, which descends with it. As soon as its teeming bulk has been pushed down to sea level, the wind is suddenly let loose into the water and stirs up all the sea, making it bubble and boil with a terrific roar.

443 It sometimes happens also that a whirling column of wind wraps itself in clouds through scraping together atoms of cloud out of the air, and mimics a *prester* let down out of the sky.

When a waterspout drops on dry land and there explodes, it disgorges a violent vortex of whirlwind and storm. But, since this happens in any case but seldom, and on land our view of it must often be blocked by mountains, the sight is more frequently encountered in the sea's wide prospect under an open expanse of sky.

451 The *formation of clouds*[45] is due to the sudden coalescence, in the upper reaches of the sky, of many flying atoms of relatively rough material, such that even a slight entanglement clasps them firmly together. The first result is the formation of separate little clouds. Then these clutch hold of one another and band together. So they grow by mutual fusion and scud before the winds, till the time comes when a raging storm arises.

Notice also what happens on towering mountain peaks. The closer they approach to the sky, the more persistently they smoke with a thick black fog of sandy cloud. This is because, when clouds are beginning to form but are still too slight to be visible to the eye, they are driven by buoyant winds against the crowning pinnacle of a mountain. Here the stage is reached in the process of accumulation at which they are sufficiently condensed to become visible, so that they are seen ascending from the summit into the clear sky. As for the prevalence of wind in these upper regions, that is proved by the evidence of our own senses when we climb high mountains.

We must reckon also with the fact that nature causes a constant stream of particles to rise up from the whole ocean, as shown when clothes hung up on the shore receive a clinging film of moisture. This suggests that the clouds may also be swollen, in no small measure, by an exhalation from the ocean's briny surge;[46] for its moisture is of a kindred quality.

Again, we see vaporous mists ascending from every river and from the land itself. These exudations, wafted up from the earth like breath, douse the sky with their blackness and build up high clouds by gradual coalescence. For[47] they encounter opposing emanations descending from above out of the heat of the starry zone of ether, which help them to condense and weave a cloudy curtain under the blue.

Lastly, it happens that atoms composing clouds and flying storm-clouds also come into this sky of ours from outside the world. I have shown[48] that the number of the atoms is numberless and the extent of space infinite, and I have explained with what velocity the atoms fly and how instantaneously they cover an incalculable distance. No wonder, then, if storm and darkness, louring from on high, are often so swift to envelop seas and lands with clouds, when through all the pores of ether on every side – as if through all the breathing channels in the great world all around – the atoms are provided with an outlet and an inlet.

Let me now demonstrate how *rain-drops*[49] condense high up in the clouds and fall to earth in a dripping shower. First, you will not dispute that many atoms of water rise up from every source together with the clouds themselves, and that the clouds and

461

469

480

490

500 whatever water is in them grow concurrently, just as our bodies grow concurrently with the blood and sweat and any other fluid that exists in our limbs. The clouds also, like dangling fleeces,[50] absorb a lot of seawater when they are swept by the winds over the wide sea. In the same way moisture is sucked up into the clouds out of every river.

509 When they are fully charged with many atoms of water amassed in many ways from all sorts of sources, the swollen clouds attempt to discharge their moisture in two ways: the force of the wind itself pushes it out, and the cloud-mass itself, under pressure of increased accumulation, crushes and squeezes from above and makes it flow out in showers. Again, when clouds are being dissipated by winds or dissolved by the descending impact of the sun's heat, they discharge a drizzle of moisture, just as wax drips freely when melting over a hot fire.

A violent downpour is occasioned when clouds are violently compressed by both forces, accumulation and the assault of wind. Long continuance and the persistency of rain occur when
519 a great many atoms of water are in motion, moisture-laden clouds are heaped one on another and come drifting up from every side, and the whole earth exhales a vaporous steam. In this setting, when the sun's rays blazing through the murky storm strike against the droplets of the storm-cloud, then there sparkles out among the black clouds the splendour of the rainbow.[51]

As for the other forms of matter that originate and grow up aloft and condense in the clouds – snow, wind, hail, icy frost
530 and the strong grip of ice that hardens waters and bridles impetuous torrents throughout their course – it is easy enough to discover and picture mentally how one and all come into being or are created, when once you have rightly grasped the properties of the elements.

Learn now *the true nature of earthquakes*.[52] First you must visualize that the earth, below as well as above ground, is everywhere full of windy caves, and bears in its bosom a multitude of lakes and pools and beetling, precipitous crags. You must also picture that under the earth's back many buried rivers with torrential

force roll their waters mingled with sunken rocks. For the plain
facts demand that earth should be of the same nature through-
out. With these things lodged and embedded in its bowels, the
earth above trembles with the shock of massive demolition
when huge caverns down below have collapsed through age.
Whole mountains topple down, and sudden tremors started by
that violent shock ripple out far and wide. Naturally enough,
when we reflect that whole buildings by the roadside are
shaken and jarred by the inconsiderable weight of a wagon; the
wagons also jump in the same way whenever a crack in the
road jolts the iron-shod rims of the wheels on either side. It
happens also, when a huge lump is dislodged from the earth by
process of time and rolled into vast and roomy gulfs of water,
that the wash of the water makes the earth reel and quiver, just
as a pot is sometimes unable to stand firm till the water in it has
stopped surging to and fro.

Again, when a concentrated wind blowing through subterra-
nean caverns has come to a head and hurls itself with all its
might against the lofty vaults, its impulsive pressure tilts back
the earth away from its impact. The houses built up above on
the surface – and the more so in proportion as they tower up
towards the sky – lean over and bulge out perilously in the
same direction, and projecting beams overhang and threaten to
crash. And yet men are loath to credit that a day of doom and
ultimate catastrophe awaits this mighty world,[53] though they
see such a colossal mass of earth tilting over. But if the winds
did not stop to recover their breath, then no power would
check the downfall of things. As it is, winds bluster and abate
alternately, now rallying to the assault, now recoiling from a
repulse. So it happens that the earth more often threatens a
collapse than executes it. It tilts over and then swings back and
after toppling top-heavily recovers its balance. This is how all
buildings totter, the top more than the middle, this in turn
more than the base and the base hardly at all.

Another cause of the same tremendous quaking is this. When
a sudden turbulent squall of wind, whether of external origin
or generated within the earth, has rushed into the subterra-
nean hollows, it first rages there tumultuously among the vast

542

549

559

570

582 caverns, swirling and eddying. Then, with intensified energy, it forces its way out and, splitting open the earth from its depths, creates a stupendous chasm. This is what happened in Syrian Sidon[54] and at Aegium[55] in the Peloponnese, when these cities were demolished by such an outrush of wind and the resulting earthquake. Many another set of battlements have been laid low by mighty earthquakes on dry land, and many cities with their citizens have been engulfed in the sea. If the wind does not 591 break out, the fury of its accumulated momentum is dissipated through a multitude of underground passages as a passing shudder that sets the earth trembling. It behaves in fact just like the cold air that penetrates our limbs and makes us shiver and shake in spite of ourselves.

So through the menaced cities men tremble with a two-edged terror. While they dread the roofs above, they are afraid that the earth may suddenly fling open her caverns below, gaping wide to reveal a yawning mouth which she will gorge in 601 her confused state with her own wreckage. Let them go on imagining that sky and earth are both indestructible and guaranteed life everlasting. From time to time the visible presence of peril stabs them in one quarter or another with a secret goad of fear that the earth may suddenly be whisked away from under their feet into the abyss and, robbed of its foundation, the whole world in a wild chaotic welter may follow it to perdition.

A point that sometimes occasions surprise is *why nature does not cause the sea to grow bigger*,[56] considering what a huge influx of 610 water it receives from all the rivers that flow into it from every side. Add to these the stray showers and flying rainstorms by which every sea and every land is sprinkled and soaked. Add the sea's own springs. And yet, compared to the total bulk of the ocean, all these together scarcely amount to a single drop. This makes it less remarkable that the vast ocean does not grow still vaster. Besides, a large proportion of this increase is subtracted by the heat of the sun. We see how dripping wet clothes are dried by the sun's parching rays. We see, too, that the oceans exposed to them are multitudinous and of huge extent. However small the quantity that the sun may absorb

from the sea at any particular point, yet over such an expanse   620
the total loss will be considerable.[57] Then, again, the winds that
scour the ocean may carry off a good deal of moisture, since we
often see roadways dried up by the winds in a single night and
soft mud hardened to a crust. Again, I have shown that the
clouds too pick up a lot of moisture drawn from the wide
ocean levels and sprinkle it over all the earth when it is raining
above the land and the clouds are blown along by the winds.
Lastly, the earth is of a porous texture and is contiguous with   631
the sea, encircling its shores on every side. Therefore, just as
water enters the sea from the land, so it must trickle into the
land out of the briny gulf. The brine is filtered out, and the
main bulk of the water flows back to reassemble in full at the
fountain-head. Hence it flows overground, a steady column of
sweet fluid marching down the highway already hewn with
liquid foot for the guidance of its waves.

I will now explain how it happens that flames sometimes shoot   640
out in such a tornado through the throat of *Mount Etna*.[58] For
it was no light matter when the fiery storm exerted its despotic
power over the fields of Sicily. The eyes of neighbouring
nations were drawn towards it, when they saw the smoke and
the sparks spread over every quarter of the sky. Their hearts
were filled with dreadful apprehension that nature might be
planning some revolutionary change.

This is a problem that calls for wide and deep contemplation
and far-ranging survey. You must remember that the universe
is fathomless and reflect how minute a part of the whole is one   650
world – an infinitesimal fraction, less in proportion than one
man compared to the whole earth. If you look squarely at this
fact and keep it clearly before your eyes, many things will cease
to strike you as miraculous. Does anyone think it a miracle if
somebody catches a fever that enflames his body, or is racked
throughout his frame by a painful disease? A foot suddenly
begins to swell. Sometimes a stab of pain grips the teeth or
pierces right into the eyes. A fiery rash[59] erupts and worms its
way through the body, burning every part it occupies as it
crawls from limb to limb. All this because there is a multiplicity

662 of atoms, and this earth and sky of ours have plagues in plenty to generate a superabundance of disease. In just the same way we must picture this earth and sky as amply supplied out of the infinite with matter to jolt the earth with a sudden shock, to set a wild tornado racing over sea and land, to make the fires of Etna erupt and the sky burst into flame. For this too happens: the heavenly regions actually blaze; and rainstorms of abnormal 672 intensity are similarly due to such casual concentrations of water atoms. 'But[60] the tumultuous burst of conflagration is too huge for such an origin.' Why, any river seems huge to one who has never seen a bigger. So does a tree or a man. The largest thing a man has seen of any sort strikes him as huge, whereas all of them together, with sky and earth and sea thrown in, are nothing to the sum total of the universe.

I will now turn to the specific question, by what means that suddenly quickened flame spouts from the stupendous furnaces of Etna. First, then, the whole interior of the mountain is 684 hollow, honeycombed with basaltic caverns. Next, in all the caves there is air and wind, the wind being produced by disturbance of the air. When this has been thoroughly heated and in its raging has heated the surrounding rocks and earth where it comes in contact and extracted their content of fire ablaze with leaping flames, it wells up and flings itself skyward by the direct route of the gaping throat. So it scatters fire and ashes far and wide, rolling dense clouds of murky smoke and discharging boulders of staggering weight. There can be no doubting that this is the work of wind at its most tempestuous.

694 Furthermore, the sea dashes its waves against a great part of the roots of this mountain and sucks back the undertow. From this sea subterranean caverns penetrate all the way to the depths of its throat. It cannot be doubted that by this channel ⟨a blend of wind and water⟩ from the open sea is forced into the heart of the mountain. From here it spouts out, shooting up flame, volleying stones and disgorging clouds of sand. For at the very summit there are *craters* or 'mixing bowls', as the Sicilians call them, which we term 'throats' or 'mouths'.

There are some *phenomena to which it is not enough to assign one*

cause: we must enumerate several, though in fact there is only 704
one.[61] Suppose you were to see the lifeless body of a man lying
some distance away. You would have to mention all the possible
causes of his death to be sure of mentioning the right one. You
could not prove that he had perished by the sword or by cold,
by sickness or by poison. But we know that whatever has
happened to him must fall into one category of this sort. And
there are many other questions that we are obliged to answer in 711
the same way.

The Nile, for instance, the only river in all the lands of Egypt,
rises and floods the fields on the threshold of summer. The
reason why it often irrigates at the height of the heat may be
because in summer there are north winds blowing against its
mouths – the winds that are said to be *Etesian*[62] or 'seasonal' at
that time. These winds, blowing against the stream, arrest its
flow. By forcing the wind upstream they raise the water-level
and hold up the current's advance. There is no doubt that these 720
breezes do run counter to the river. They blow from the cold
stars of the Pole. The Nile, on the other hand, comes out of the
torrid south, rising in the heart of the noonday region among
races of men whose skin is burnt black.[63]

It is also possible that a great sand bar is heaped against the
river mouths in opposition to the current when the windswept
sea drives the sand shoreward. In this way the river has less
freedom of egress, and the downflow of its current loses momen-
tum.

Or again, it is possible that at this season heavier rains[64] fall 729
near its source, because then the Etesian blasts from the north
concentrate all the clouds in those parts. It may be assumed
that, when these southward-driven clouds have massed in the
noonday region, they are eventually accumulated there and
squeezed against high mountains.

Lastly, it may be that a spate of water forms in the heart of
the Ethiopian highlands when gleaming snows[65] are forced
to flow down into the plains by the liquefying beams of the
all-irradiating sun.

738   Let me now explain the nature of those *lakes and such like that
are called Avernian*. First they owe the name Avernus to the fact
that they are inimical to all birds:[66] when the line of their flight
has brought them over such places, they rest on their oars, furl
their plumy sails and tumble headlong with nerveless necks
outstretched. So they fall to earth, if the lie of the land so
determines, or into the water, if it be a lake of Avernus that lies
outspread below them. There is such a spot near Cumae, where
747   hills give off an acrid fume of sulphur, fed by hot springs.
There is another within the walls of Athens, on the very crest
of the Acropolis, by the temple of the beneficent virgin Pallas
Athene, to which cawing crows never wing their bodies, no
matter how the altars smoke with burnt offerings. Not that
they are really in such dread of Pallas' dire displeasure, which
they had brought on them by their wakeful observation, as
Greek bards have sung;[67] but the nature of the place produces
this effect spontaneously. In Syria,[68] too, there is said to be a
756   spot that evidently possesses a similar property, affecting even
quadrupeds: as soon as they set foot within it, the potency of
the place causes them to fall down flat, as though they were
suddenly sacrificed to the gods of the Underworld.

All these phenomena occur in the course of nature, and the
causes from which they spring are plain to see. There is firstly
no need to imagine that these places are gateways to the
Underworld, or indulge in the further fancy that by this route
spirits are drawn into the infernal regions by the infernal gods,
as light-footed stags are commonly supposed to draw serpents
from their lairs by the breath of their nostrils.[69] How far this is
767   from reality you may now learn, for I am setting out to give
you the true explanation.

I will begin by repeating what I have often said before, that
in the earth there are atoms of every kind. Many of them, those
that serve as food, have vitalizing powers; many are such as to
instil disease and hasten death.[70] I have already shown that
substances vary in their power to promote life in various living
species, owing to differences in their nature and structure and
their atomic shapes. Many hurtful particles enter through the
ears; many noxious particles which are rough to the touch slip

in through the nostrils, and not a few are to be avoided by the 779
sense of touch or shunned by sight, or are disagreeable to taste.

Next, it is plain to see how many things in their action on
human senses are intensely nauseating and harmful. Certain
trees[71] are possessed of a shade so oppressive that they often
provoke a headache in one who lies outstretched on the grass
beneath them. Among the high hills of Helicon there is even a
tree[72] with the property of killing a man by the baleful scent of 787
its blossom. Obviously, the reason why all these grow out of
the soil is because the earth contains many seeds of many things
mixed together in many ways which are sifted out and then
passed on.

Again, when a night lamp,[73] newly extinguished, assails the
nostrils with its pungent reek, an epileptic prone to fits of
foaming and falling is overcome with drowsiness. The heavy
scent of beaver musk makes a woman droop in slumber and the
bright embroidery slip from her dainty hands, if she smells it at
the time of menstruation. And there are many other things that 797
enervate and slacken the limbs throughout the body and unsettle
the vital spirit in its inmost recesses.

Again, if you loiter too long in a hot bath after a heavy meal,
how easily it often happens that you collapse in the middle of
the bathtub of steaming water. How easily the drowsy fume
and scent of charcoal[74] passes into the brain, unless we have
taken water beforehand. When parching fever has gripped the
limbs, then the scent of wine is like a knock-out blow.

In the earth itself you often see sulphur generated and
bitumen congealing with its vile stink. When men are following 808
veins of gold and silver, groping with their picks in the bowels
of the earth, what fumes are emitted from the pits of Scapte
Hyle![75] What malignant breath is exhaled by gold mines! How
it acts upon men's features and complexions! Have you not
seen or heard how speedily men die and how their vital forces
fail when they are driven by dire necessity[76] to endure such
work? All these vapours, then, are given off by the earth and
blown out into the open, into the unconfined spaces of the air.

So also these Avernian places must send up an effluence
deadly to birds on the wing. As this rises from the earth into

820 the winds, it poisons a certain tract of air. No sooner has a bird
winged its way into this tract than it is caught and halted by the
invisible venom. Down it tumbles in a sheer fall on the very
course in which the vapour rises. Once it has fallen here, the
action of the same vapour expels the remnants of life from all
its limbs. The first reaction, of course, is a sort of vertigo.[77]
Then, when they have fallen into the very fountain-head of the
829 poison, they can do nothing there but cough up life itself,
enveloped as they are in a cloud of the deadly stuff.

It also happens sometimes that this force and vapour from
Avernus dispels all the air that lies between the birds and the
earth, so that this space is left almost void. When their flight
has brought them straight into such a place, the upthrust of
their pinions is forthwith lamed and baffled, and all the efforts
of either wing are nullified. Since they can no longer support
themselves by resting on their wings, nature of course compels
them to drop to earth by their own weight. Lying in the midst
839 of almost total vacuity, they dissipate their vital spirits through
all the pores of the body.

Let us now consider *why it is that well water is warmer in winter
and cooler in summer*. This happens because in summer the earth
opens up its pores with the warmth and any particles it may
contain of its own heat are dispersed into the air. The more the
earth is drained of heat, the colder grows the water embedded
in it. Conversely, when all the earth is compressed by cold and
contracts and virtually congeals, it naturally happens that in
847 contracting it squeezes out any heat it may contain into the
wells.

It is said that next to the temple of Egyptian Ammon[78] there
is a spring that is cold through the daylight hours but warm at
night. By this spring men are unduly impressed. Some suppose
that it heats up from the sun's ardour below the earth, when
night has shrouded the lands in dreadful darkness. This theory
is very wide of the mark. When water cannot be warmed from
above by the sun's touch on its naked body, for all the blazing
incandescence of the light raised above us, how can the same
sun bake through the solid substance of earth from beneath so

as to drench the same water with its boiling heat? Why, the sun   858
with its fiery rays can scarcely gain admission for its heat into a
shuttered house. What then is the explanation? Evidently the
earth surrounding the spring is of looser texture than other
earth, and there are many particles of fire near the body of
water. When the dewy waves of night flow over the earth, the
soil is immediately chilled through and condensed. So it happens
that, as if it were squeezed in the hand, it forces out into the   867
spring all the particles of fire it contains; and it is these that
make the water warm to touch and steamy. Then, when the
risen sun has loosened and relaxed the earth with the interpen-
etrating heat of its rays, the atoms of fire return to their former
positions and all the warmth of the water passes into the earth.
That is why the spring is cool by daylight. Besides, the spring-
water exposed to the impact of sunbeams is rarefied at daybreak
by the pulsating radiance. This causes it to lose all the particles
of heat it possesses, just as water often loses its content of ice,
melting and dissolving its bondage.   879

There is also a certain cold spring[79] such that a piece of tow
placed above it is normally quick to catch fire and burst into
flame. Similarly, a torch floating in its waters is set alight and
blazes wherever the breezes drift it. The reason obviously is
this. There are in the water a great many atoms of heat; and
particles of fire must rise out of the depths of the earth all
the way through the spring and so escape by exhalation into
the air. There are not, however, so many of them as to heat the
spring. Besides they are forcibly impelled to burst out suddenly
through the water disconnected and unite on the surface. We   890
may compare that spring of fresh water at Aradus,[80] which
wells up in the sea and dispels the salty waves that surround it,
and those many other places where the sea provides a welcome
refreshment to thirsty mariners by spouting out fresh water
amongst the salt. So in this spring the fiery atoms may well up
and spout out. When they cluster together on the tow or cling
to the body of the torch, they readily catch fire there and then,
because tow and the swimming torches also contain many seeds
of fire. You must have noticed, again, how a newly extinguished
wick, when you bring it near to a night-burning lamp, catches

902 light before it has touched the flame. A torch behaves in the same way. And many things besides are kindled at a distance by mere contact with heat before they are actually dipped in the fire. This, then, is what we must picture as happening also in this spring.

At this point, I will set out to explain what law of nature causes iron to be attracted by that stone which the Greeks call from its place of origin *magnet*,[81] because it occurs in the territory of the Magnesians.[82] Men look upon this stone as miraculous. They are amazed to see it form a chain of little rings hanging from it. Sometimes you may see as many as five or more in pendent succession swaying in the light puffs of air; one hangs from another, clinging to it underneath, and one derives from another the cohesive force of the stone. Such is the permeative power of this force.

919 In matters of this sort it is necessary to establish a number of facts before you can offer an explanation of them. This may mean approaching the problem by a very roundabout route. For this reason I beg you to lend me your ears and your mind with particular attentiveness.

In the first place, it must be a fact that all visible objects emit a perpetual stream and shower of particles that strike upon the eyes and provoke sight.[83] From certain objects there also flows a perpetual stream of odour, as coolness flows from rivers, heat from the sun, and from the ocean waves a spray that eats away walls round the seashore. Sounds of every sort are surging incessantly through the air. When we walk by the seaside, a salty tang of brine commonly enters our mouth; when we watch a draught of wormwood being mixed in our presence, a bitter effluence touches us. So from every object flows a multiform stream of matter, rippling out in all directions. The stream must flow without rest or intermission, since our senses are perpetually alert and everything is always liable to be seen or smelt or to provoke sensation by sound.

Let me now re-emphasize, what is made crystal clear in my first book, the extreme looseness of the structure of all objects.[84] A knowledge of this fact is relevant to many problems. In

tackling the problem with which I am now confronted, it is   939
especially necessary to establish that there is no perceptible
object that does not consist of a mixture of matter and vacuity.
In the first place, we find that in caves the rocky roofs sweat
moisture and drip with trickling drops. Similarly in our own
bodies sweat oozes from every surface; hairs grow on the chin
and on every limb and member; food is diffused through every
vein, building and sustaining the most outlying parts right   947
down to the tiny nails. So also, when we hold full drinking
vessels, we feel that cold and heat pass through bronze and
through gold and silver. The stone partitions of houses are
pervious to voices[85] and to scent and cold and the heat of fire,
which penetrates also through hard iron. Even the cuirass of the
sky that encloses us is not proof against the invasion of tempest
and pestilence from without. Storms that are born of earth are
duly allayed by absorption into the sky; and those of celestial
origin into the earth. In short, there is nothing in existence that
does not have a porous texture.
                                                                  959
   Add to this that not all the particles thrown off by objects
are identical in their effect[86] on the senses or on particular
substances. The sun bakes and dries out the earth; but it melts
ice, and its rays cause deep drifts of snow on the high hills to
thaw.[87] Wax, too, is liquefied by exposure to its heat. Similarly,
fire liquefies bronze and melts gold; but it shrivels skins and
flesh and makes them shrink. Water hardens iron coming fresh
from the fire; but it softens skins and flesh that heat has
hardened. To bearded goats wild olive is as delicious as if it
were redolent of ambrosia and steeped in authentic nectar; yet
to man there is no plant growing whose foliage is more   972
unpalatable.[88] Pigs fight shy of marjoram and shrink from
perfume in general; what seems to us on occasion a welcome
restorative is dire poison to their bristly bodies. On the other
hand filth that nauseates and revolts us is evidently delectable
to pigs, so that they are never weary of wallowing[89] in it from
head to tail.
   There is one more point that clearly ought to be made be-
fore I embark on the matter in hand. The innumerable pores
that exist in different objects must be possessed of mutually

983 dissimilar[90] natures, each having its own peculiarities and its own system of passageways. In living creatures, for instance, there are various senses, each of which affords an entry for its own specific object.[91] We see that sound penetrates into one organ of sense, the savour of juices into another, the smells of an odour into a third. It is evident too that one thing seeps through stone, another through wood, another through gold, while yet another leaks through silver or glass. One medium is
993 pervious to sight, another to heat. The same medium is traversed by different elements at different speeds.[92] This, of course, results inevitably from the great diversity, to which we have just alluded, in the nature of their internal passageways, due to differences in the nature and texture of substances.

So much by way of preface, to posit and establish the necessary premises for our argument. On this basis it will be easy to elucidate the problem and lay bare the whole cause of the attraction of iron. First, this stone must emit a dense stream or emanation of atoms, which dispels by a process of bombard-
1003 ment all the air that lies between the stone and the iron. When this space is emptied and a large tract in the middle is left void, then atoms of the iron all tangled together immediately slide and tumble into the vacuum. The consequence is that the ring itself follows and so moves in with its whole mass. No other substance is so rigidly held together by the intertanglement of its elemental atoms as cold iron, that stubborn and benumbing metal. No cause for wonder, then – indeed this could be inferred from the atomic structure – if a cluster of particles
1014 from the iron cannot drop into the void without the whole ring following. This it does, and continues to follow till it actually reaches the stone and clings to it by invisible ties. This happens in any direction in which there is a vacuum, whether the immediately adjoining particles move into it sideways or upwards. Of course they cannot rise up into the air of their own accord; but they are impelled by blows from other quarters.

The process is facilitated and the movement helped on by a contributory cause: as soon as the air in front of the ring is rarefied and the space fairly well emptied and evacuated, it thereupon happens that all the air situated at the back of the

ring pushes and shoves it forward from behind. For objects are 1027
always being pelted by the surrounding air; but in this case it
happens that the iron is pushed by the pelting because in one
direction there is a vacuum ready to receive it. This air of
which I am speaking creeps nimbly in through the many
porosities in the iron and comes up against its tiny particles so
as to push and drive it along as sails and ship are driven by the
wind. 1034

Again, all objects must contain air within their bodies, since
all are of loose texture and all are encompassed and bounded by
air. Accordingly the air that lies hidden in the core of the iron
is perpetually surging to and fro in a restless motion. By this
means, no doubt, it keeps on battering the ring and unsettling
it from within. And by the same means the ring is, of course,
kept moving in the same direction in which it has once launched
itself by its plunge into the vacuum.

It also happens at times that iron moves away from this
stone; its tendency is to flee and to pursue by turns. I have even 1044
seen Samothracian[93] rings of gilded iron dance and iron filings
rage madly inside bronze cups when this magnet stone was put
under them. So eager, it seemed, was the iron to run from the
stone. The reason why the interposition of bronze causes such a
turmoil is doubtless this. After the effluence of the bronze has
first taken possession of the open passageways in the iron and
occupied them, along comes the effluence of the magnet and
finds everything full in the iron and so has no way of passing
through as before. It is therefore compelled to pelt and batter
the texture of the iron with its stream. In this way it spews 1055
away from itself the iron and through the bronze it drives away
what otherwise it normally attracts.

There is no need to be surprised that the effluence from this
stone has no power to impart a similar motion[94] to other
substances besides iron. Some are held fast by their weight, for
instance, gold. Others cannot be moved anywhere, because their
loose texture allows the effluence to pass through intact; a clear
example of this class is wood. Iron, which by its nature lies midway
between the two, needs only the addition of some particles of
bronze and then it yields to the current from the Magnesian stones.

1065

These phenomena are not so different from others that I cannot find plenty of parallels to adduce, in which a unique relation exists between two substances. First, you see that stones are held together only by mortar. Wood, on the other hand, can be joined only by means of bulls' glue; and then it more often happens that cracks in boards gape open through a flaw in the wood than that the bovine bonds relax their grip.

1073

The juices of the vine will mix with spring water when ponderous pitch and buoyant olive oil refuse. The crimson dye of the murex[95] combines only with wool, and that so firmly that it can never be parted: not though you should labour with Neptune's flood to restore it; not though all the ocean with all its waves wished to cleanse it. Again, is there not one thing[96] only that will alloy gold to gold? Is not bronze soldered to bronze by nothing but tin? How many other examples might be found! But to what purpose? There is no need for you to follow such a roundabout route to your goal, nor for me to expend such

1083

labour on the point. Better to sum up a long argument in a few brief words. When the textures of two substances are mutually contrary, so that hollows in the one correspond to full sections in the other and vice versa, then connection between them is most perfect. It is even possible for some things to be coupled together, as though interlinked by rings[97] and hooks. And such, it would rather seem, is the linkage between iron and magnet.

I will now explain *the nature of diseases*[98] and the source from which the sickly power of pestilence is able to breathe a sudden

1091

death-dealing plague upon the tribes of men and herds of beasts.[99] In the first place, I have shown[100] above that there are certain atoms of many substances that are vital to us, and that on the other hand there must be countless others flying about that are a cause of disease and death. When these, by some chance, have accumulated and upset the balance of the atmosphere, the air becomes infected. This crop of pestilence and plague either comes in through the sky from outside, like clouds and mists, or very often springs from the earth itself when it has been rotted by drenching[101] with unseasonable rains and pelting with sunbeams.

You should note also how unaccustomed climates and   1103
waters[102] affect those who venture far from home and country
because of the wide range of variation in things. For what are
we to say is the difference between the climate that prevails
among the Britons and that of Egypt, where the celestial axis is
tilted askew, or between Pontus[103] and Cadiz and right on to
the land where the skins of men are burnt black?[104] As we see
these four regions mutually distinguished by the four winds   1111
and quarters of the sky, so their inhabitants are markedly
distinct in complexion and features and in their susceptibility to
particular diseases. There is elephantiasis,[105] for instance, which
is bred in the heart of Egypt on the banks of the Nile and
nowhere else. In Attica the feet are attacked; in Achaia it is the
eyes that suffer.[106] To other members and organs other regions
are adverse. This is brought about by variations in the air.

Let us suppose, then, that some atmosphere that chances to
be uncongenial to us is set in motion. The baleful air begins to
creep. Like mist and cloud it glides and, wherever it comes, it   1122
sows disorder and change. When at length it makes its way into
our region, it contaminates the atmosphere there, making it
conformable to itself and unfriendly to us. So, without warning,
this new plague and pestilence either falls upon the water or
settles right on the growing wheat or on other human food or
pasturage of animals; or else it remains suspended in the air
itself so that, when we inhale the polluted atmosphere, we
cannot help sucking in the sickness right into our bodies. It is
in much the same way that a plague often falls on cattle or a
distemper on bleating sheep already enfeebled. It makes no   1133
odds whether it is we who move into unpropitious regions and
change the atmospheric garment that enwraps us or whether
nature brings to us a tainted atmosphere, or something else to
which we are unaccustomed, to menace us with the advent of
the unfamiliar.

Of this nature[107] was the fatal tide of pestilence that once
laid waste the Athenian[108] fields, turning the highways into
deserts and draining the city of citizens. From its well-spring in
the heart of Egypt it traversed a wide expanse of air and the
swimming plains of the sea and swooped at length upon all

1144 the people of Pandion.[109] Then they began to surrender, battalions at a time, to sickness and death. First they would find their heads enflamed with feverish heat and their eyes bright with a bloodshot flush. Then the throat would turn black and sweat internally with blood; the pathway of the voice became blocked and constricted by ulcers; the tongue, the mind's interpreter, enfeebled by pain, grew troublesome to move and rough to 1151 touch and began to ooze blood. Then, when the sickness passing down the throat had filled the victim's chest and flowed into his sad heart – then indeed all the bolts of life began to shake. The breath coming through his mouth began to roll out a foul odour like the stench that rises from corpses thrown out to rot. The vigour of the mind as a whole and all the body began to wilt, now on the very threshold of death. The intolerable sufferings were unremittingly attended by the torture of anxiety and wailing mixed with groaning. The sufferers were shaken night and day by incessant retching that 1162 convulsed every limb and sinew and broke them down, exhausting the already exhausted.

You would not observe any excessive heat in the surface regions of the body; rather, it felt tepid to the touch of the hands. At the same time the whole body reddened, as though branded with ulcers. It looked as though every limb were inflamed with a spreading fire of erysipelas.[110] But the inner parts of the victims were ablaze to the very bones. A flame was blazing in their stomach as though in a furnace. It was no good applying anything, however light and flimsy, to their limbs, except 1172 continual cooling and ventilation. Some of the sufferers would immerse their fevered limbs in chilly streams, flinging their bodies naked into the waves. Many hurled themselves headlong down from a height into the water of a well, their mouths gaping wide before they got there. The quenchless parching thirst in which their bodies were immersed made a thorough drenching no more satisfying than a few drops of water.

There was never any easing of the suffering. The body lay exhausted. Medicine muttered, too scared to speak out. But still those staring eyes, ablaze with fever, rolled and tossed and never closed in sleep.

Then many signs of death began to appear: the mind delirious   1182
with agony and terror; the brow contracted; the features wrung
with madness and energy; the ears tortured by incessant noises;
the breath coming in short gasps, or heavy and laboured: a
glistening stream of sweat trickling down the neck; a thin
phlegm in little drops, tinged with yellow and tasting of salt,
painfully ejected from the throat by a hoarse cough. The sinews
of the hands began to twitch, the limbs to tremble, and from   1191
the feet a persistent chill spread very gradually upwards. Then
the last hour drew on, heralded by pinched nostrils, the tip of the
nose narrowed to a point, hollow eyes, sunken temples, skin
cold and hard to the physician's touch, forehead bulging and
distended. After this it was not long before the limbs stiffened
in death. About the eighth kindling, or the ninth, of the sun's
daily torch they gave up the ghost.

If the victim, as might happen, stopped short of this fatal
extremity, before long by way of loathsome ulcers and a black
torrent pouring from the bowels he was overtaken none the   1201
less by decay and death. Or else, in many cases, he was seized
by a flow of putrid blood through choked nostrils accompanied
by a violent headache, and through this channel all the strength
of his body ebbed away.

If he survived this malignant stream of foul blood, the
disease had still to make its way into his joints and sinews and
right into the genital organs. Some in their overwhelming
dread of death[111] saved their lives by having their male organ
cut off with a blade. Others stayed alive after a fashion minus
hands and feet or with the loss of their eyesight: so completely   1212
were they mastered by the dire dread of death. There were even
some who fell a prey to total forgetfulness, so that they could
no longer recognize themselves.

While many corpses lay unburied[112] on the ground, heaped
one upon another, yet carrion birds and beasts of prey either
kept well away from them, repelled by the disgusting stench, or
having tasted were stricken with a speedy death. In those days
scarcely a bird was to be seen, nor did the sad species of wild
beasts emerge from the forests. Most of them were stricken
with the plague and died. In particular, man's strong and trusty

1223 animals the dogs lay stretched in every street, battling vainly for the life that was dragged out of their limbs by the power of the pestilence.[113]

Lonely funerals were raced without a mourner to the grave. No reliable remedy was found for general application. The treatment that had allowed one to draw the breath of life into this throat and remain a spectator of the starry vault proved in other cases a minister of death.

1230 One especially distressing symptom was this: as soon as a man saw himself enmeshed in the malady, he lost heart and lay in despair as though under sentence of death. In expectation of death, he gave up his life there and then.

Without a pause the contagion of the insatiable pestilence laid hold of victim after victim, as though they had been fleecy sheep or horned cattle, and this was one of the main factors that heaped death on death. Those whose excessive love of life and dread of death made them shrink from tending their own

1241 sick were punished before long by slaughtering Neglect[114] with a death as painful as it was disgraceful, unbefriended and destitute of aid. Those, on the other hand, who stood by the deathbed were overcome by contagion and the exertions imposed on them by their sense of honour and the appealing voice of the exhausted with its intrusive note of fretfulness. This, then, was the fate that overtook the finest characters.

⟨...⟩ and[115] upon each other, struggling to bury the vast crowd of their dead. Then back they would go, exhausted with tears and lamentation. Many were driven by sorrow to the sick-

1251 bed. The times were such that not a soul could be found untouched by death or sickness or mourning.

Meanwhile shepherd and herdsman and the sturdy pilot of the curved plough were among the victims. Within the cottage, body lay heaped on body, consigned to death by poverty[116] and pestilence together. Sometimes you might see the lifeless bodies of parents stretched above lifeless children, or children in turn gasping out their lives above the corpses of their prostrate parents. To no small extent did the affliction flood in from the countryside into the city by the concentration there of the plague-stricken peasantry from every district,[117] who crowded

land and lodgings. Here, all the more because of the stifling   1262
heat, death piled high his heaps of victims. Along the roadside
by the drinking fountains sprawled the bodies, prostrated and
bowled over by thirst, of multitudes in whom the breath of life
had been cut off by the excessive sweetness of the water.
Exposed in streets and public places you might see many a
wasted frame with limbs half dead begrimed with filth and
huddled under rags, dying in squalor with nothing to cover the   1270
bones but skin, well-nigh buried already in loathsome sores and
dirt. Every hallowed shrine of the gods had been tenanted by
death with lifeless bodies – yes, all the temples of the Heavenly
Ones, which their overseers had filled with guests, were left
occupied by crowds of corpses.[118] In this hour reverence and
worship of the gods carried little weight: they were banished by
the immediacy of suffering.

The mode of burial that had hitherto always been in vogue
was no longer practised in the city. The whole nation was
beside itself with terror. Each in turn, when he suffered   1281
bereavement, put away his own dead hastily, as time allowed.
Many unpleasant expedients were inspired by poverty and the
suddenness of the event. Men would fling their blood-relatives
amid violent outcry on the pyres built for others and set
torches under them. Often they shed much blood in these
disputes rather than abandon their dead.[119]

NOTES

BOOK ONE

1. See Appendix A for the interpretation of this prologue.
2. The metaphor in 'unleashed' suggests the myth of the winds locked in the cave of Aeolus as in Homer, *Odyssey* 10.19–27.
3. The title of the poem is a Latin translation of the Greek *peri physeos*, the title of the chief work of Epicurus and also the title of a poem by Empedocles.
4. On Memmius, see Appendix B.
5. See Introduction.
6. Epicurus.
7. L. attacks the theory that the gods cause thunder and lightning in 6.379–422.
8. At Aulis (in Boeotia) Iphigeneia was sacrificed by her father, the Greek general Agamemnon, to placate Artemis (the virgin goddess) and cause the wind to blow the fleet to Troy – to fight the Trojan War.
9. Early Roman poet (239–169 BC), believer in reincarnation, who at the beginning of his *Annales* claimed that his soul had 'been' Homer and Pythagoras in previous existences.
10. Mountain in Boeotia where the Muses were said to live.
11. Early Greek epic poet said to have composed the *Iliad* and the *Odyssey*.
12. Latin lacked the technical philosophical and scientific vocabulary of Greek: see L.'s problems with the Greek term *homoeomeria* below (830 ff.).
13. Friendship was especially praised by Epicurus as both an ethical ideal and as one of the highest pleasures available to man.
14. This argument proceeds as a *reductio ad absurdum*: since absurd inferences can be drawn from a proposition, it must itself be absurd.
15. Throughout this argument note how L. proceeds from our own empirical experience.

16. One of L.'s favourite analogies – letters make up words just as atoms make up objects. Cf. 823ff.

17. The examples chosen hint at feats of Greek gods and giants: Poseidon strides from Samothrace to Aegae in three steps (Homer, *Iliad* 13.20–21), the giant Polyphemus tears the top off a mountain (Homer, *Odyssey* 9.481), and of course gods do not die.

18. On this passage see D. West, *The Imagery and Poetry of Lucretius* 4–7.

19. That is, empty space for the atoms to exist and move in.

20. Most Greek philosophers, from Empedocles on, accepted the theory of *antiperistasis* here derided: cf. Plato, *Timaeus* 80c, Aristotle, *Physics* 213b–216b, Strato of Lampsacus fr. 63 Wehrli, Barnes, *The Presocratic Philosophers* 397–426.

21. That is, that there is condensed air between them which expands naturally as they separate.

22. That is, Helen of Troy, abducted from her husband Menelaus by Paris, thus starting the Trojan War. L. is perhaps attacking the Stoics, but on this see Furley, *Bulletin of the Institute of Classical Studies* 13 (1966) 13–14. Facts about the past are difficult for Epicurus: the indubitable fact 'Paris raped Helen' seems to exist although the matter of which it *was* an attribute (i.e., the bodies of Helen and Paris) no longer exist. Facts thus seem to exist independent of either matter or void.

23. Helen.

24. This only applies to the atoms themselves: if two atoms touch with no space in between them they can still be separated.

25. The four elements of Empedocles.

26. As argued by, e.g., Empedocles (see 753–8) and Anaxagoras (see 847–58).

27. A difficult paragraph. L. is probably still thinking of Anaxagoras' theory of *homoeomeria* (see below, 830–920), arguing that as no known substance is hard enough to withstand eternal battering, atoms cannot be made up of any known substance.

28. For the background to, and difficulties in, L.'s theory of minimal parts, see Appendix C.

29. Heraclitus (floruit 500 BC). L. is hardly fair in his attack: H. is selected a) to represent the extreme Monist school of thought (and so his subtle theories of flux and concord are not considered), and b) to attack his more immediate rivals the Stoics, who were heavily influenced by him.

30. Heraclitus was nicknamed 'the Riddler' because of the obscurity of his language – obscurity well parodied in L.'s Latin here – note especially the synaesthetic metaphor 'dyed with . . . sound.'

31. The impossibility of 'creation out of nothing' has already been established at 149–214. L. merely has to use the phrase ('creation out of nothing') to remind the reader of the earlier argument, cf. 757.

32. Stresses the neutrality of the atoms to prepare us for his attack on Anaxagoras' theory of *homoeomeria* below (830–920).

33. On the primacy and veracity of sense-experience see below Book 4.478–521.

34. Anaximenes of Miletus (floruit *c.* 546 BC).

35. Thales of Miletus (*c.* 625–545 BC).

36. A belief of some popular currency, according to Aristotle, *Metaphysics* 989a. It rounds off the four elements well.

37. Empedocles of Sicily (*c.* 493–433 BC) also wrote a didactic poem with the equivalent Greek title as Lucretius' poem. He is here chosen to represent Pluralism; as with Heraclitus, L. gives a partial and one-sided account of Empedocles' thought, omitting, for example, the vital doctrine of 'love and strife'.

38. That is, the south-western coast of Italy, near to the Aeolian islands. Rhegium is said to have been founded by Iocastus, son of Aeolus.

39. The whirlpool vividly described in Homer, *Odyssey* 12.101–110.

40. Explained fully at 6.639–702.

41. See Appendix C.

42. That is, neutral in substance, as opposed to, for example, Anaxagoras' elements (830–920).

43. The 'transformationist' theory mentioned is not Empedo-clean, but is similar to one apparently held by Aristotle, *On Coming into Being and Passing Away* 2.4, the Stoics (Cicero, *On the Nature of the Gods* 2.84) and contains more than a hint of Heraclitus' 'upward and downward path'.

44. An axiomatic concept: cf. 2.750–54.

45. Pluralism is thus not complex enough to explain the wide variety of nutrition. On this topic see below 4.633–72; 6.959–78, Sextus Empiricus, *Outlines of Pyrrhonism* 1.40–61.

46. A common analogy to the atomic theory, appropriate for a writer: cf. 2.688–90.

47. Anaxagoras was born in Clazomenae in Asia Minor in about 500 BC and died in Athens in 428. He spent much of his life in Athens, where he was associated with Pericles and Euripides; he was however condemned and exiled from Athens on a charge of impiety when he asserted that the sun was not a divinity but rather a lump of red-hot stone. On this passage see R. D. Brown, *Classical Quarterly* 33 (1983) 146–60.

48. That is, Heraclitus (see 658) and Empedocles and his followers (746–52).

49. A conventional poetic metaphor (cf. 4.450), but appropri-ate here to describe the hidden seeds of flame bursting out of the branches in the manner of flowers out of stalks.

50. L. uses the jingle *ignis* – *lignum* to illustrate the point verbally: the word he uses for 'letters' (*elementa*) can also mean 'particles'.

51. The Muses were the goddesses of literature and the arts, worshipped at Pieria, on the slopes of Mt Olympus, and Mt Helicon in Boeotia. This passage (926–50) is repeated almost verbatim at 4.1–25.

52. *Pace* Cicero (*Tusculan Disputations* 4.6–7), who claims that Epicureanism has 'taken over the whole of Italy'. For the appeal of Epicureanism see Introduction.

53. This would suggest that the poetry is of secondary, cos-metic significance compared to the philosophy being ex-pounded. See on this Introduction and Appendix A.

54. Ancient 'books' were lengthy scrolls to be unwound sideways from one end to the other: L.'s verb *evolvamus* suggests the act of unrolling the scroll of the book further.

55. Cf. Locke, *Essay on Human Understanding* 2.13.21.

56. The observable downward force of gravity throughout infinite time would have dragged matter to the 'bottom' of a finite universe.

57. Gods are also made up of atoms and void like everything else. On Epicurean theology see Introduction.

58. L. opposes teleology on every possible occasion: cf. 4.823–42, 5.416–508.

59. L. argues that finite matter would have dispersed out of all its atomic combinations throughout an infinite universe during infinite time. Again, the argument is: if P, then Q: not Q, therefore not-P.

60. One answer to the previous note: finite matter might be pushed together towards the centre of the universe. This theory can be found in Parmenides, Plato, the Peripatetics and the Stoics. L. is attacking the theory itself rather than any one exponent of it, but his contemptuous *stolidis* (1068) suggests *Stoicis* and was doubtless deliberate.

61. A gap of eight lines appears in the manuscript here: the translation supplies the minimum required to connect the lines we have. L. appears to have argued that if fire and air can escape to travel away from the earth, then other matter can do so also, and we thus face the dire consequences described. It may be, however, that this is a more substantial lacuna and that L. is here returning to the earlier argument for the infinity of matter, as Munro argued.

62. In the description of destruction, L. closes the book with a strong contrast to its opening paean of praise to the creative force of nature: just as the whole poem ends on a 'destructive' note.

BOOK TWO

1. For the apparent *Schadenfreude* of these lines see Introduction.

2. The life of futile relentless and even criminal struggling is often contrasted with the peaceful life of the wise man: cf. 3.62–93, which finishes with a repetition of 2.55–61.

3. The three classes of pleasure are here adumbrated: the necessary ones to remove pain, the natural but unnecessary ones to provide 'pleasure', 'delight' (*delicias*), and then the empty ones which, being neither necessary nor natural, are to be avoided altogether. This interpretation is not agreed by all editors, some of whom – e.g., Munro – see a straight split between removing pain (good) and all forms of unnecessary pleasures (taking line 22 with what follows). On Epicurus' classification of pleasure see Introduction.

4. The description of the opulent household derives from Homer, *Odyssey* 7.100–102.

5. A truism often repeated by later writers of Epicurean sympathies, e.g. Horace, *Epistles* 1.2.47, *Odes* 3.1.25–48.

6. The Plain of Mars, much used for army exercises, contained an altar of Mars in early times from which it derived its name.

7. The imagery of the light of truth against the darkness of superstition recurs many times: e.g. 3.1ff. Lines 55–61 are repeated at 3.87–93 and 6.35–41.

8. This notion of universal constancy in mutability will later be applied to human life, which has to give way to new generations by dying (3.964–71).

9. The metaphor is of handing on the torch in a relay race: cf. Plato, *Laws* 776b.

10. The two causes of atomic movement. Epicurus postulated a universal downward movement in opposition to Aristotle's thesis of objects tending towards the centre of a spherical world – an argument rejected at 1.1050–1113.

11. It is axiomatic that atoms are constantly on the move because void can offer no resistance to their motion.

12. At 1.958–1007.

13. A traditional Atomist illustration: cf. Democritus fr. 200–203, 206, Aristotle, *On the Soul* 1.2.404a.

14. No atoms are visible, so L. has to postulate this 'snowballing' idea of cumulative force (cf. 4.193-4, 6.340-42) to explain the visibility of the movement of the particles.

15. Aristotle (*Physics* 215a24-216a21) had argued that the speed of moving bodies was 'determined by the ratio of their weight to the density of the medium' (Long and Sedley, *The Hellenistic Philosophers* vol. i p. 50): the zero density of void would leave no possibility of any such ratio, and would further leave all atoms moving at the same speed. Epicurus countered that the speed of atoms may be immeasurably great but that it is less than infinite, and that atomic speed *is* uniform (*Letter to Herodotus* 46-7, 61-2).

16. That is, the atoms are made up of minimal parts but remain units as these minimal parts cannot be separated. See 1.599-634, Appendix C.

17. This paragraph argues against the Stoic (and Platonic) view of divine – and anthropocentric – creation of the world, citing the imperfection of the world as evidence: for the Stoic teleological view see, e.g., Cicero, *On the Nature of the Gods* 2.37-9, 75-6.

18. This follows at 5.156-234.

19. Cf. 1.1092-3.

20. Cf. 4.1049-51.

21. Cf. 6.219-378.

22. On this vital topic and its implications, see Introduction.

23. This was a popular fallacy, and L. is not thinking of anybody in particular.

24. See note 17 above.

25. The Latin *minimum* translates Epicurus' term (*elachiston*) for the 'minimum magnitude' (see Appendix C, and Cicero, *On Ends* 1.19).

26. That is, the deterministic causation of, for example, Democritus and later the Stoics (cf. Cicero, *On Fate* 39-43).

27. The mechanics of this are more fully explained at 4.877-906.

28. The looseness of L.'s use of terms like 'mind' and 'heart' will be tightened up in the analysis of Book Three.

29. L. has not explained precisely *how* this happens, beyond postulating atomic indeterminacy to mirror the psychological indeterminacy we call free will.

30. This paragraph restates the principles of 1.159–264: despite the apparent flux of atomic motion, the universe is constant.

31. Answering the 'sunbeam' image of 112–41, where L. showed atomic movement in what is apparently still, he now demonstrates stability in matter, for all that it is made up of constantly moving atoms.

32. The following two sentences present an epic picture: cf. Homer, *Iliad* 2.457–8, 19.362–3; *Odyssey* 14.267–8.

33. A weak argument. Epicurus (*Letter to Herodotus* §42) has a much stronger point when he argues that the obvious variety in the world could not be produced if all atoms were of the same shape. Nor is there any reason why an infinite number of atoms should not all be identical.

34. This famous passage shows L. at his most moving. Notice how the single scientific point (the calf is recognizably unique, hence individuals do differ) is expanded into a picture of immense artistry and power.

35. L. moves from the high pathos of the calf to lighter examples of the same phenomenon – note the humorous point that lambs on occasion go for the wrong udder.

36. A full account of lightning and thunderbolts is given below at 6.160–422.

37. L. imagines a lamp made of horn 'carried on a wet night' (M.F. Smith).

38. This point does not square well with Epicurus' belief that atoms were invisibly small – and anyway L. has already demolished the view that oil is not made up of 'oil' atoms, as Anaxagoras held (see above 1.830–920): either L. means 'atomic clusters' here, or else the persuasive power of the illustration outweighs its consistency with what has gone before.

39. Cf. 4.615–72.

40. The adjective 'stinking' suggests cremation rather than sacrifice of freshly slaughtered victims. For the smell of the dead cf. 6.1217.

41. Cilicia was famous for producing saffron – a solution of which was sprinkled in the Roman theatre: cf. Horace, *Epistles* 2.1.79. L. also uses the theatre for an analogy at 4.75–89.

42. The axiomatic statement of Epicurean epistemology. Cf. 4.26–215.

43. To be fully explained and commented on at 4.1037–1287.

44. L. has already accounted for degrees of weight and density by the proportion of void within the matter (1.358–69; 2.100–108). He is now examining the degrees of fragility/hardness by arguing that atoms are either sharp or smooth and also either hooked or not. Surface hardness is caused by degrees of 'hookedness'.

45. This conclusion is forced by Epicurus' refusal to believe in infinite divisibility of matter: if there is a lower limit (minimal parts 1.599–634; see Appendix C), then each atom would contain a finite number of parts: infinity would extend the other way, causing atoms to be visible – and of even infinite size! – which we know that they are not.

46. A town in Thessaly famous for the opulent purple murex dye obtained from shellfish.

47. An interesting argument, working on the principle that things possess qualities to a greater or lesser degree: it is theoretically conceivable for qualities to be possessed to an infinite degree, unless there is only a finite number of atomic shapes that form the things possessing the qualities in question.

48. Cf. 1.1008–51.

49. See 569–80 below.

50. There is no other evidence for this ivory wall in classical literature.

51. For the moral aside on the folly of sailing the seas cf. 5.1004–6, Aratus, *Phaenomena* 110–11, Virgil, *Georgics* 1.136f., Ovid, *Metamorphoses* 1.94ff.

52. Matter is infinite, but nature observes a balance of forces, an equilibrium (*isonomia*) such that creation and destruction balance each other out: we infer this from the stability of the world around us, neither expanding nor shrinking.

53. Cf. nature's rebuke to the man reluctant to die at 3.964–8.

54. Cf. 6.639–711.

55. L. 'demythologizes' popular belief but here finds a philosophical justification for it.

56. The Great Mother, Cybele, was a Phrygian goddess whose priests were called Corybantes, most of whom were said to be castrated (cf. Catullus 63 for self-castration in worship of Cybele). Her worship was brought into Rome in 205–204 BC, the Corybantes becoming confused with the Curetes of Crete, partly because both Crete and Phrygia have a Mount Ida.

57. Cf. St Augustine, *City of God* 7.24.

58. After Mount Ida in Phrygia. For the title of Idaean Mother cf. Livy xxix.10.5

59. For the tale cf. Herodotus ii.2 and Dover's note on Aristophanes *Clouds* 398.

60. Cf. Catullus 64.261–4.

61. That is, a pruning-knife used for the castration of the frenzied devotee.

62. Jupiter's mother Rhea hid him in a cave on Mount Dicte in Crete when his Father Saturn learned that he was destined to be overthrown by one of his children: for fuller details see Graves, *The Greek Myths* vol. i pp. 39–44.

63. Especially the Stoics: see Cicero, *On the Nature of the Gods* 1.15.40. Of course L. himself can use the divine names for poetic purposes, e.g., 2.472, 3.221, 6.1076: the point being made is the reminder to avoid superstition.

64. Cf 4.1209–32.

65. But homogeneous: it was Anaxagoras' belief that the atoms are heterogeneous that L. has argued against at 1.830–920.

66. The mechanics of sensation will be analysed in Book 4.

67. Cf. 1.823–5.

68. Most obviously the legendary Centaurs, half man and half horse, whose non-existence is argued for at 5.878–924.

69. The Scylla, a sea-monster with six heads, twelve feet and the voice of a dog (Homer, *Odyssey* 12.85ff.), later endowed with a girdle of dogs' heads around her waist (Virgil, *Eclogue* 6.74–5): see 5.893.

70. The Chimera was a fire-breathing beast with the head of a lion, the body of a she-goat and the rear of a snake. Cf. 5.905–6, Homer, *Iliad* 6.181–2.

71. Cf. 1122–43.

72. Not only in excretion, but also in respiration and perspiration.

73. A good example of the way L. can pass quickly from the microscopic to the telescopic, stressing the unity of the world.

74. Size, shape and weight are the primary qualities of atoms: other qualities – the sensory qualities of colour, taste, smell, heat, cold, sound – are secondary as they only apply to atomic compounds, not to individual atoms. He did not follow Democritus in regarding these secondary qualities as 'merely' subjective – on the veracity of sense-impressions see 4.469–521. The distinction between primary and secondary qualities is also not equivalent to that between sensory and non-sensory, as the primary qualities of size, weight and shape are also sensory, even if in practice the atoms are too small to be perceived.

75. A deliberately stark statement: if colours can change, and atoms have colours, then atoms can change. If atoms can change they are not the permanent changeless foundation of matter, and the universe is no longer stable.

76. This was probably the view of Anaxagoras.

77. This is exactly the argument used against Anaxagoras' *homoeomeria* theory (1.875–96) applied to his theory of colours.

78. L.'s reasoning for this perceptive argument is that the beams of light cause the atoms to rearrange themselves and so display a different colour.

79. L. does not explain why ravens *are* black: but see for example 4.1209–32 and 5.883–924 on the consistency of species.

80. E.g. wind and water, the devastating effects of which have been graphically described at 1.265–97 in proving their atomic nature.

81. Atoms cannot emit anything from themselves as they are indivisible: but L. is here confusing the qualities (heat, cold etc.) with the atomic emissions that communicate those qualities to our senses.

82. Cf. Plato, *Timaeus* 50e.

83. This is essential to the argument of Book 3 that the 'soul' is made up of insentient atoms which disperse at death and so kill all our conscious identity.

84. Spontaneous production of animate from inanimate matter was attested by Aristotle (*de generatione animalium* 762a8ff.) and reflects deep uncertainty about the dividing-line between the animate and inanimate. On this see W. Capelle, 'Das Problem der Urzeugung bei Aristoteles und Theophrast und in der Folgezeit', *Rheinisches Museum* 98 (1955) 150–80, Guthrie, *History of Greek Philosophy* vol. vi pp. 236, 288–91.

85. Cf. 1.900 Here, as there, L. is probably arguing against Anaxagoras.

86. In the next book L. will tackle the difficult question of the difference between the – apparently identical – living body and the corpse.

87. Anaxagoras again: at least the theory here attacked fits his *homoeomeria* theory perfectly (1.830–920).

88. L. will go on to argue in the next book that sensation is communicated through the *anima* spread throughout the body.

89. L.'S opponent here is usually seen as a Stoic, but see Furley, *Bulletin of the Institute of Classical Studies* 13 (1966) 24–5, for qualification of this. There is also perhaps a

reminiscence of the theory of spontaneous generation of life, on which see note 87 above.

90. This paragraph anticipates Book 3, especially 3.592–606 (fainting) and 476–86 (drunkenness).

91. Cf. 434–41, 4.858–69. This sort of pleasure is kinetic pleasure, on which see Introduction.

92. Cf. 1.919–20. L. as often creates a *reductio ad absurdum* to refute his opponents.

93. Cf. 1.250–61, 5.795–836. L. uses the language of myth to great effect in this summary passage.

94. As will be explained in Book Three.

95. Cf. Cicero, *On the Nature of the Gods* 2.38.96.

96. At 1.958–1001.

97. Cf. Epicurus, *Letter to Herodotus* 45. The purpose of the argument here is at least partly to refute the idea of any being, even divine, being able to direct an infinity of worlds. Interestingly, the concept is not used to deny the anthropocentric nature of the universe.

98. L. expressly denies all forms of teleology: cf. 4.823–57, 5.156–234 and 837–77. There remains the problem that L. appears to be stressing the random operation of chance in creating worlds, when the Atomists as a school preached iron determinism, with the caveats of Epicurus' notion of swerve and free will: L. presumably intends us to read the passage stressing the *purposeless* nature of the collisions, denying the volitional purposes of a creating deity.

99. That is, male and female.

100. Cf. 2.167–83, 5.110–234 and 6.379–422: Epicurus, *Letter to Herodotus* 76, for the Epicurean anti-theological viewpoint.

101. All these points are repeated and expanded at 6.379–422: see notes to pp. 176–8.

102. The whole of this final passage is based on the idea that worlds are organisms like all others and so are subject to birth, growth, decay and death. The destruction of the world is as certain as our own death, cf. 5.91–415 and 6.601–7.

103. Cf. 4.858–69.

104. L. appears to end the book with a pessimistic note of degeneration reminiscent of the 'Golden Age' idea found in, for example, Hesiod, *Works and Days* 109–201, Aratus, *Phainomena* 96–136, Ovid, *Metamorphoses* 1.89–150. Epicureanism of course denied the myth of primitive paradise, but L. stresses our *moral* backwardness until enlightened by Epicurus: cf. 3.59–86, 5.988–1010.

105. Cf. Homer, *Iliad* 8.19, Plato, *Theaetetus* 153c.

106. As held by, e.g., Anaximander cf. 5.793–4.

107. As does, e.g., Nestor in Homer, *Iliad* 1.260–73 and Virgil, *Aeneid* 12.900.

108. The image of the ship going aground on the rocks echoes the words with which the book began, where the wise man surveys serenely the plight of the foolish mariner in rough seas.

BOOK THREE

1. Epicurus. L. begins Books 1, 3, 5 and 6 with panegyric of this sort.

2. Epicurus was not the inventor of the Atomic theory, in fact. Cf. Introduction.

3. Imagery of light of truth versus dark of ignorance and superstition: cf. 1.146–8, etc.

4. The following description of the gods' abode is inspired by Homer, *Odyssey* 6.42–6. (See West, *The Imagery and Poetry of Lucretius* 31–3.) On the serenity of the gods, see Introduction.

5. Acheron was one of the rivers of the Underworld.

6. L. gives a quick resumé of the first two books before launching into this one.

7. As ever, the ethical purpose is all-important, the philosophy is expounded to eradicate the fear.

8. For example, Empedocles and Anaximenes respectively (on whom see Barnes, *The Presocratic Philosophers* 472–507). 'The whim' suggests, however, that L. is referring to people who wear their materialistic ideas without any deep philosophical commitment.

9. The pose of being a tough-minded materialist is thus shown up for what it is.

10. For the diatribe against contemporary society cf. Sallust *Catiline* 10.3–5, Catullus 64.397–408 and Fowler in Griffin and Barnes, *Philosophia Togata* 135ff.

11. L. is clearly alluding to Rome's contemporary civil strife: see Introduction.

12. L. here appears to be offering a more altruistic reason for adopting Epicureanism: not just to benefit the individual, but also to inculcate moral responsibility.

13. 'Mind' is the closest word in English to L.'s *animus*, the rational part of the soul.

14. For this belief see, e.g., Plato, *Phaedo* 86b, Aristotle, *On the Soul* 407b27ff., Barnes, *The Presocratic Philosophers* 488–92.

15. 'Possession' of harmony simply means an arrangement of its parts so as to appear harmonious: it is of course not the same as possessing a heart or a leg.

16. Whereas, if the soul were simply a condition of the body, it would have to feel the same as the body.

17. Cf. 4.907–1036 for the analysis of sleep.

18. *Anima*, the irrational part of the soul. L.'s clinching argument against the *harmonia* theory is saved until this paragraph: if the soul is a condition of the whole body, then why do bodies die when they have lost only wind and heat? (cf. 211–15 below).

19. *Harmonia* was a term used in music to describe the tuning of the strings of a lyre: it is not accidental that one of the chief exponents of the 'harmony' theory of the soul was the musician Aristoxenus (Cicero, *Tusculan Disputations* 1.10.19).

20. But L. only shows it to be the apparent seat of the emotions, not the intellect. For the 'soul within the breast' cf. Homer, *Iliad* 1.188–92, 9.255–6.

21. Cf. Sappho fr. 31, Catullus 51.

22. Cf. 2.381–97.

23. A double contrast is to be set up: poppy-seeds are light

and smooth, contrasted to the heaviness of stones and the spikiness of corn respectively.

24. Cf. 1.331.

25. That is, wine.

26. That is, wind, air and heat; wind and air are seen as separate entities partly to fit the psychological 'types' L. will go on to infer from them (288–322). Air gives placidity, fire gives anger, wind gives fear ... but what gives sensation? The nameless fourth element.

27. Whereas before (122) L. had the spirit leaving through the mouth.

28. L. is apologizing, as Kerferd suggests, for the absence of a Latin term for the Greek *krama* (blending). Cf 1.136–9, 832.

29. The blending is so complete that the atoms of the four substances are combined into a new substance.

30. The 'fourth element' rules the spirit, and the spirit rules the body.

31. L. first describes temporary changes in mood caused by temporary changes in the prominence of the four elements (282–93): he then describes permanent temperaments caused thus (294–322).

32. This attempts to counter the obvious objection that if our nature is atomically predisposed as he argues, then we cannot change ourselves to become Epicureans as he would like. Again, the determinism of the Atomists has to be tempered by Epicurus to make our 'conversion' possible. On divine serenity, see Introduction.

33. A good example, as the matter would *look* the same (as the corpse can look alive), but it would have ceased to have the essential properties of incense: unlike water losing its secondary quality of heat (339–40).

34. L. is in this paragraph at his most dogmatic, stating rather than proving his contentions.

35. Cf. the argument against Scepticism at 4.469–99.

36. As did, apparently, Heraclitus (Sextus Empiricus, *Against the Professors* 7.129) and especially the Stoics (Cicero, *Tusculan Disputations* 1.20.46).

37. Democritus of Abdera (*c.* 460–*c*.356 BC), the founder of the Atomic theory. For L.'s respect for his predecessor, cf. his words on Empedocles at 1.730.

38. Cf. 179–230.

39. Cf. 278.

40. The gaps between spirit atoms must be greater than the tiniest phenomena mentioned here.

41. This is of course fallacious. All conscious people are alive, but not all living people are conscious.

42. This demonstrates that the person can survive the loss of part of the spirit (*anima*) spread through the limbs, but not the loss of the mind (*animus*) in the breast.

43. Alcmeon of Croton, a younger contemporary of Pythagoras, medical expert and philosopher, is said to have dissected an eye: the gruesome detail here may suggest this great Presocratic thinker to the reader, especially as Alcmeon argued strongly for the immortality of the spirit. L. is thus using Alcmeon's own techniques against his own theories. See Barnes, *The Presocratic Philosophers* 114–20, 478–9.

44. In fact this begins the next major section of the book (417–829), the 29 proofs of the mortality of the spirit.

45. This is not idle rhetoric. Plato argued for the pre-existence of the soul before birth (*Phaedo* 70c–77d) as did also the Orphics, Empedocles, Pythagoras, Posidonius, Varro and Aristotle. On this see 670ff. L. here means that the spirit is unique to this body, born with it and dying with it.

46. See Appendix B on Memmius.

47. 177–230.

48. L. will analyse the mechanics of perception through images at 4.45–521 and 722–857.

49. For the image of the vessel cf. 6.17–23. For the notion of the body as the prison or tomb of the soul cf. Plato *Gorgias* 493a.

50. As does the earth itself: cf. 2.1144–52, 5.91–415, 6.601–7.

51. L. has a scathing portrayal of mourners later in the book (894–911).

52. Cf. 1024–52.

53. The 'Sacred Disease' well analysed by Hippocrates, and suffered by Julius Caesar (Suetonius, *Julius Caesar* 45).

54. The Greek medical writers ascribed diseases such as epilepsy to a surfeit of one of the 'humours' in the body (bile, phlegm and serum). Cf. 4.664, Plato *Timaeus* 82e.

55. Greek writers seeking to display madness often used some of the symptoms of epilepsy (frothing mouth, rolling eyes, etc.): cf. Euripides, *Heracles* 931–4, *Medea* 1173ff., *Bacchae* 1122–3.

56. Anything that can be altered can be killed: not a watertight argument, but resting on the vital atomic characteristic of 'impassivity' (cf. Barnes, *The Presocratic Philosophers* 345–6) and the axiomatic statement of 519–20 (cf. 1.670–71, 792–3, 2.753–4). The same argument that proved the immortality of the atoms now proves the mortality of the soul.

57. Reminiscent of the slow death of Socrates (Plato, *Phaedo* 117e–118a).

58. A weak ending to the argument. The *body* is stripped of life, to be sure, but the spirit may be thus kept intact.

59. Cf. 94–7 and 136–40. This is L.'s simplest line of attack; the spirit is part of the body, and the body is patently mortal, ∴ the spirit is mortal.

60. A weaker analogy, as the vessel does not have the sort of atomic interweaving with its contents that the spirit and body have (cf. 323–349). None the less L. continues the analogy into the picture of the 'bodily envelope' later.

61. Another Lucretian *reductio ad absurdum*; cf. 367–9 above, 727–8 below.

62. A staggering *non sequitur*. The dissolution of the body will not impress those who believe that it is merely the tomb from which the soul has happily escaped (cf. 612–14).

63. L. now has slightly stronger inductive reasons – so long as one accepts the analysis of the spirit as spread throughout the body.

64. For example, Polygnotus (*c.* 475–445 BC), who painted a

fresco of Odysseus talking in the Underworld with Tiresias.

65. For example, Homer, *Odyssey* Book 11, where Odysseus visits the underworld and talks with the dead.

66. That is, the poet does not claim to have seen the Oriental tactic of using scythed chariots for himself. For their effects see Livy 37.41, Xenophon, *Anabasis* 1.8.10.

67. That is, climb up on to the chariot to attack the driver.

68. Unless the separate parts instantly become independent beings with their own spirits.

69. After arguing against survival of death, L. now turns to the theory of the pre-existence of the soul: see note 45 above.

70. As claimed by, for example, Empedocles (fr. 117, Diogenes Laertius 8.77: 'I have already been a boy and a girl, a bush, a bird and a leaping fish'). Plato attempts to prove this memory (*anamnesis*) at *Meno* 81ff.

71. On this argument see Barnes, *The Presocratic Philosophers* 492–5.

72. A reference perhaps to the Pythagorean doctrine *soma sema* (the body is the tomb ⟨of the soul⟩).

73. For the theory of spontaneous generation of living out of inanimate matter see 2.871–3 and note 87.

74. There follows a series of comic questions to ridicule the theory of his opponent. For this tactic cf. 6.387–422.

75. Alluding perhaps to the idea that the child is formed entirely by the father, the mother being merely a receptacle for its growth. Cf. Aeschylus, *Eumenides* 657–66.

76. Renowned for their ferocity and believed to have interbred with tigers (Aristotle, *Natural History of Animals* 8.607a). Hyrcania is on the Caspian Sea.

77. Again, mocking questions to ridicule the opponent, as at note 75 above.

78. Cf. 1.881–4. L. is here setting up the impossible scenario that belief in immortality would necessitate, a hyperbolic rhetorical device known as the *adynaton*: cf. e.g. 6.1076–7.

79. The following passage is repeated (with minor changes) at 5.351–63.

80. The first half of this paragraph suggests the carefree eternity of the gods (cf. 18–24): the second half is a sharp reminder of the grim reality of human frailty, its defects both physical and moral.

81. Here begins the final diatribe against the fear of death which closes the book. The axiom that death is nothing to us is from Epicurus himself (*Key Doctrines* 2).

82. That is, in the Punic Wars, especially the second (218–201 BC). By L.'s day the war had been turned into high epic poetry by Ennius, and some of L.'s phrasing here suggests parody of the earlier poet.

83. A sharp reminder that we are no more than the temporary union of atoms.

84. As suggested by e.g. Pythagoras, the Stoics (see, for example, Nemesius 309.5–311.2) and, much later, Nietzsche (see Barnes, *The Presocratic Philosophers* 503–7).

85. It is difficult to see how L. could deny this, having established infinity of time and the randomness of atomic collisions in Books One and Two.

86. Perhaps a reference to the custom of the Persian Magi who exposed corpses to beasts and birds of prey (Cicero, *Tusculan Disputations* 1.45.108).

87. Exactly the fate that befell Polynices in Sophocles' *Antigone*, in which the eponymous heroine gave up her life to see him buried. The Epicurean would see her sacrifice as pointless.

88. Honey was often used for embalming the dead. L. is here effectively pointing out that *all* methods of disposal of corpses are equally disgusting when imagined. For discussion of the relativity of burial customs – and a bizarre example – see Herodotus 3.38.

89. A much admired and imitated passage, for all the irony of L.'s writing. Cf. Virgil, *Georgics* 2.523–4, Gray's 'Elegy Written in a Country Churchyard' 21–4. That the sentiments expressed are conventional is shown by Lattimore *Themes in Greek and Latin Epigraphs* (1962) 172–7.

90. An obvious example of exactly this scene is found at Petronius, *Satyricon* 34.6–10: the theme becomes a com-

monplace of later 'sympotic' poetry, e.g., Horace, *Odes* 1.11, Propertius 2.15.

91. Personification of abstract forces (*prosopopeia*) is a common rhetorical device: cf. 6.1241–2 ('Negligence'), Plato, *Crito* 50a–54d (the Laws), Cicero, *Catilinarian Orations* 1.7.18 (Rome). L.'s personification of nature is also to be found at e.g. 6.226 and 1135. See Brown, *Lucretius on Love and Sex* 229.

92. Cf. 1003–10, 6.20–21.

93. Epicurus addresses a similar challenge to pessimists at *Letter to Menoeceus* 126–7, although the wise man will 'keep his share in life' even if he lose his eyes (Diogenes Laertius 10.119), unlike the Stoic acceptance of suicide (Diogenes Laertius 7.130)

94. Perhaps a reference to the myth of the centaur Chiron, who was granted immortality but ended up begging for death: some say because he was in agony after being shot by an arrow from Heracles, others that he was sick of his long life (Graves, *The Greek Myths* 2.113).

95. Cf. 1.263–4, 2.71–9. The eternal atoms are needed constantly and are only borrowed for a time.

96. This section allegorizes superstitious myths in moral terms. The Homeric version of the myth shows Tantalus standing in a pool of water that recedes when he tries to drink it, with fruit-trees above him that the wind blows out of reach whenever he tries to grasp them: in this version he is punished for stealing the nectar and ambrosia of the gods by having a stone suspended over him. (Pindar, *Olympian* 1.55–64, Virgil, *Aeneid* 6.602–3).

97. A giant who tried to rape the goddess Leto. His punishment was to have his liver eaten by vultures (cf. Homer, *Odyssey* 11.576–81).

98. Sisyphus betrayed Zeus' abduction of Aegina to her father, the river-god Asopus, and was punished by being made to roll a boulder uphill that would never reach the top (cf. Homer, *Odyssey* 11.593–600, Graves, *The Greek Myths* 1.216–18).

99.   The Danaids, who murdered their husbands and were condemned to draw water in sieves.

100.   Three-headed dog who guards the gates of the underworld.

101.   Primeval beings, female in form, who avenge crimes especially of bloodshed within the family: cf. Aeschylus' *Eumenides*.

102.   Tartarus was that part of the Underworld where the wicked suffer their punishment.

103.   The Tarpeian Rock at the south-western corner of the Capitoline Hill, from which criminals sentenced to death were flung.

104.   Ancus Martius was the fourth King of Rome. The sentence is in imitation of the line of Ennius (*Annales* 149v): 'after good Ancus left the light with his eyes'.

105.   Xerxes King of Persia built a bridge of boats across the Hellespont in 480 BC (Herodotus 7.33–7).

106.   Publius Cornelius Scipio Africanus Major, who defeated Hannibal at the battle of Zama in 202 BC.

107.   Early Greek poet and traditionally seen as the author of the *Iliad* and the *Odyssey*.

108.   Democritus (cf. note 37 above) is said to have starved himself to death (Diogenes Laertius 9.43).

109.   The only mention of Epicurus by name in the whole poem and the culmination of the catalogue of great men.

110.   That travel by itself does not free men of themselves became a commonplace: cf. Horace's famous line 'those who run across the sea change the climate but not themselves' (*Epistles* 1.11.27: cf. *Odes* 2.16.18–20).

111.   The satirical portrait is unmistakably Roman.

112.   Cf. Plato, *Republic* 352a, Aristotle, *Nicomachean Ethics* 1166b. 13–14: but whereas they speak of the wicked, L. speaks of the 'sick' man whose sickness could be cured with the knowledge granted by Epicureanism.

113.   For the simple reason that infinity minus x is still infinite, for any value of x except infinity.

BOOK FOUR

1. The opening 25 lines are a repetition of 1.926–50.
2. In Book Three.
3. Cf. Epicurus, *Letter to Herodotus* 46–52.
4. This establishes a link with the previous book. Indeed it could even be seen that the whole theory of perception here discussed is there mainly to rebut the apparent 'proof' of survival of death afforded by ghosts.
5. The argument is *a fortiori*. If visible matter leaves bodies, and invisible matter moves more easily than visible, then there must be even more invisible matter leaving bodies.
6. Briefly at 56 – in more detail below at 90–94.
7. This sort of awning was first used in 78 BC: cf. 6.109–12 and West, *The Imagery and Poetry of Lucretius* 38–41.
8. Cf. 150–54, 269–323.
9. Epicurus argued that all perceptions are true: he now has to show how what are apparent perceptions of monsters do not 'prove' their existence. Cf. 732–48, 5.878–924.
10. The jingle *res. respondent* makes better sound than science: elsewhere L. argues that we do not see *objects* but only the images of them (but see 256–68 for qualification of this).
11. For the need to overcome the superstitious fear of storms, see 6.48–91.
12. The swan was said to sing a beautiful song before it died; cf. 3.6–8, Theocritus 5.136.
13. A minute impetus will produce immense speed as L.'s theory of kinetic force sees it as cumulative, not constant; cf. 6.340–42.
14. *A fortiori* argument again.
15. Cf. the atomic proofs resting on the phenomenon of erosion at 1.311–21, 326.
16. Hardly a watertight inference.
17. We do not in fact have any sensation of air pushed through our eyes like this, and so this theory can only be stated dogmatically. L. does not deal with the problem of how we can receive elephant-sized films in our small eyes.

18. L. here attempts to explain how an aggregate of invisible films can be visible: he works on lines similar to those advanced in Book One, where individual atoms are too tiny to be seen but they amass in sufficient numbers to be felt and seen.

19. Analogy rather than proof of the preceding statement: the 'surface ... colour' is misleading, as the stone may be the same colour all the way through, and anyway L. means the 'coloured surface'. It is analogous in that the solidity of the whole is conveyed by our contact with the topmost surface, just as the topmost surface, when it has flown off the object as a film, causes us to see the whole object.

20. That is, concave mirrors.

21. That is, the angle of reflection is equal to the angle of incidence.

22. L. now begins a section on optical problems in answer to the challenge of Scepticism (on which see Introduction).

23. Cf. Sextus Empiricus, *Outlines of Pyrrhonism* 1.44.

24. A standard argument of the Sceptic (cf. Sextus Empiricus, *Outlines of Pyrrhonism* 1.32, Annas and Barnes, *The Modes of Scepticism* 105–6) and a commonly observed phenomenon (cf., e.g., Plato, *Republic* 602c–d, Euripides, *Ion* 586–7.

25. Just as successive static images appear cinematically as moving figures to us (768–76), so do their 'negatives' the shadows.

26. This is Epicurus' answer to the apparent proof of the mendacity of the senses: see Introduction.

27. Cf. Sextus Empiricus, *Against the Mathematicians* 7.414, Cicero, *Prior Academics* 2.25.81. L. typically embellishes these illusions to hyperbolic lengths.

28. Cf. Sextus Empiricus, *Outlines of Pyrrhonism* 1.118.

29. Cf. Sextus Empiricus, *Outlines of Pyrrhonism* 1.118.

30. The bent oar was another favourite example of illusion: cf. Sextus Empiricus, *Outlines of Pyrrhonism* 1.119, Annas and Barnes, *The Modes of Scepticism* 106–9. Notice L.'s high epic style of describing the phenomenon.

31. Cf. Sextus Empiricus *Against the Mathematicians* 7.192,

Outlines of Pyrrhonism 1.47. A more common cause of this illusion is drunkenness: cf. Petronius, *Satyricon* 64.

32. Dreams are an obvious example of illusory experience: cf. 962–1036 for further description and analysis.

33. Epicurus' *to prosdoxazomenon*, the premature judgement based on inadequate evidence.

34. L. now attacks the full Sceptic position thus; if no proposition can be known, then the proposition that no proposition can be known cannot be known either.

35. Epicurus' *perikato trepesthai*: see Burnyeat, *Philologus* 122 (1978) 197–206.

36. For the argument from our conception of truth and falsehood cf. 5.181–6, 1046–9. For the logical position cf. Aristocles' criticism of Melissus (Barnes, *The Presocratic Philosophers* 298–302).

37. L. argues that as the senses operate in different ways, they cannot refute each other (for all that they all operate through touch 2.434–5), and also that we have no reason to prefer one sense over another. He concludes that all senses – and the reasoning based on them – is either totally false or totally true. Our experience rules out the first possibility, so they must all be true. The possibility that *some* perceptions are false is ruled out because we have no means of discriminating true from false – except through the senses. See Annas and Barnes 69–73.

38. L. may be making fun of the Roman orators who would filibuster bills in the Senate.

39. The analysis of speech is not strictly necessary, but is of interest to a wordsmith such as L.: and words are analogous to the images he has described in that a tiny phoneme can summon up the image of a gigantic object at once (785).

40. If visual films can bounce off mirrors (269–323), then sounds can also bounce in echoes.

41. L. never misses a chance to mock superstition; for comparable material cf. Herodotus 6.105, Pindar, *Pythian* 3.79, Dodds, *The Greeks and the Irrational* (California, 1951) 117 & n. 87.

42. Satyrs were attendants of the god Dionysus – grotesque, partly bestial and in a permanent state of sexual arousal. The Roman general Sulla was believed to have captured one and brought it back to Rome in 83 BC (Plutarch, *Sulla* 27).

43. Fauns were nature-spirits, similar to satyrs.

44. A goat-like deity of nature, in particular of flocks and shepherds, originating in Arcadia; inventor of the Pan-pipes and would-be lover of nymphs.

45. The phenomenon of relativity in food was another weapon of the Sceptics: see Annas and Barnes, *The Modes of Scepticism* 31–65.

46. Perfect balance: what is in his mouth kills us, what is in our mouths kills him. Cf. Pliny, *Natural History* 7.2.15; Aristotle, *Natural History of Animals* 607a.

47. Cf. Sextus Empiricus, *Outlines of Pyrrhonism* 1.57, Diogenes Laertius 9.80, Galen, *On Temperaments* IV 684K.

48. Cf. 1.814–29, 895–6, 2.333–80.

49. Cf. Sextus Empiricus, *Outlines of Pyrrhonism* 1.92, Seneca, *Letters* 109.7.

50. For the tale of the geese of Juno saving the Capitol from the invading Gauls in 387 BC see Livy 5.47.1–4, Virgil, *Aeneid* 8.655–6.

51. Cf. Sextus Empiricus, *Outlines of Pyrrhonism* 1.58, who tells us that elephants cannot face rams, sea-beasts cannot bear to hear beans pounded and tigers cannot stand hearing drums.

52. The mind is material, and so thought must also be material, caused like perception by the images. There are problems with abstract ideas, with free volition of thought, and L. does not attempt to explain how there could be an image of 'void'.

53. Cf. 129–42; 2.700–717; 5.878–924.

54. Cf. 2.704 and note ad loc.

55. Cf. 3.1011.

56. This is important as it proves that the images enter through the pores and not through the eyes which are of course shut.

57. Exactly as in cartoon animation.

58. L. is careful not to split time into an infinite number of parts, as, e.g., Zeno had done in his notorious paradoxes. See Appendix C.

59. As already suggested at 465 above, the misinterpretation of perception is the fault of the mind, not the senses.

60. Another passage attacking the theological view of the world as held by Aristotle and the Stoics; cf. 2.167–83, 644–60, 5.110–234, 1183–1210, 6.379–422.

61. That is, man himself is a teleological being, but nature is not.

62. This looks forward to the scathing moral contrast of primitive vs. 'civilized' at 5.925–1010.

63. L. passes from the mechanics of the desire for food to the less easily explained free volition which makes us choose, for instance, to read this book.

64. Thus the mind is a two-way transmitter: it feels the movement of the spider crawling on the skin and then tells the hand to squash it.

65. One of L.'s more extravagant – and less convincing – images.

66. The essential nature of sleep is anaesthesia: the mind is still seeing images and dreaming, the involuntary motions of the body carry on undisturbed, but the external senses perceive nothing.

67. Cf. 180–82.

68. As the spirit is responsible for receiving sensory stimuli, its dislocation will suspend sensation.

69. L. does not explain how we ever manage to wake up. Cf. Schrijvers in *Études sur l'épicurisme antique* I (1976) 247.

70. L.'s dreams are suitably naturalistic, unlike the inspirational poetic dreams of, e.g., Propertius 3.3.

71. Roman games lasted between seven and fourteen days (Carcopino, *Daily Life in Ancient Rome* (Harmondsworth, 1991) 224–5).

72. To prove that dreaming is a purely natural, rather than supernatural, activity, L. looks at the dreams of animals.

73. It is impossible, of course, to be sure of other people's dreams simply from their movements while asleep.

74. The dreams mentioned are mostly anxiety dreams, allowing L. another chance to explore human insecurity (cf. 2.1–61, 3.59–86). Most of the 'literary' dreams known to L.'s readers are of this morbid/revelatory form: e.g., Herodotus 1.108, Sophocles, *Electra* 417–23.

75. As, for instance, in the arena. See Carcopino, *Daily Life in Ancient Rome* 260–61.

76. Cf. 5.1158–60, Polybius 18.15, 23.10.

77. Perhaps falling from the Tarpeian Rock: cf. 3.1016.

78. L. again tilts at the folly of acquiring luxuries: cf. 2.20–36.

79. The phenomena of bedwetting in children and nocturnal emissions in adolescents are superficially similar; what matters here is their connection with dreams.

80. The sexual urge is an atomic mechanical response beyond our control; cf. Aristotle, *On the Movement of Animals* 703b5ff., Furley, *Two Studies in the Greek Atomists* (1967) 221–2. Observe also that the beloved may be of either sex (cf. 1053).

81. Democritus and Epicurus held that sperm is drawn from the whole body; cf. Hippocrates, *On Generation* 8.

82. Poets had long used the metaphor of the 'battle of love' (see, e.g., Ovid, *Amores* 1.9, E. J. Kenney in *Mnemosyne* 23 (1970) 380–85): L. deromanticizes the flowery metaphors into crude reality.

83. Casual pederasty seems to have been accepted in Rome (cf. Propertius 2.4.17–22, Petronius, *Satyricon* 64.5–6, J. Griffin in *Journal of Roman Studies* 66 (1976) 100–102): the boy here referred to is clearly a surrogate female ('womanish limbs').

84. The irrational nature of sexual desire is plainly expressed in the crude statement of desire; cf. Euripides, *Trojan Women* 990, where Aphrodite (goddess of love) is punned with *aphrosyne* (irrationality).

85. A loaded word in this book: if the lover can only have insubstantial atomic images, he is doomed to unhappiness.

86. The ejaculation of sperm releases frustration: it is the retention of sperm by the lover that will thus cause pain.

The locked-out lover will also harbour fatuous illusions about his beloved (1153–91).

87. Love as a sickness is a theme in classical poetry: cf. Sophocles, *Trachiniae* 445, Euripides, *Hippolytus* 477.

88. The essence of madness for the Greeks and Romans was hallucination (cf. Sophocles, *Ajax*, Euripides, *Heracles* and *Bacchae*): the lover who is deluded about his beloved is thus mad.

89. Food and drink are natural and necessary pleasures (cf. 858–76), whereas sex is natural but not necessary (cf. Introduction).

90. Cf. 1272–3, Adams, *The Latin Sexual Vocabulary* (London, 1982) 82–5.

91. The Latin word *caecus* means both 'blind' and also 'unseen'. Cf. Virgil, *Aeneid* 4.1–2.

92. And a woman's, at that. For the indignity of enslavement to a woman cf. Democritus: 'the worst insult for a man would be to be governed by a woman' (B 111 D–K). This may be a reference to the 'slavery of love' as paraded by the elegists (cf. Lyne, *Classical Quarterly* N.S. 29 (1979) 117–30, Kenney, *Mnemosyne* 23 (1970) 389).

93. For Sicyon as a source of luxury goods see A. Griffin, *Sikyon* 32 n. 2, Lucian, *Conversations with Prostitutes* 14.2.

94. Cf. Cicero, *Verrine* 2.176, 4.103, 5.27.

95. Cf. Horace, *Satires* 1.2.101–2, *Odes*, 4.13.13, Propertius 4.2.23, Griffin, *Journal of Roman Studies* 66 (1976) 92 & n. 1.

96. For the carefree love-life of the young cf. Cicero, *Pro Caelio* 42.

97. Cf. Plato, *Phaedrus* 255c.

98. The famous catalogue of euphemisms is derived from Plato, *Republic* 474d – a passage that Plutarch (*Moralia* 56d) tells us was a favourite passage of Plato in later antiquity; cf. also Sextus Empiricus, *Outlines of Pyrrhonism* 1.108. Many of the terms used are Greek, suggestive of the Hellenism that was rife in Rome at this time.

99. L. is as irrationally contemptuous of the girl as the lover is irrationally besotted.

100. The figure of the 'locked out lover' (*exclusus amator*)

serenading the beloved on her doorstep is familiar in Roman elegy and lyric poetry (e.g. Propertius 1.16.17–44, Ovid, *Amores* 1.6, Tibullus 1.2, Horace, *Odes* 1.25: see Copley, *Exclusus Amator*) and is parodied in Horace, *Epode* 11.

101. L. now moves into the acceptable form of sexual companionship based on seeing the truth.

102. For the comparison of human and animal behaviour, see note 74 above.

103. Heredity is through the stronger seed: cf. Hippocrates, *On Generation* 7.8, Aetius 5.11.3. The sex of the child is not always determined thus, however – see 1227–32.

104. The 'random' assortment of available characteristics denies any divine involvement, of course: but once the atoms have combined, there is no more 'chance' but only effects determined by their nature.

105. As, e.g., in Homer, *Iliad* 9.453–7.

106. The excess of the language here mocks the superstitious: cf. 1.84–101, 2.352–4 etc.

107. Divorce being common in Rome, at least in the upper classes. Infertility was also a common reason for divorce.

108. For the idea of children as an investment for the future cf. Homer, *Iliad* 24.540, Euripides, *Medea* 1033.

109. Not a rude remark against frigid wives, but simply the observation that wives generally want children and so do not need the lascivious movements that (he suggests) inhibit conception.

110. Agricultural metaphors are common in sexual contexts: cf. 1107, Adams, *The Latin Sexual Vocabulary* 24–5, 82–5.

111. For the importance of habit see 880, Aristotle, *Nicomachean Ethics* 1104b3–13.

BOOK FIVE

1. For the praise of Epicurus cf. 1.63–101, 3.1–30, 6.1–42.

2. Epicurus was mortal (cf. 3.1042), but his philosophy enabled him (and us) to 'live a life worthy of the gods' (3.322) and exceeded the benefits conferred on men by the 'real' gods.

3. Cf. 2.1–4.

4. Regarded by the Stoics as the ideal hero, and so ideal material for L. to denigrate. L. lists eight of his twelve 'labours' (see Graves, *The Greek Myths* 2.100–158).

5. In, for example, his lost treatise 'On the Gods' (Diogenes Laertius 10.27).

6. Cf. 4.757–76.

7. L. mocks the Aristotelian teleological view of the world many times: cf. 156–234, 2.167–82, 4.823–57, 6.379–422.

8. For the pathetic indignity of the superstitious cf. 1.62–4.

9. See Appendix B.

10. Cf. 2.1144–5.

11. The conflict of chance and necessity in Epicurus is a thorny problem (discussed in Rist, *Epicurus* 51–2). Here he would presumably argue that chance can cause/prevent the atomic collision, but that once the collision has happened, disaster is inevitable. See Introduction.

12. Epicurus, like a prophet, reveals to men what is true but hidden: this knowledge is however available to all and does not rely on the superstitious apparatus L. mocks here. Cf. Diogenes Laertius 10.12.

13. Who attempted to scale the heights of Olympus and were punished by being buried under the earth: cf., e.g., Ovid, *Metamorphoses* 1.151–62, Horace, *Odes* 3.4.42ff.

14. It is said that Anaxagoras was punished for his impiety in denying the divinity of the sun (Diogenes Laertius 2.12, Plato, *Apology* 26d).

15. For the hyperbolic *adynaton* figure cf. especially 1.881–92, 3.784–6 (with note ad loc.).

16. Thales had claimed that magnets have spirits (cf. Barnes, *The Presocratic Philosophers* 5–9), and the belief extended to other inanimate objects: hence L.'s lengthy attack on the principle here and his lengthier account of the magnet at 6.906–1089.

17. Atomic contact between the rarefied gods and our grosser world is proved impossible by the way gods can only be seen by the mind and not the senses.

18. L. does not fulfil this promise – unless the whole of

Books Five and Six are taken as proving the points necessary to establish the divine incompatibility with the known world.

19. For the serenity of the gods see Introduction and 3.18–24.

20. Cf. Theognis 425–8, Sophocles, *Oedipus Coloneus* 1225 for the full tragic view that non-existence is preferable to life: and see Diogenes Laertius 10.126 for Epicurus' criticism of this.

21. That is, a mental blueprint of a class of phenomena formed by our past experience of objects belonging to it: for this 'mental image' (*notities*, *prolepsis*) see 1046–9, 4.473–7.

22. For the diminishing returns from this sort of labour see 2.1160–74. Throughout the book L. opposes the Golden Age theory of primitive paradise.

23. Cf. [Plato] *Axiochus* 366d, Empedocles (B124 D–K) etc.

24. The word *infans* literally means 'speechless' as well as 'infant'.

25. This merely suggests that animals are better suited to their environment than we are to ours and does not refute the teleological approach to animal life.

26. The four elements of Empedocles, rejected as the ultimate constituents of matter at 1.705–829 but here seen as four types of atomic compound observable in the world.

27. NB the atoms themselves are eternal, as proved at 1.215–64: what L. refers to are the atomic compounds (*concilia*) that dissolve into their component atoms and reform as new compounds.

28. Cf. Aeschylus *Libation Bearers* 127, Thucydides 2.43.3 ('the whole earth is the tomb of famous men'). For Mother Earth cf. 795–836, 1.251.

29. For the pun whereby *radiis* means both 'rays' and also 'shuttles' see West, *The Imagery and Poetry of Lucretius* 82.

30. Cf. 2.473–7.

31. L. is presumably thinking of, for example, the eroding action of wind on soil.

32. A famous dictum of Heraclitus (*panta rhei*): L. accepts the

complete mutability of atomic compounds, but not the atoms themselves.

33. For the phenomenon of shadows cf. 4.364–78.

34. The examples are well chosen: the gods may be eternal, but their temples are not; and however great while alive, the tombs of famous men crumble to dust. For the thought cf. Shelley 'Ozymandias'.

35. For the Trojan War cf. Homer's *Iliad*: the Theban war was told of in the now lost *Thebais*. Horace developed the notion of poetic immortality ('many brave men lived before Agamemnon . . .' *Odes* 4.9.25–6).

36. The inference is invalid: and L. has earlier claimed that the world is 'past its prime' and old (2.1150–74).

37. Yet Cicero claims that Amafinius was first to write about Epicureanism in Latin (*Tusculan Disputations* 4.6, *Letters to his Friends* 15.19.2).

38. The sort of disaster that L. goes on to predict will one day destroy the earth: cf. 2.1144–9 etc. If a total destruction is possible, then partial destruction is *a fortiori* more likely.

39. If atomic collisions are random, then the equilibrium (of, for example, heat vs. water) obtaining could be upset by a random preponderance of one side or the other.

40. L. narrates the tale in parody of epic, only to dismiss it as nonsense (406). Cf. Ovid *Metamorphoses* 1.750–2.400.

41. L. mocks the 'divine' use of thunderbolts as weapons at 6.379–422.

42. E.g., Aeschylus and Euripides.

43. The tale of Deucalion (e.g., Ovid, *Metamorphoses* 1.253–415, Graves, *The Greek Myths* vol. 1.138–43).

44. L.'s main purpose here is again to deny any theological/teleological design to the world: he thus stresses the randomness of events.

45. Infinite, in fact, as the atoms are eternal: hence every possible combination will in turn be formed, including our world.

46. L. states this dogmatically – there is no evidence he can adduce to prove it.

47. Cf. Empedocles (B37 D–K).

48. A beautiful analogy: note how the 'morning' of the world is compared to the dawn of day.

49. The ancients believed that the Black Sea always flowed into the Sea of Marmora (Propontis) and never the other way.

50. Direct observation being difficult, L. offers alternative theories that at least do not contradict the known facts of atomism.

51. A difficult argument. L. seems to be asserting that the dense matter of the base of the earth blends imperceptibly into ever less dense matter, which eventually becomes fine air: hence the earth 'rests' on this 'other substance' and does not drop through the void.

52. Cf. 4.877–906.

53. An idea much ridiculed in antiquity; cf. Cicero, *On Ends* 1.6.20. The argument rests partly on Epicurus' assertion that sense-perception must be reliable, partly on the analogy of earthly fires.

54. Cf. 4.353–63. Images on their way to our eyes are roughened and blurred at the edges so that, for example, square towers look round.

55. Cf. 3.371.

56. This 'other possibility' actually attempts to answer the *second* problem posed, i.e., the reason for the sun's ecliptic course from Cancer to Capricorn. On this difficult passage see Bailey's commentary vol. iii. 1416–20.

57. As asserted by Heraclitus (B6 D–K), Xenophanes (A33 D–K) and Metrodorus of Chios (A4 D–K).

58. That is, Mount Ida in Phrygia. Matuta is the goddess of morning light, associated with Aurora.

59. Cf. 637–42 for the theory that wind currents affect the path of the sun.

60. As held by Anaximander (A22 D–K) and Xenophanes (Aetius 2.28.1).

61. Cf. Epicurus, *Letter to Pythocles* 94.

62. L. is referring to Berosus, the Chaldaean, who wrote in the third century BC and introduced much Babylonian astronomy to the Greeks. Cf. Aetius 2.28.1, 25.12, Vitruvius 9.2.1.

63. An ancient Italian goddess of fertility and flowers: she had a temple near the Circus Maximus, her own priest and games (*Ludi Florales* in late Spring).

64. Goddess of crops and the generative power of the earth.

65. Northern winds which move south for about 40 days after the rising of Sirius on 23 July. Cf. 6.716.

66. God of wine (*inter alia*).

67. A south-east wind.

68. Cf. Epicurus, *Letter to Pythocles* 96, Empedocles (B42 D–K), Anaxagoras (A42 D–K).

69. On the assumptions that a) the sun, earth and moon are (at the moon's eclipse) in a straight line, and b) that the sun is as small as it looks from the earth (564–74) and thus the massive earth casts a divergent conical shadow.

70. As asserted by Empedocles (Aetius 5.26.4)

71. Cf. Empedocles (B82 D–K).

72. A gross parody of the Stoic theory: cf. 2.1153–4.

73. As held by, e.g., Anaximander (A30 D–K).

74. Cf. 2.871 (& n. 87), 899 etc.

75. An idea attributed to Epicurus by Censorinus, *On the Birthday* 4.9 (Usener 333), but already found in the fifth-century BC thinker Archelaus (A1, A4 D–K).

76. The cold, frost and winds were as young and feeble as the living things. Cf. 925–87, Virgil, *Georgics* 2.338.

77. Cf. 2.1150–74.

78. In the absence of all teleological direction, the random collisions of atoms would produce every possible form, of which only some could survive.

79. The same three species are endowed with the same qualities at 3.741–3; cf. Aristotle, *Natural History of Animals* 488b15.

80. L. – ever ready to refute superstition – now proves biologically what he has already shown in atomic terms at 2.700–717 and in phenomenological terms at 4.732–48.

81. Cf. 4.732, Ovid, *Amores* 3.12.21.

82. Cf. 4.640–41, 6.970–72.

83. The name Chimera means 'she-goat' in Greek. Cf. 2.705, Homer, *Iliad* 6.181–2.

84. Primitive man was bigger (925–30), but not ludicrously large as the mythical Giants were. L. here refers to Atlas.

85. On L.'s view of early man and the concept of progress see Introduction.

86. An idea developed later 1019–25.

87. L. takes a lot of trouble to refute a theory for which we have no evidence earlier than this passage. The fanciful idea of men fearing eternal night is contrasted with the far more realistic fear of being eaten in the dark.

88. A vital paragraph in L.'s ethical theory; see Introduction.

89. Something of a cliché: cf. Aeschylus, *Seven against Thebes* 1020–21, Gorgias (B5a D–K), Ennius, *Annales* 138–9v, etc.

90. Cf. 2.557–9. For the folly of sailing cf. Virgil, *Georgics* 1.254. Propertius 3.7.37.

91. A textually corrupt line: the reading translated offers a double contrast between self-inflicted accident and deliberate homicide.

92. Often called the 'social contract' theory of justice: cf. Plato, *Republic* 2.358–9, and contrast the theory of inborn justice found in, for example, Cicero, *On Duties* 1.157–60.

93. Cf. Epicurus, *Letter to Herodotus* 75–6, Diodorus Siculus 1.8.3–4.

94. As suggested by, e.g., Democritus (B26 D–K), Plato, *Cratylus* 388e–390e, *Protagoras* 322a5–6.

95. *Notities, prolepsis*: see 181–6 & note 21, 2.745.

96. From Epirus in north-west Greece: good hunting and sheep-dogs.

97. Cf. Horace, *Odes* 3.17.12–13.

98. And not Prometheus stealing it from the gods, as in the myth. For the analysis of lightning see 6.160–218.

99. Here follows one of L.'s few ethical passages: cf. 2.1–61, 3.59–73, 830–1094.

100. Cf. Sisyphus at 3.995–1002.

101. Metaphorically speaking, of course: L. (in Book 3) has proved that the Underworld (Tartarus) does not exist as a place of torment.

102. *Lathe biosas* ('live in secret') was one of Epicurus' most famous slogans.

103. Which are the only 'true' sources of our knowledge of the world: see 4.478–521.

104. This sentence has more ethical than historical truth: the pride of kingship *is* humbled, but many societies have never abandoned their monarchies.

105. L.'s language here suggests that laws were a compromise, justice being (on balance) a lesser irritant than injustice.

106. In Glaucon's tale of Gyges and his ring (Plato, *Republic* 2.359d–360d), where Gyges becomes invisible and so can always escape detection for his crimes, it is assumed that even just men will seek to commit unjust acts if they can be sure of escaping detection. L.'s answer to this is simply to deny that any man ever could be *sure* of escaping detection, and that the consequent fear would upset his tranquillity.

107. Cf. 4.1018–19.

108. Epicurus did not doubt their existence – the truth of our perceptions of them assures that (*Letter to Menander* 123) – but urges against fear of them.

109. Cf. 6.76–7, Sextus Empiricus, *Against the Mathematicians* 9.25, Cicero, *On the Nature of the Gods* 1.46.

110. Cf. 4.788–801.

111. Cf. Empedocles B124 (D–K).

112. Cf. Diogenes Laertius 10.10 and see 1203, 6.68–78 for a definition of real Epicurean worship of the gods.

113. As placed at crossroads or boundaries; cf. Theophrastus, *Characters* 16.5.

114. As faced first by the Romans in 280 BC when Pyrrhus (319–272 BC) used them at Lucania (cf. 1302).

115. The ceremonial rods and axes carried by the lictors (attendants of senior state officials), here standing for the power itself.

116. For the explanation of earthquakes see 6.535–607.

117. *Aes* can mean both 'copper' and 'bronze', but L. almost certainly means the alloy from here onwards in his description of the uses of the metal.

118. Note how L. plays repeatedly on the parallel military and agricultural uses of metals.

119. In fact chariots preceded cavalry.

120. Cf. 3.642.

121. Elephants, so called because they were first seen in Pyrrhus' army in Lucania (Pliny, *Natural History* 8.16).

122. A difficult and brutal paragraph reminiscent at times of the Roman games rather than ancient warfare.

123. L. suddenly undermines the whole detailed picture he has created: the hyperbole of the battle-scene is now deflated by common sense.

124. For this common ancient view cf. Plato, *Republic* 455c.

125. Cf. Democritus (B154 D–K) for the theory that we learnt the arts from nature – weaving from the spider, etc.

126. Cf. 2.29–33. L. seems to be equating the life of primitive man with the ideal Epicurean life.

127. That is, once the pain of need has been satisfied, pleasure can be varied but not increased. On the Epicurean doctrine of pleasure, see Introduction.

128. Cf. 326–7.

BOOK SIX

1. The prologue depicts Athens as mother of crops and good things: the epilogue sees Athens as place of disease and death (1138–1286).

2. Cf. Cicero, *For Flaccus* 26.62.

3. Epicurus: for his 'oracular' powers cf. 1.738–9, 5.111–12.

4. Cf. Homer, *Odyssey* 8.74.

5. As the wise man will be contented with a little: cf. 2.20–36.

6. A metaphor for the mind of man; cf. 3.1003–10.

7. That is, pleasure – but see Introduction for discussion of this concept.

8. Cf. 5.195–234.

9. 35–41 = 2.55–61 = 3.87–93.

10. 5.91–770.

11. Probably imitating Parmenides (B1 D–K).

12. Cf. 1.63, 69, 5.1200.

13. See 3.18–24.

14. As in the legends of, for example, Niobe, Arachne, Pentheus.

15. The Etruscans divided the sky into sixteen areas and then observed the movements of, for example, lightning in the different zones.

16. The Muse especially associated with epic poetry (cf. Empedocles B131 D–K). See Appendix A.

17. It was portentous if it did: cf. Horace, *Odes* 1.34.5–8, Virgil, *Aeneid* 9.630. For Epicurus' analysis of thunder see *Letter to Pythocles* 100.

18. Cf. 4.75–83.

19. Cf. Aristophanes, *Clouds* 404ff.

20. Cf. 1.271–97.

21. The simile is based on Homer, *Odyssey* 9.391–3.

22. The famous oracle of Apollo at Delphi.

23. For Epicurus' explanation see Diogenes Laertius 10.1012.

24. Cf. Homer, *Odyssey* 5.490, Virgil, *Aeneid* 6.6–7.

25. 124–9.

26. Cf. 306–7, Aristotle, *On the Heavens* 289a19–26, Virgil, *Aeneid* 9.588, Livy 28.37.6.

27. L. is thinking of the beasts penned up to be used in the hunting-displays in the arena.

28. For Epicurus' analysis see Diogenes Laertius 10.103–4.

29. Cf. 1.489–90, 4.595–614.

30. Cf. Pliny, *Natural History* 2.51.137.

31. 251–4 is modelled on 4.170–33.

32. Cf. Homer, *Iliad* 4.275–9.

33. 206–10.

34. The image is of a Cyclopean workshop: cf. Apollonius Rhodius, *Argonautica* 1.730–34.

35. As in the myth of Deucalion (5.411–15, Ovid, *Metamorphoses* 1.313–415).

36. Cf. 178–9.

37. On the 'snowballing' theory of kinetic energy cf. 4.193–4.

38. As autumn and spring have a natural mixture of heat and cold.

39. Cf. 86–8. There follows another anti-theological passage: cf. 2.167–82, 4.823–57, 5.110–234.

40. Often called simply 'the Thunderer' (*Tonans*).

41. Cf. Hesiod, *Theogony* 820–80, Virgil, *Aeneid* 1.44.

42. For the rationalist questions which follow cf. 2.1102–4, Cicero, *On Divination* 2.19.45, Aristophanes, *Clouds* 401–2.

43. The rhetorical climax; cf. Aristophanes, *Clouds* 401.

44. See Diogenes Laertius 10.104–5 for Epicurus' explanation of this phenomenon. Cf. also Aristotle, *Meteorology*. 369a10ff.

45. Cf. Diogenes Laertius 10.99.

46. Cf. Xenophanes fr. 30, Hippocrates, *Airs Waters Places* 8.

47. L. is now answering the unspoken question 'What stops the clouds from ascending indefinitely into the limitless sky?'

48. 1. 958–1051.

49. Cf. Diogenes Laertius 10.99–100.

50. L. has only just (471–2) shown clothes hanging out and absorbing moisture: now he compares the clouds to fleeces hanging out.

51. Cf. Diogenes Laertius 10.109–110.

52. Cf. Diogenes Laertius 10.105–6.

53. Shown at 5.91–109, 235–415.

54. In the fifth century BC: cf. Strabo 1.3.16.

55. In 373–372 BC the towns of Helice and Buris, near Aegium, were destroyed by an earthquake.

56. An abrupt change of topic – the following paragraph may be out of place in the manuscript.

57. That is, the sun only takes a small part of any area of the sea, but the total area of the sea is so vast that the sun must take up a vast amount of water in all.

58. The most famous active volcano known to L.'s readers, having erupted in 475 BC, 396 BC and 122 BC (when the whole city of Catana was destroyed: cf. Cicero, *On the Nature of the Gods* 2.38.96). It was also invested with superstitious tales of giants buried underneath it: cf. *Oxford Classical Dictionary* s.v. 'Giants'.

59. Erysipelas, linked by Celsus (5.28.4) with herpes.

60. For the trick of putting words into the mouth of the imaginary opponent cf. 3.894–9. L.'s answer is based on Sextus Empiricus *Outlines of Pyrrhonism* 1.142.

61. Where empirical evidence is unavailable to decide between them, and so long as they do not conflict with empirical evidence which we do have. See Long and Sedley, *The Hellenistic Philosophers* 90–97.

62. Cf. 5.742: north winds which move for about 40 days after the rising of the dog-star Sirius on 23 July. For the theory cf. Thales A16 (D–K), Herodotus 2.20.

63. Cf. Herodotus 2.22.

64. As first asserted by Democritus (A99 D–K).

65. Seneca (*Natural Questions* 4.2.17) ascribed this idea to Anaxagoras.

66. In Greek, *aornos* means 'birdless'. Lake Avernus is near Cumae and was regarded by some as the entrance to the Underworld (cf. 762–3).

67. Cecrops' three daughters disobeyed Athena's command and opened the chest containing the infant Erichthonius: a passing crow saw and reported this to the goddess, who punished the crow by banishing all crows from the area for ever. See Graves, *The Greek Myths* vol 1.96–100. The 'Grecian bards' include Callimachus, *Hecale* fr. 260.

68. Not otherwise attested.

69. For this interesting theory see Pliny, *Natural History* 28.42.149, who attributes the same power to elephants.

70. For the relativity of different foods see 4.633–72.

71. Cf. Virgil, *Eclogues* 10.76. Mynors on Virgil, *Georgics* 1.121.

72. Not otherwise attested.

73. Cf. Aristotle, *Natural History of Animals* 604b29ff. For epilepsy see 3.489 and note.

74. Cf. Aristotle, 5.444b31 *On Perception and the Perceptible*.

75. A town in Thrace famed for its mines: see Herodotus 6.46.3. The mines became Athenian property when Thasos was taken in 464/3 BC (Thucydides 1.101).

76. The workers were slaves.

77. The Latin word *aestum* here means 'exhalation' as well as 'vertigo' – *aestus* will cause *aestus*.

78. An Egyptian sky-god: on this spring see Herodotus 4.181.

79. At Dodona in Epirus in Northern Greece, a place famous for the oracular oak tree of Zeus, a speaking dove and the spring here described: cf. Herodotus 2.55.7, Pliny, *Natural History* 2.103.228.

80. An island off the coast of Phoenicia: Pliny, *Natural History* 2.102.227, Strabo 16.2.13.

81. L. devotes a good deal of time to this because of the superstitious wonder it aroused: Thales has declared that magnets 'have souls' because they can move. (Diogenes Laertius 1.24); see also Plato, *Timaeus* 80c, *Ion* 533d–e.

82. In Lydia.

83. As explained in Book 4.

84. 1.329–69.

85. Cf. 4.595–614.

86. Relativity of effects was a favourite argument of the Sceptics: cf. 4.469–521, Long and Sedley, *The Hellenistic Philosophers* 1.468–88.

87. Cf. Sextus Empiricus, *Against the Mathematicians* 9.246–51.

88. Cf. Diogenes Laertius 9.80, Annas and Barnes, *The Modes of Scepticism* 57–65.

89. Sextus Empiricus strengthens the contrast by having the pigs actually eat the excrement they wallow in (Diogenes Laertius 9.80).

90. Cf. 4.643–72.

91. As discussed in Book 4: hearing at 4.524–614, taste at 4.615–72, smell at 4.673–705.

92. Cf. 4.176–215, 2.62–332, Rist, *Epicurus* 46–52, Long and Sedley, *The Hellenistic Philosophers* 1.46–52.

93. An island in the north of the Aegean Sea, not especially noted in antiquity for making iron rings: but its old name Electris reminds us of *electrum* – amber, linked with magnets by, for example, Plato, *Timaeus* 80c.

94. That is, repulsion, not attraction.

95. Cf. note 46, p. 208.

96. That is, chrysocolla ('Gold-glue').

97. A reminder of the ring image with which the passage on the magnet began (910–11).

98. Relevant here both because they can arise from the air and because the superstitious ascribe their origin to the gods.

99. As often, the fact that beasts suffer as well as men indicates the atomic, non-theological cause: cf., e.g., 4.984–1010.

100. 769–80.

101. For the link between disease, heat and moisture cf. Hippocrates, *Epidemics* 1.

102. Cf. Hippocrates, *Airs Waters Places*.

103. In northern Asia Minor, famed as the home of Mithridates whose ambitions had provoked three wars with Rome in the previous generation.

104. The four points of the compass are represented by Britain (West), Egypt (East), Pontus (North) and Cadiz downwards (South).

105. Elephantiasis – produces grotesque swelling and unsightly skin. Cf. Pliny, *Natural History* 26.2.8.

106. No other ancient evidence links Attica and Achaea especially with foot and eye diseases.

107. For discussion of the difficulties of interpreting the epilogue to the poem see Appendix E.

108. L. bases his account on that of Thucydides 2.47–52. This book ends, as it began, with Athens.

109. Legendary king of Athens.

110. Cf. 660.

111. One of L.'s main ethical themes: but the mutilated wretches here cannot be equated with the ignorant fools of 3.31–90.

112. Breaking a strong taboo in ancient thought: cf. Sophocles, *Antigone*.

113. For animals suffering the plague cf. Homer, *Iliad* 1.48ff. – but the pathos is original in L.

114. Personified: cf. Nature in 3.931–51.
115. It is arguable that lines 1247–51 should be transferred to the end of the poem to provide a more complete sense of an ending.
116. Poverty caused lack of space, which increased the risk of infection.
117. The rural poor came into Athens to escape the Spartans ravaging their land.
118. A grim sentence: the gods' temples were perhaps crowded with the superstitious seeking divine cures – and the attendants who normally looked after living guests found their 'guests' were corpses.
119. The final sentence is chilling: the living are injuring themselves to bury the dead (in vain as the dead cannot be helped by their efforts), showing us a picture of humanity still racked with futile pain and fear.

The Prelude to the Poem

The opening of any long work of literature is bound to be important in our interpretation of the whole. The openings of Homer's *Iliad* and *Odyssey*, for instance, in their different ways set the tone and the themes for all that is to come. When we look at the opening to this poem, however, we immediately encounter problems that concern the entire work.

The problems are basically twofold. In the first place, how can Lucretius dare to pray to the goddess Venus to become his ally in composing verse when the whole thrust of his anti-theological arguments later on will deny any possibility of the gods intervening in human life? Second, what is Lucretius doing writing verse at all, when Epicurus seems to have advised against poetry? Above all, why is Lucretius composing this sort of poetry – full of myth, hymn-formulas and richly ornamented language?

I will examine the two problems in reverse order, beginning with Epicurus' antipathy to poetry. 'Sail past it with stopped ears, as from the Sirens' song' (Plutarch, *de poetis audiendis* 15d) he is said to have said. He insisted on the use of simple and appropriate language:

> The terms he used for things were the ordinary terms, and Aristophanes the grammarian credits him with a very characteristic style. He was so lucid a writer that in the work *On Rhetoric* he makes clearness the sole requisite (Diogenes Laertius 10.13).

The two faults with conventional poetry were its form and its content: the luxuriously unnecessary ornamentation of its language and the mythological lies it told about the world and the gods. We see a glimpse of the first point in 3.131–4:

> drop this name 'harmony' that was passed down to the musicians from the heights of Helicon – or else perhaps they

fetched it themselves from some other source and applied it to the matter of their art, which had then no name of its own.

The word for 'applied' (*transferre*) almost certainly translates the Greek μεταφέρειν, from which our word 'metaphor' derives, and suggests that Lucretius is consciously rejecting what Kenney (in his note on 3.133–4) calls 'second-hand metaphor'. Epicurus seems to reject poetry because it sets up words that deliberately confuse the reader with metaphorical imagery that is patently untrue. It cannot be accidental that when Lucretius is describing the origins and growth of music and poetry he places it in a solidly simple rustic context: 5.1379–1411 explicitly draws the comparison between the artistic pleasure of primitive man and the more 'cultivated' accomplishments of today – in good Epicurean terms, the pleasure can only be varied, not increased, and there is distinct disapproval emerging of the 'new' as unnecessary and decadent (1412–35). This would suggest that, just as bread is easier to obtain and therefore preferable to caviare, so also whistling on a reed is preferable to getting hold of an epic poem on Epicureanism. Poetry is perhaps not always anathema to the Epicurean in all circumstances – it may after all contribute to our serenity and it would fall under the class of pleasures that are natural but not necessary, like sex – but we have still not begun to answer the two main criticisms of poetry advanced by Epicurus, namely its deliberately obfuscating use of metaphor (instead of clear speech) and its encouraging of beliefs in the silly stories of the gods. The prelude to this poem seems to break both rules.

One answer given to this problem is that of Waszink ('Lucretius and Poetry' *Mededelingen der koninklijke Nederlandse Akademie van Wetenschappen* 17 (1954) 243–57), who urges that Lucretius was heavily influenced by Empedocles – whom it was customary for Epicureans to despise – and Parmenides, seeing their choice of poetry and in particular their equation of poetry with light and light with truth as inspiration for his own efforts. At all events, says Waszink, the 'mission' to convert is central, the poetry being very much the means to that end and not the end in itself. Following a similar line, Classen ('Poetry and Rhetoric in Lucretius' *T.A.P.A.* 99 (1968) 110–18) urges that Lucretius' first duty was to the 'mission' to convert us from fear of the gods and fear of death, and that he was prepared to use all possible means to achieve this, even ones of which Epicurus might not have approved. In other words, Lucretius was far too original and talented a writer to have been tied slavishly to every letter of what Epicurus had said. Epicurus is praised lavishly in the prologues to books 3, 5 and 6: but so is Empedocles (1.716–33), who wrote his philosophy in didactic verse and gave it the same title as this poem: so also is Ennius (1.117–26), whose ideas on our survival of death may have been wrong but whose verse was 'everlasting'. So also is Homer (3.1037–8). Lucretius used the ideas of Epicurus as scientific justification for his ethical precepts, but his beliefs transcended and developed those of the master, not least in this matter of their exposition.

We are still left with the 'mythology' of the prelude – especially when we are presented with an anthropomorphic picture of Venus and Mars reclining together and thus bringing about the peace that the poet prays for. The abrupt insertion of the 'correct' view of Epicurus' gods (2.646–51) after 1.43 – if not an interpolation by a waggish scribe or a puzzled reader – was done by the poet to disabuse us of the philosophical errors while leaving the power of the poetry undiminished. One thing is of course clear. Whatever interpretation we arrive at, we cannot sensibly ignore the contradiction and see this presentation of the gods as simply theology. There must be more to it than that.

One obvious line of inquiry is to see Venus as a symbolic figure representing the 'force of nature', which by its reproductive delight brings into being all the myriad life-forms we see around us. Lucretius several times uses a personification of Nature (e.g., 3.931–51, with Brown, *Lucretius on Love and Sex* 229) just as elsewhere he plays on the mythical figure of Mother Earth (e.g. 5.795–836): it may be that Venus is at one level a personified force in the same way. A further look at her character makes this more compelling.

Venus is at once glossed as 'delight/pleasure of men and gods, life-giving' (1.1–2). It is not coincidental that the highest good in Epicurus' moral system is pleasure, and that the poet is thus fixing his moral colours to the mast right away. The passage goes on to describe Venus' activities in terms of sunlight, life, warmth, spring, and Venus is seen as the force behind all of this – *Venus physica* to the Romans – in a way calculated to dispel at once any suggestion that this Epicurean atomism is a gloomy picture of the world in which cold dark atoms collide in a futile random manner and we might as well – and could as well – be dead. The rest of the poem will demonstrate that there is no theological purpose to the collisions of atoms, and that the source of everything we know is simply atomic movement, which in turn is blindly caused by weight: but in this burst of poetry we see the poet rejoicing in the free gift that is life and joy, recognizing that within the breasts of living things there is undeniably a *force*, an instinct towards warmth and reproduction which is the source of our creative joy and survival. This force may be atomically determined and blind – but the opening paean of the poem is a celebration of it. This sort of allegorical address to Venus (Aphrodite in Greek) had already been done in, for example, the *Homeric Hymn to Aphrodite* 1–5, Euripides, *Hippolytus* 447–50, 1272–81, Parmenides B12.3–6 (D–K) and Empedocles B17, 22, 35, 71 (D–K), Lucretius himself addresses Nature as 'creatress of the universe' at 1.629, 2.1117, 5.1362. What is more, Venus is exactly what the poet calls the sexual urge in Book Four. This sort of allegory is mentioned at 2.655–60 as being allowable, provided that the reader 'genuinely refrains from polluting his mind with the foul taint of superstition.'

This line of argument becomes more difficult to sustain when the allegory becomes too specific and mythological – in particular when Mars enters and reclines with the goddess, and the poet then prays for peace to be granted (31–2): 'for you alone have power to bestow on mortals the blessing of quiet peace'. It is all very well to see Venus as symbolizing pleasure, peace and life, but now we have to see Mars as the contrary force of death, pain and war and pray the one to beguile the other into submission. The two forces of Empedocles spring to mind, where Love and Strife fight it out for supremacy of the universe – and we have seen how great an admiration Lucretius has for Empedocles – but the identification is left to be inferred with no help from the poet.

If pressed, Lucretius would perhaps have defended his 'hymn' as follows: prayer is a perfectly proper activity in which to engage, so long as it is recognized that it will not produce reactions from the gods. We contemplate the divine images (*simulacra*) of gods (6.58–79) and are ourselves shaped ⟨by the impact of the images⟩ to resemble those perfect paragons of serenity. The poet thus transforms the images being contemplated from a rampant god of War to a pacified god of War being embraced by Venus, thus inculcating the sort of contemplation which *will* bring us peace if we allow it to shape our minds.

Bignone (*Storia della letterature latina* vol. 2 134–342) has further argued ingeniously that, as Venus is pleasure, she is first of all (1–20) the kinetic sexual pleasure which reproduces ourselves, but then switches to the katastematic pleasure of serenity, peace, friendship. It is as the embodiment of the latter sort of pleasure that she is in a position to represent the peace and serenity that Lucretius needs to write the poem and Memmius needs to read it. The incongruous lines 44–9 would then find a place as explaining how the gods practise this serenity which Venus has by now come to represent. This is surely going too far. We must not forget that this is a prelude to a poem, not an epilogue, and that the first-time reader cannot be expected to pick up detailed points about the nature of Epicurean pleasure in cryptic form without any explanation.

A simpler form of allegory is produced if we examine the polarity in lines 21–43 between peace and creativity on the one hand and war and death on the other. Lucretius elsewhere (2.569–72) speaks of the opposing forces of 'destructive motions' and 'generative and augmentative motions', and points to the equilibrium between the two, the cry of infants mingling with the wailing of those mourning the dead. Here in this passage he assumes that life has the upper hand (temporarily?)

over death, Venus over Mars, creation over destruction, peace over war: such is the interpretation of Giancotti. There are, however, still other factors to be introduced.

Venus is amongst other things the patron goddess of at least one branch of the Memmii family (see Appendix B) and appeared on coins of the family. More important, Venus is addressed at once as *Aeneadum genetrix* (Mother of the sons of Aeneas) before she is given her proper name, an epic title referring back to Ennius *Annales* 52 and the whole mythology that saw the Roman race as descended from the Trojan prince Aeneas, himself the son of Venus. Any doubt that this is going to be an epic poem is dispelled before it can arise and – more important still – it is going to be a quintessentially Roman poem. No mere copy or translation of a Greek original but a new creation for Roman readers, referring to Roman figures and Roman life: see, for example, the references to 'this evil hour of my country's history' (41), the named references to Roman people such as Scipio (3.1034) and Ennius (1.117–26) and the frequent allusions to features of Roman life from Etruscan scrolls (6.381) to hunting-dogs (4.991–7) to the locked-out lover pining on the doorstep (4.1177–84). The hymn-formula of the prelude may be Greek and traditional, but the contents are pure Roman.

There is one final point to be made here. Some commentators have spoken of the prelude – as they have of the epilogue – as 'l'anti-Lucrèce chez Lucrèce', as showing the poet's 'real' religious feelings emerging through the clenched teeth of his affected atomism, and have pointed to the prayer to justify that allegation. I hope to have shown that it is at least arguable that Lucretius intends us to see Venus in symbolic terms as the source of vitality in the world, as the representative in particular of the Roman race and its burgeoning growth and expansion – at which point the 'evil hour of my country's history'(41) takes on a sharper focus – and as the sign that the poem which is about to unfold will be epic in the grand style. It remains however to be explained why he did not address the Muse(s) as was customary in the epic tradition, and as he himself does at 6.92–5. After all, Homer and Hesiod address the Muses and such an invocation would have occasioned none of this agonizing about the 'sincerity' of the poet's beliefs but would simply have been seen as a trademark of the genre. What did Venus have to offer which made her preferable to the ancient Muses?

One possible answer, I think, lies in the resonance of the word Venus and its derivatives *venustas/venustus*. The word means 'charm', especially charm in appearance and style, and used to describe people and writing displaying the key facets of elegance, style, even sex-appeal. The link between Venus and *venustus* is made explicitly in Catullus (e.g., 3.1–2; 86) and the qualities implicit in the word *venustas* – along with words such as *lepidus* (cf. *lepore* in line 15 and asked for explicitly at 28) are precisely those espoused by the so-called 'New Poets' of Catullus and his generation. Catullus, for example, uses *lepidus* at 1.1 and 6.17, where he applies the term to his poetry; the word may be derived from the Greek *leptos* used in important Hellenistic programmatic texts such as the preface to Callimachus' *Aitia* 24 – the etymology is not watertight but at least the similarity of sound is there. It may be far-fetched to suggest that Lucretius is here making a claim to the same aspirations as those of the New Poets – he would not, for instance, agree to their aim of 'art for art's sake' but sees art as ancillary to philosophy (4.18–25) – but the correspondence between Venus and *Venustas* and the typically neoteric appeal for *leporem* cannot be overlooked and cast doubt on the traditional picture of Lucretius as a literary loner. To open a poem in the late republic – the age of the New Poets – addressing Venus and asking for 'her' to grant *leporem* (grace) to the poetry – rather than the traditional address to the Muses followed by a 'syllabus' of content – is arguably a sign that this poet was heavily influenced by the notions of poetic technique and refinement so typical of the Hellenistic poets such as Callimachus and by the movement of young poets centred around Catullus whom we call the New Poets.

Memmius

Much of ancient poetry was dedicated to a named individual, in a long tradition of literary patronage. Virgil dedicated his *Georgics* for instance to Augustus' friend and political associate Maecenas, Horace dedicated his poems to a wide range of friends and patrons. This poem is repeatedly addressed to a certain Memmius, and it must be worth examining what we know about this figure. It is worth saying at the outset, however, that Lucretius' dedication of the poem is not simply an empty convention. The poet did not compose the work and then find a name on which to pin it: on the contrary, the poet addresses Memmius many times in the course of the poem in terms which suggest that the desire to convert the addressee is at least one main reason for writing the poem in the first place.

The Memmius addressed is usually agreed to be Gaius Memmius who married a daughter of the dictator Sulla. He was quaestor to Pompey in Spain in 77, tribune in 66 and praetor in 58 BC. It was in that year of street violence and political uncertainty that he attacked Caesar in the Senate (Suetonius, *Julius Caesar* 23); in the following year he went to Bithynia as governor, returning to Rome to stand for the consulship with the support of that same Caesar whom he had attacked as praetor in 58. His failure to secure election was the result of an electoral scandal in which he attempted to do a deal with the consuls of 54 to secure his election for 53 (on which, see Cicero, *Letters to his Brother Quintus* 3.2.3; 8.3., and E. S. Gruen, 'The Consular Elections for 53 BC' in J. Bibauw, *Hommages à Marcel Renard*). It failed, and he was convicted of bribery and went into exile in Athens in 52. We do not know if he ever came back to Rome before his death sometime before 46.

His literary tastes are well known. He was apparently something of an expert in Greek literature but contemptuous of Latin (Cicero *Brutus* 70.247) and would have been a formidable orator if he had not avoided 'the labour not only of speaking but even of thinking'. When he was governor in Bithynia he was accompanied by the poets Catullus and Helvius Cinna – that famous 'Cinna the poet' whom Shakespeare shows us being murdered by the mob after Caesar's death (*Julius Caesar* III.3). This encouragement of young poets was not unparalleled – Tibullus, for instance, was going to join the staff of Messala in the East (Tibullus 1.3.2). Memmius' own attempts to write love poetry are mentioned by Ovid (*Tristia* 2.433) and Pliny (5.3.5). His private life was also well known, and was scandalous in an age not easily scandalized: he tried, for instance, to seduce the wife of Pompey the Great by sending her an amorous letter (Suetonius, *On Grammarians* 14), and his wife Fausta was also famous for the number of her lovers.

His relations with the Epicureans in Athens where he settled in exile were not good: he acquired the ruins of Epicurus' old house and declared his intention of demolishing them and erecting a new building on the site. The head of the Epicurean group in Athens, Patro, met Cicero and asked him to intervene with Memmius for the safety of the house. The letter which Cicero wrote to him is preserved (*Letters to his Friends* 13.1) and makes fascinating reading, not least because it contains not a single word about Lucretius or any debt of obligation which the dedication of this great literary work could have occasioned in Memmius. (It is even suggested, for example by D.P. Fowler, 'Lucretius and Politics' in Griffin and Barnes, *Philosophia Togata*, 122, that Cicero apologizes for the poem; he pleads with Memmius: 'if your feelings have been hurt, however little, by the unreasonable behaviour of certain persons ...' referring perhaps to the unwelcome mockery caused by dedicating an Epicurean epic to so unphilosophical a man as Memmius.) Or, alternatively, one might conjecture that the patron had failed to encourage the poet, causing Lucretius (and his circle, if he had one) to grumble about the ingratitude of the patron – leading Cicero not to mention Lucretius by name but to refer to the 'behaviour of certain people'. All this is pure speculation, of course, attempting to fill the gaps in our knowledge about the relations between poet and patron.

There is, at any rate, something odd about a poet dedicating a major epic to a man whose life and character put him out of sympathy with the philosophy being expounded. Would the rake and scoundrel actually *read* the thing?

The references in the poem to 'an illustrious scion of the house of Memmius' (1.42–3), or the poet's desire that his verses should be 'worthy of your calling and character' probably put the identification of the well-known patron beyond doubt. What we know of his ruthless unscrupulous political tactics, his notorious sex drive and his intellectual laziness make him an ideal subject for persuasion – Lucretius was not intending to preach to the converted or to tilt at windmills. M.F. Smith has argued interestingly (Loeb xlvii–xlviii) that Memmius may perhaps have expressed interest in Epicureanism when he heard that it elevated pleasure to the highest good, only to lose heart when he discovered that it required disciplined philosophical study rather than simply physical gratification. Lucretius appears to tire of his addressee as the poem progresses (Wormell, 'The Personal World of Lucretius' in Dudley, *Lucretius*, 42), and it has been shown that the frequency with which Memmius is personally named diminishes in the course of the work (see Townend, 'The Fading of Memmius', *Classical Quarterly* 28 (1978) 267–283). It has further been urged – more speculatively – that Lucretius originally dedicated the work to Caesar, changing to Memmius later on (Louise Adam Hollands, *Lucretius and the Transpadanes* 101–115). All these in their different ways point to the same phenomenon: Memmius is more than merely a token dedicatee, but he is not kept centre-stage throughout; and the poem is not written exclusively for him. To some extent this is in itself not surprising, since most ancient poems stand or fall by other criteria than simply their suitability for the named addressee. If not, then reading poems might become a form of legal eavesdropping.

A superficially more promising line of inquiry would use Memmius to help explain the use of Venus in the prelude to the poem (on which see Appendix A): it has been pointed out (by Munro, vol. 2, 121) that coins of the Memmii in the Galeria tribe have Venus on them: one might add that Virgil, *Aeneid* 5.117 (explicitly linking Memmius with the Trojan Mnestheus) gives an excellent reason for opening the poem addressed to him with the title 'Sons of Aeneas'. Alas, the evidence of the coinage is not watertight – our Memmius may belong to a different part of the family than the Memmii on the coins (Wiseman, 'The Two Worlds of Titus Lucretius' in *Cinna the Poet*, 38–9 & nn.). It can still be urged, however (as, for example, by M. F. Smith, Loeb edition xlix–l), that Lucretius uses Memmius almost as an excuse to compose the sort of poetry which Epicurus would have despised, to suit the patron whom he wished to convert: the poetry is more than once described as the honey on the cup to trick the reader into drinking the (otherwise bitter) medicine (1.921–50, 4.1–25), and an addressee of literary taste but dubious moral and intellectual gifts would therefore need precisely this sort of an enticement to read on. This may indeed help to explain the choice of poetry to persuade Memmius, but it only pushes the question further back: why not choose to address a more philosophical and worthy man, and thus keep faith with both patron and master? Did the poet 'sell out' to the un-Epicurean world of politics in his recognition that 'at such a crisis (Memmius) cannot withhold his service from the common weal' at 1.41–3? Does he contradict his thesis that gods do not listen to our prayers by praying to Venus simply as a bouquet to Memmius' patron deity? It is difficult to imagine Lucretius letting the tail wag the dog in this way, and further thoughts on the famous prelude are to be found in Appendix A.

Smallest Parts

The atomic theory as developed by Epicurus postulates, as we have seen, that matter can be split into tiny invisible indivisible particles. These atoms cannot be divided any further, but they, like everything else, have parts, in that one could (with sufficient magnification) point to 'the part nearest the right' or 'the top half' of an atom, especially in view of the fact that they are three-dimensional. These 'parts' are obviously not perceptible to the naked eye, and can thus only be logically inferred. It may be wondered why Lucretius bothers to mention them at all (1.599–634), and to what extent Aristotle was right to see them as a surrender to the arguments of Zeno of Elea.

Let us begin with Zeno. The famous paradoxes that bear his name seek to prove such apparently absurd statements as 'motion is impossible' or that Achilles will never overtake the tortoise in his race if the tortoise is given a start, however small. Most of them rest on the notion of infinite divisibility or dichotomy. So, for instance, if I wish to travel from A to B, I must move along the whole distance AB. But the line AB consists of an infinite range of points {p1, p2, p3 . . . pn} and to reach B I must pass each of these points. Thus I need to perform an infinite number of tasks to reach B, as each point on the way is logically a separate task, and an infinite series of tasks will take me an infinite amount of time. I do not have an infinite amount of time. I will therefore never reach B.

This sort of dichotomy becomes more relevant to our enquiries when applied to matter itself. A point, we are told, has location but no magnitude: but Epicurus' atoms are not points for the very reason that the aggregate of atoms makes matter but the aggregate of points without magnitude would add up to nothing. Now if an amount of matter has magnitude, it can be divided, as there is no number that cannot be halved. What, then, is to prevent us splitting the atoms themselves – with mathematics if not with a knife? Just as space, in the first paradox, is imagined to be continuous and Euclidean, so in this case matter is also seen as continuous. Now a primary argument of Epicurus is that if matter is infinitely divisible, then nothing would exist – as the destruction of atomic compounds is always easier than building them up, and so destruction would always have the upper hand (*Letter to Herodotus* 40–41): furthermore (in Zenonian terms) it would take an infinite number of tasks to make anything, and the time since the world began has not been infinite. Furthermore, an infinite array of parts each of which possesses magnitude would add up to an infinite magnitude, which would mean that each atom was the size of the whole universe itself (1.615–26 and Epicurus, *Letter to Herodotus* 57), which is patently not the case. Therefore there must be a minimum magnitude, and hence matter and space must be in some sense 'granular' – like, say, the squares on a chess board – and not continuous. This theory, however, has grave consequences for geometry.

For if, say, a cone is bisected and the surface planes on the underside of the top half and the top of the bottom half are compared, they must be of different magnitudes, or else the cone would be a cylinder. But if thus is true, then our apparently perfect cone is in fact corrugated and not geometrically continuous. If our geometry is thus shown to be fatally flawed, how can we formulate a system that will be true to reality?

The reasons why epicurus developed this idea of notional smallest parts in an indivisible whole atom are thus several. One reason is to be found in Aristotle's *Physics* 231a21–b10, where he demonstrates that partless magnitudes cannot touch each other since touching is of either whole to whole, whole to part, or part to part. If it were the first of these then the two magnitudes would be totally co-extensive – which would be impossible for three-dimensional atoms to achieve – and the other two are ruled out because partless things have no parts. The atoms undoubtedly do touch, and so they must have parts: but the atoms cannot be splintered into these parts without surrendering their indivisibility and so running out of the frying pan of Aristotle into the fire of Zeno. Hence the need to work out a balance between these two positions, and hence the doctrine of smallest parts.

A more basic reason is simply this: atoms do not differ in substance, but in size and shape. It was the rejected *homoeomeria* theory of Anaxagoras, which argued that atoms of hair make up hairs etc., and Lucretius laughs this out of court at 1.830–920. Instead he posits differences in size and shape that demand the existence of a finite number of minimal parts in each atom, whose number and configuration will cause the size and shape of the atom (1.631–3, 2.481–99). Again, the atom is indivisible and so these minimal parts have no motion of their own but only as parts of the whole (on the reasoning that a smallest part cannot move by itself without incurring the possibility of crossing a boundary between places, and this would involve it having one part on each side of the boundary, which, being partless, it could not do). What is more, he also posits minimal quanta of time, the smallest unit of time being that required for an atom to hop from one minimal quantum of space into the next. These theories surely show that Epicurus believed that if he did not postulate the non-continuous, 'granular' nature of matter, time and space, then he would be hauled over the coals of Zeno's infinite divisibility. He could have perhaps argued that the fact that a magnitude can be mathematically subdivided does not alter the fact that space and matter *in fact* cannot be divided to infinity – not that that is any answer in logic. He could also have suggested that a finite space/magnitude can only be likely to be divided into an 'infinite' number of parts if these parts are unequal and thus form a convergent series such as: $\{\frac{1}{2} + \frac{1}{4} + \frac{1}{8} + \ldots \infty\}$ whose sum will never be greater than 1: thus fears that gnats will be the size of elephants are somewhat premature; except that that particular line of reasoning, while valid in its own terms, is no answer to the skilled Zenonian, whose infinite parts are not a convergent series but an array where each part is simultaneously divided into an infinite number of equal parts . . .

The argument goes on, and the curious and the brave are referred especially to Furley, *Two Studies in the Greek Atomists* and Barnes, *The Presocratic Philosophers* pp. 231–95, 352–60, and other further reading suggested in the bibliography. The significance of the theory of smallest parts cannot be overstated, as it brings up the question of the fundamental nature of matter, space and time – whether they are continuous or granular – and demands an answer on which the mathematician, the logician and the theoretical physicist could agree. I doubt that we will find one.

The Text

Like all classical texts, our editions of Lucretius rely mainly on
manuscripts (MSS) that go back to the Middle Ages. By a
detailed comparison of the different MSS – especially their
mistakes – it is possible to argue a case for their relative
antiquity and reliability – although 'older' does not always
mean 'better', as the intelligent scribe emended as he copied,
either from his own head or by consulting other MSS.

The actual text L. wrote is lost. So are all the copies made of
it for the first few hundred years after its composition, as the
earliest MSS date from the ninth century – a gap of eight
hundred years between composition and earliest text, the sort
of gap between (say) Chaucer and ourselves.

The archetype or source of the MSS we have, then, has not
survived. It is, however, known in greater detail than that of
almost any other Latin text. In his edition of 1850 the great
scholar Lachmann deduced that the archetype was written in
capitals in the fourth or perhaps the fifth century. The symmetry
of the passages omitted in one major manuscript and stuck in at
the end – each of them fifty-two lines long – shows that the
pages were of a standard twenty-six-line length, the fifty-two-
line gaps being the result of a whole leaf falling out of place.
(Cf. for example 4.299–322, misplaced after 323–47 because a
leaf of the archetype had fallen out and been replaced the
wrong way round.)

The earliest sources for the text are the two Leiden manu-
scripts O and Q: three sets of loose pages (*schedae*) are also
extant from the same century, known as G, V and U. After
OQGVU there is a further gap of about 400 years until the next
MS.

In 1417 the scholar Poggio Bracciolini discovered a text of L.
(known as π) and sent it off to Niccolo Niccoli to be copied:
Niccoli's copy survives in Florence and is known as L, and a
host of other MSS exist copied from Poggio's text and known

collectively as 'Itali'. The consensus of the best of them is known as P (for Poggio) and is the best reconstruction possible of that long lost manuscript π found in 1417. The comparison of P against OQGVU suggests that Poggio's text derives from O, although there are occasions where P agrees (rightly and wrongly) with Q against O, and although some scholars argue that the Itali derive from an MS tradition independent of OQ. The 'family-tree' of MSS (the *stemma*) as suggested by recent research looks like this:

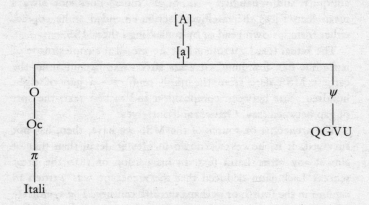

Below are listed the places where the text translated differs from the Oxford Classical Text of Bailey. Where the text is certainly corrupt but no emendation has been devised that is acceptable, then the corrupt words are printed with the so-called obelus (†), before and after them.

BOOK ONE

14	insert comma after *ferae*.
44–9	omitted by Bailey, as it is repeated at 2.646–51, but translated here.
599–600	Bailey notes a lacuna, filled in the translation by Munro's conjecture:

> *corporibus, quod iam nobis minimum esse videtur*
> *debet item ratione pari minimum esse cacumen*

On this see Furley, *Two Studies in the Greek Atomists* 31–3, and for a different view, Long and Sedley, *The Hellenistic Philosophers* vol. 2 p. 36.

657   Bailey prints †*Musa*†. The translation reads Merrill's *quae sint* (cf. 4.510).

721   Bailey's *Italiae* is the easier reading, altered by him in his own 1947 edition to my own reading *Aeoliae*, referring to South Italy, close to the Aeolian islands and near Rhegium, which was said to have been founded by Aeolus' son Iocastus.

744   Bailey reads *ignem* with the manuscripts, but altered it in his later edition to *imbrem*, which nicely completes the four Empedoclean elements.

860–61   Lambinus noted the lacuna and supplied the supplement, which I translate:

   et nervos alienigenis ex partibus esse

873–4   Munro noted the lacuna and Diels transposed 873–4 to produce sense: the translation fills in with the suggested supplement of Bailey in his 1947 edition.

998–1001   Bailey puts these lines in between 983 and 984: the translation restores them to their original place.

1013–14   lacuna: translation follows Bailey's suggested supplement.

1068–75   defective in the manuscripts as a page has obviously been torn, removing the ends of these lines. The translation attempts to reconstruct the sense from the words remaining.

1093–1102   Manuscript O has a lacuna of eight lines. The translation supplies the minimum required to join the two ends together, but the lacuna may be considerably longer than eight lines.

BOOK TWO

42   †*epicuri*† OCT. I read *et equum vi* (Munro).

43   †*itastuas*† OCT. Read Bernays' *pariter*, omitted by

	haplography. No need for the line composed by Bailey as 43a.
159	read *unum* (OQ), not *una* (OCT).
252	read *motu* (OQ), not *semper* (OCT).
356	read *quaerit* (Bailey) for OCT †*non quit*†.
462	read Grasberger's *sensibu' dentatum* for OCT's †*sensibu' sedatum*†.
515	read *hiemum usque* (Munro) for OCT †*hiemisque*†.
529	read *ostendens* (Munro) for OCT †*ostendam*†.
600–601	No lacuna as marked in OCT.
630	read Diels':

> *quos memorant, Phrygias inter si forte catervas*

instead of OCT reading:

> *quos memorant Phrygios, inter se forte ⟨quod armis⟩*

681–2	lacuna. Supply Munro's:

> *quis accensa solent fumore altaria divom*

748–9	lacuna filled by Bailey's:

> *corpora prima omni semper privata colore*

749–50	lacuna. 749 should read *et omnis*, then the lacuna should be filled by Bailey's:

> *res sese mutat, mutat quaecumque colorem*

805	OCT reads *curalium* (red coral) as suggested by Wakefield. OQ reading *caeruleum* better.
903–4	lacuna filled by Munro:

> *ipsi sensilibus, mortalia semina reddunt*

1082	*geminam* (OQ) preferable to Marullus' *genitam*.
1174	OCT †*scopulum*† is correct, not to be emended.

BOOK THREE

84	OCT †*suadet*† I translate Lambinus' reading *fundo*.
97–8	The lacuna is filled by Bailey's:

at quidem contra haec falsa ratione putarunt

240 OCT †*quaedamque mente volutat*† I translate the reading of T. J. Saunders (*Mnemosyne* 28 (1975) 296–8): *et quaecumque ipsa*.

377 I place a comma before *dumtaxat*, not after as in OCT.

444 MSS have †*incohibescit*†. Read Woltjer's emendation *incohibens sit*.

492 OCT reads *vis*. I read *vi* (Brieger).

493 OCT has †*animam spumans*†. I read *anima spumas* (Tohte).

658 The MSS reading *utrumque*, obelized in OCT, is at least arguably correct and has been translated 'both ends of . . .'

823 The lacuna is filled by Bailey's:

hoc fieri totum contra manifesta docet res

962 I read Marullus' *iam aliis* for OCT's †*magnis*† 1012–13. There is no need to postulate a lacuna as marked in OCT.

BOOK FOUR

26–53 OCT attempts to make sense of the lines by transposing groups of lines. I translate the lines in the MSS order and mark where the duplication of thought indicates that the second proem should be discarded.

79 OCT obelizes the MSS reading †*patrum matrumque deorum*†. I translate Konrad Müller's *personarumque decorem*.

127–8 Munro argued that a whole leaf of the text is missing here – a loss of 52 lines of verse. The translation supplies the minimum required to complete the sense.

133–42 No need for Bailey's transposition of 141–2 as in OCT: but Lambinus' transposition of 135 after 132 is correct.

144–5	Lacuna to be filled with a line such as 2.66: *expediam: tu te dictis praebere memento*.
166	Voss' *omnis* makes better sense than *oris* (Q) printed in OCT.
289–90	Lacuna filled by Bailey's: *hoc illis fieri, quae transpiciuntur, idemque*.
437	OCT prints Lachmann's *undae*: better sense is provided by the reading of F *undis*.
546–7	One of the major cruces in the text. The OCT reads:

> et reboat raucum †retro cita† barbara bombum,
> et †validis necti tortis† ex Heliconis

Many attempts to emend the lines have been made: I have finally gone for Büchner's *buxus cita* in 546 and Richter's *gelida volucres nocte hortis e fruticosis*, both argued for in my edition of Book 4 *ad loc*.

632	OCT prints Lachmann's *umidulum* (MSS read *umidum*). Better by far is Orth's emendation *validum*. Sturdy stomachs, not digestive juices, are called for here.
638	OCT prints the MSS reading †*est itaque ut*†. The smallest change required is Howard's *et* for *ut*, and I have translated this.
858–76	is printed within square brackets in OCT, but there is no strong reason to doubt the authenticity of the passage.
990	OCT obelizes the MSS reading †*saepe quiete*†, obviously copied mistakenly from 991. I read Richter's *fundere sese*.
1026	OCT's *puri* is weak, much improved by *parvi* (Clarke).
1130	OCT reads *atque Alidensia* (OQ), although the only place corresponding to the word (Alinda in Caria) would not give that adjective and did not produce the goods referred to either. A much better reading is Lambinus' *ac Melitensia*. Similarly

Chiaque (OQ) ought surely to be emended to *Coaque* – Coan garments were *de rigueur* for the elegant ladies of fashion. (Griffin J.R.S. (1976) 92 –n.1).

1271 The OCT reading *pectore* is nonsense, the best emendation being *corpore* (Clausen).

BOOK FIVE

29–30 The OCT reading is correct to posit a lacuna here and to transpose 29 and 30. The translation supplies the minimum sense to fill the intervening gap.

312 OCT reads †*quaerere proporro sibi cumque senescere credas*†: better with *cumque* emended by Munro to *sene* (omitted by the scribe by haplography *sene sene-*).

396 OCT reads *superat et lambens*: better to read the MSS reading *superavit* and emend *lambens* to *ambiens*.

412 Purmann's *vitas* is wrong: the MSS *multas* needs simply to be altered to *multos* to make sense.

571 I read the MSS *fulgent* instead of Lachmann's *mulcent* adopted in the OCT.

704–5 Lacuna noted by Munro, best filled with Bailey's suggestion: *pluribus e causis fieri haec qui posse putarunt* (cf. 752).

948 OCT *vagi* (Lachmann) should be restored to the MSS reading *vagis*.

1012–13 OCT marks lacuna noted by Marullus, filled by Munro's: *hospitium ac lecti socialia iura duobus*.

1094 OCT prints Marullus' *incita*; better to restore the MSS *insita*.

1442 OCT prints the MSS reading †*propter odores*†: better to emend to *navibus altum* with Merrill.

1451 Emend OCT's *polire* (131) to *polita* (Bergk).

BOOK SIX

47–8 a difficult crux: the translation merely plugs the lacuna.

56–7	is 90–91, which is 1.153–4: OCT omits the lines here but prints them at 90–91. These lines are identical to 56–7 and 1.153–4 and should be omitted.
131	Voss' *magnum* is preferable to the MSS reading *parvum*.
242	The OCT obelizes *ciere*: but it is a possible reading either in the simple sense of 'displace' or perhaps to suggest the 'summoning forth' of the dead from their tombs.
453	OCT reads Lachmann's *moris*: better to read *modis* (OQ).
490	OCT †*montis*†: I prefer Richter's *nebulis*.
550	OCT obelizes †*es dupuis*†: the whole line should read: *nec minus exsultant, fissura ubicumque viai. Fissura* was first proposed by Rusch.
608–38	Bracketed by Lachmann and OCT because of the abrupt transition in thought. L. might have placed the lines elsewhere in the revision that the poem evidently lacks.
697–8	Munro first noted the lacuna and filled it with:

fluctibus admixtum vim venti: intrareque ab isto.

712	Removing OCT's comma after *terris* makes better geographical sense, as the Nile was not the only river to flood in summer.
762	OCT †*poteis*†. Emend to *primo his* (Richter).
778	The MSS reading *tactu* (obelized in OCT) is still the best reading available.
804	OCT prints MSS corrupt †*fervida servis*†. Much better is Lambinus' emendation *fervida febris*.
839–40	Lachmann argued that a whole page of the archetype had fallen out between these lines: but the lacuna has not been universally accepted.
870	Read *miscente* (OQ) for OCT/Wakefield's unnecessary *gliscente*.
899	OCT prints Bernays' *latentis* for the unexciting MSS reading *tenentes*. I prefer to read Romanes' *natantes*, agreeing with *taedae*.

927   The MSS reading *auras* is preferable to Lambinus' emendation *auris* printed by OCT.

954–5   The lacuna was first noted by Brieger. I translate Bailey's suggestion to fill the gap:

corpora nimborum penetrant et semina nubis

971   OCT reads *ambrosia*: I prefer Avancius' *ambrosiam*.

972   OCT prints Lachmann's *frondeat esca*: I prefer the recent suggestion of M. L. Clarke, *fronde virescat*.

1135   OCT prints †*corumptum*†, easily emended to *coruptum* with the Itali.

1195   OCT prints: *in ore truci rictum*: a better reading is Richter's *in archiatri tactum*.

1281   OCT prints *pro re ⟨compostum⟩*. I prefer Housman's *propere pro tempore*.

The Ending of the Poem

It has often been noted that there is a stark contrast between the eulogistic paean with which this poem opens and the dismal threnody with which it ends. The symmetrical contrast between the opening of the poem in the address to Venus – full of hope, life and joy – and the closing account of the plague at Athens with its despair, death and misery, is puzzling, if the purpose of the poem is thought to be positive and encouraging. The closely argued pages of Thucydides' *History of the Peloponnesian War* (2.47–55) are either translated directly or reworked into a rhetorical and chilling account of the suffering, both mental and physical, of the Athenian plague of 430 BC.

The problem of the ending of the poem is actually no less controversial than that surrounding the ending of Virgil's *Aeneid*, but there seems to be general agreement about one thing: L. intended to finish his poem with the plague – it is the longest piece of descriptive writing in the poem and well suited to bring the work to a climax, Athens being both familiar and unfamiliar, a distant foreign capital but also one where many a Roman – such as Memmius the dedicatee – spent years of his life. The problem is simply that of understanding why this poet proclaiming the good news of Epicurean serenity and happiness freed from fear should leave us with this dreary saga of pain and futile death. Some critics have seen it as the arch-example of 'l'anti-Lucrèce chez Lucrèce' whereby the poet's 'real' melancholy won over his attempts to hide it under a façade of facile optimism – this, linked with the apparent neurosis of his denunciation of romantic love in Book Four and St Jerome's tales of Lucretius' love-potions and suicide, gives a picture of L. as a sick recluse losing a long battle with depression. It has something to recommend it if we avoid patronizing psychoanalytic terms but see it instead as the poet's ultimate recognition that optimism has to be tempered with insight into the tragic side of life. The ending of the poem thus becomes a display of the real suffering to be faced – remember Epicurus' own painful death (Diogenes Laertius x.15) – and a reassurance to the reader of the way true philosophy can endure even this. Death is after all 'nothing to us' (3.830), and the true Epicurean would even be happy when being roasted to death in the bronze bull of Phalaris, compared with which a plague is relatively commonplace!

There are however other possible lines of argument. Minyard sees it as a form of satire against Athenian life: a demonstration that the old-style world of the Greek city-state would fail until the day Epicurus appeared with his truth. (*Lucretius and the Late Republic* 60–61.) Müller ('Die Finalia der sechs Bücher des Lukrez' in *Lucrèce* (Fondations Hardt Entretiens 24,220), on the other hand, is surely right to stress the universal nature of the plague as something that could recur at any time as part of the nature of the world as we know it. Besides, Minyard's account would make Lucretius promote the apolitical side of Epicureanism by using the plague as a 'proof' that political societies do not work: it attempts to turn the Hippocratean catalogue of symptoms into 'satire', which it patently is not: and it is inconceivable that L. would have left the 'before and after' point so obscurely drawn if that were the point of the whole passage.

The theory is not wholly without merits, however. The ending of Book Five shows us the growth of 'civilization' and the way that even now mankind is still racked with fear and superstition: the poet is concerned neither to praise progress nor to sentimentalize primitivism, but simply to argue that material progress will only improve our lives if we listen to Epicurus. Turn to the opening of Book Five and we find Lucretius praising Epicurus in contrast to the great 'benefactors' of mankind such as Hercules: once again, the progress made in material terms is futile until we hear the message of Epicurus. The plague, seen in these terms, is an extreme example of the opposite point: not the futility of the 'good' things without Epicurus, but the bleak nihilistic pain which is all that 'bad' things give us – without Epicurus. The connection is not explicitly drawn – perhaps as a result of the unfinished state of the poem – but this would at least link the plague with the rest of the poem and with Lucretius' evangelistic mission in general.

It has also been suggested (for example, Arragon, 'Poetic Art as a Philosophic Medium for Lucretius', *Essays in Criticism* 11 (1961) 386–7) that the 'artist' in L. got carried away with the experience of describing the plague and 'forgot' the distressing moral effect on the reader. More perceptively Commager ('Lucretius' interpretation of the plague' *Harvard Studies in Classical Philology* 62 (1957) 105–18) has shown how the so-called 'mistranslations' of Thucydides' account of the plague are in fact re-interpretations of physical symptoms in more psychological terms, brought about by the way the picture of 'a diseased population burning with an insatiable and self-destructive thirst ... may have obscurely reminded Lucretius of his own image of man'. We all suffer from the inner plague of weariness, anxiety and thirst for contentment, and the plague thus has a symbolic and paradigmatic function far beyond the mere recital of gory symptoms. It is thus, as Segal argues (*Lucretius on Death and Anxiety* 234), a sort of moral allegory of our need for Epicurus' teaching in facing death and a historical allegory of the failure of society to cope with suffering. The disease, in short, is symbolic of a spiritual malaise that only Epicurus can cure.

This 'optimistic' reading of the epilogue, it seems to me, goes too far the other way: at the end of the poem this symbolism is not made explicit, the allegory is not unpacked, and the whole thrust of the passage is that the plague killed *everybody*, good and bad alike – the good by their heroic caring for the sick, the bad despite their craven refusal to care for them (1240–46). There is no distinction drawn between 'good death' and 'bad death' – there is only death – and the squabbling selfishness of the wretched survivors shows us not the stock picture of the 'unenlightened' but simply the moral effects of the sickness on human behaviour. The plague was an extraordinary event that made people behave in an extraordinary way: Lucretius' lines afford insight into their plight and above all deep compassion for their pain, rather than a cryptic sermon for our own lives to be deciphered. That would after all remove all the humane sympathy from the passage and turn it into a lame tract pruriently dwelling on the suffering of the sick and wallowing in Epicurean *Schadenfreude* and self-righteousness. Lucretius has been accused of that in, for example, 2.1ff. and also 3.59–86, but in both cases he points the Epicurean message in contrast to the anxiety and frustration of human striving. This differs utterly from the malady described here, an agony without any cure.

A further point that has not, to my knowledge, been stressed adequately before is this: Lucretius chooses to finish his poem with the plague for the same reason as he chose to finish Book Four with the similarly 'pessimistic' attack on the passion of love – in both passages man is 'sick' (*aeger*) and 'wretched'. The purpose in both is to bring the 'atomic' demonstrations of impersonal nature back to the experience of man himself and to prove once and for all that the atomic theory is not just a pretty set of arguments, but that what it describes and explains actually *matters* to us. The Epicurean may choose to dwell in his little garden but he is no ivory-tower recluse with no knowledge of the world: the very theory itself tells him the awful truth of human imperfection (cf. 6.12–23) and the fact that the world is not a kind place (5.195–234) – indeed some of the atoms flying around are harmful and cause plague (1090ff.). There would be less cause to seek the serenity of the garden if there were not ghastly realities of life such as the great plague of Athens. We can never give a conclusive answer to the question of what Lucretius might have done with the end of a probably unfinished poem: but the final lines of this book do succeed in bringing the somewhat recondite physics of the earlier sections very much into the field of human experience – with the decisive twist, however, that whereas we now understand the mechanics of plague and (being good Epicureans) would not dream of either blaming the gods for the disease or of seeking their help in dealing with it, this understanding does not in fact make the pain hurt any the less. The ending of the book is abrupt, and Martin accordingly proposed the transposition of 1247–51 to the end of the book to give something of a rounded ending. The fact remains, however, that there is nothing in the text that offers any crumb of consolation to the philosopher, no glimmer of serenity available in the agony and the *angst*.

The only shred of pleasure left is of course the pleasure of the poetry itself, which conveys the pain so beautifully – indeed Arragon points out well that this passage is not conventionally beautiful poetic imagery to sweeten the sour doctrine, but rather it is the doctrine which sweetens the sourly painted truth in the poetry. The plague thus encapsulates the tragic insight into human existence that is necessary to offset what may seem facile optimism: it expounds the working of a particularly sensational 'divine' event in purely mechanical atomistic terms, thus reinforcing one more time the anti-theological view the poem has proclaimed throughout: and it leaves the poetry alone, when the values of human joy and society are dead, as of indestructible beauty, setting out the central dilemma of human life with no facile attempt to resolve it, the only harmony available emerging from the artistic perfection of the means of its exposition. No lesser aim would be sufficient to end this great poem.

INDEX

This index is not intended to be exhaustive. Authors cited only for comparison are not usually included, and the synopsis of the poem (pages 3–9) will be of help in finding the major topics of the poem.

READ MORE IN PENGUIN

In every corner of the world, on every subject under the sun, Penguin represents quality and variety – the very best in publishing today.

For complete information about books available from Penguin – including Puffins, Penguin Classics and Arkana – and how to order them, write to us at the appropriate address below. Please note that for copyright reasons the selection of books varies from country to country.

In the United Kingdom: Please write to *Dept. EP, Penguin Books Ltd, Bath Road, Harmondsworth, West Drayton, Middlesex UB7 ODA*

In the United States: Please write to *Consumer Sales, Penguin Putnam Inc., P.O. Box 999, Dept. 17109, Bergenfield, New Jersey 07621-0120.* VISA and MasterCard holders call 1-800-253-6476 to order Penguin titles

In Canada: Please write to *Penguin Books Canada Ltd, 10 Alcorn Avenue, Suite 300, Toronto, Ontario M4V 3B2*

In Australia: Please write to *Penguin Books Australia Ltd, P.O. Box 257, Ringwood, Victoria 3134*

In New Zealand: Please write to *Penguin Books (NZ) Ltd, Private Bag 102902, North Shore Mail Centre, Auckland 10*

In India: Please write to *Penguin Books India Pvt Ltd, 210 Chiranjiv Tower, 43 Nehru Place, New Delhi 110 019*

In the Netherlands: Please write to *Penguin Books Netherlands bv, Postbus 3507, NL-1001 AH Amsterdam*

In Germany: Please write to *Penguin Books Deutschland GmbH, Metzlerstrasse 26, 60594 Frankfurt am Main*

In Spain: Please write to *Penguin Books S. A., Bravo Murillo 19, 1° B, 28015 Madrid*

In Italy: Please write to *Penguin Italia s.r.l., Via Benedetto Croce 2, 20094 Corsico, Milano*

In France: Please write to *Penguin France, Le Carré Wilson, 62 rue Benjamin Baillaud, 31500 Toulouse*

In Japan: Please write to *Penguin Books Japan Ltd, Kaneko Building, 2-3-25 Koraku, Bunkyo-Ku, Tokyo 112*

In South Africa: Please write to *Penguin Books South Africa (Pty) Ltd, Private Bag X14, Parkview, 2122 Johannesburg*

PENGUIN AUDIOBOOKS

A Quality of Writing That Speaks for Itself

Penguin Books has always led the field in quality publishing. Now you can listen at leisure to your favourite books, read to you by familiar voices from radio, stage and screen. Penguin Audiobooks are produced to an excellent standard, and abridgements are always faithful to the original texts. From thrillers to classic literature, biography to humour, with a wealth of titles in between, Penguin Audiobooks offer you quality, entertainment and the chance to rediscover the pleasure of listening.

You can order Penguin Audiobooks through Penguin Direct by telephoning (0181) 899 4036. The lines are open 24 hours every day. Ask for Penguin Direct, quoting your credit card details.

A selection of Penguin Audiobooks, published or forthcoming:

Little Women by Louisa May Alcott, read by Kate Harper

Emma by Jane Austen, read by Fiona Shaw

Pride and Prejudice by Jane Austen, read by Geraldine McEwan

Beowulf translated by Michael Alexander, read by David Rintoul

Agnes Grey by Anne Brontë, read by Juliet Stevenson

Jane Eyre by Charlotte Brontë, read by Juliet Stevenson

The Professor by Charlotte Brontë, read by Juliet Stevenson

Wuthering Heights by Emily Brontë, read by Juliet Stevenson

The Woman in White by Wilkie Collins, read by Nigel Anthony and Susan Jameson

Nostromo by Joseph Conrad, read by Michael Pennington

Tales from the Thousand and One Nights, read by Souad Faress and Raad Rawi

Robinson Crusoe by Daniel Defoe, read by Tom Baker

David Copperfield by Charles Dickens, read by Nathaniel Parker

The Pickwick Papers by Charles Dickens, read by Dinsdale Landen

Bleak House by Charles Dickens, read by Beatie Edney and Ronald Pickup

PENGUIN AUDIOBOOKS

The Hound of the Baskervilles by Sir Arthur Conan Doyle, read by Freddie Jones

Middlemarch by George Eliot, read by Harriet Walter

Tom Jones by Henry Fielding, read by Robert Lindsay

The Great Gatsby by F. Scott Fitzgerald, read by Marcus D'Amico

Madame Bovary by Gustave Flaubert, read by Claire Bloom

Mary Barton by Elizabeth Gaskell, read by Clare Higgins

Jude the Obscure by Thomas Hardy, read by Samuel West

Far from the Madding Crowd by Thomas Hardy, read by Julie Christie

The Scarlet Letter by Nathaniel Hawthorne, read by Bob Sessions

Les Misérables by Victor Hugo, read by Nigel Anthony

A Passage to India by E. M. Forster, read by Tim Pigott-Smith

The Iliad by Homer, read by Derek Jacobi

The Dead and Other Stories by James Joyce, read by Gerard McSorley

On the Road by Jack Kerouac, read by David Carradine

Sons and Lovers by D. H. Lawrence, read by Paul Copley

The Prince by Niccolò Machiavelli, read by Fritz Weaver

Animal Farm by George Orwell, read by Timothy West

Rob Roy by Sir Walter Scott, read by Robbie Coltrane

Frankenstein by Mary Shelley, read by Richard Pasco

Of Mice and Men by John Steinbeck, read by Gary Sinise

Kidnapped by Robert Louis Stevenson, read by Robbie Coltrane

Dracula by Bram Stoker, read by Richard E. Grant

Gulliver's Travels by Jonathan Swift, read by Hugh Laurie

Vanity Fair by William Makepeace Thackeray, read by Robert Hardy

Lark Rise to Candleford by Flora Thompson, read by Judi Dench

The Invisible Man by H. G. Wells, read by Paul Shelley

Ethan Frome by Edith Wharton, read by Nathan Osgood

The Picture of Dorian Gray by Oscar Wilde, read by John Moffatt

Orlando by Virginia Woolf, read by Tilda Swinton

READ MORE IN PENGUIN

A CHOICE OF CLASSICS

Armadale   Wilkie Collins

Victorian critics were horrified by Lydia Gwilt, the bigamist, husband-poisoner and laudanum addict whose intrigues spur the plot of this most sensational of melodramas.

Aurora Leigh and Other Poems   Elizabeth Barrett Browning

Aurora Leigh (1856), Elizabeth Barrett Browning's epic novel in blank verse, tells the story of the making of a woman poet, exploring 'the woman question', art and its relation to politics and social oppression.

Personal Narrative of a Journey to the Equinoctial Regions of the New Continent   Alexander von Humboldt

Alexander von Humboldt became a. wholly new kind of nineteenth-century hero – the scientist–explorer – and in *Personal Narrative* he invented a new literary genre: the travelogue.

The Pancatantra   Visnu Sarma

The Pancatantra is one of the earliest books of fables and its influence can be seen in the *Arabian Nights*, the *Decameron*, the *Canterbury Tales* and most notably in the *Fables* of La Fontaine.

A Laodicean   Thomas Hardy

The Laodicean of Hardy's title is Paula Power, a thoroughly modern young woman who, despite her wealth and independence, cannot make up her mind.

Brand   Henrik Ibsen

The unsparing vision of a priest driven by faith to risk and witness the deaths of his wife and child gives *Brand* its icy ferocity. It was Ibsen's first masterpiece, a poetic drama composed in 1865 and published to tremendous critical and popular acclaim.

READ MORE IN PENGUIN

A CHOICE OF CLASSICS

Sylvia's Lovers Elizabeth Gaskell

In an atmosphere of unease the rivalries of two men, the sober tradesman Philip Hepburn, who has been devoted to his cousin Sylvia since her childhood, and the gallant, charming whaleship harpooner Charley Kinraid, are played out.

The Republic Plato

The best-known of Plato's dialogues, *The Republic* is also one of the supreme masterpieces of Western philosophy, whose influence cannot be overestimated.

Ethics Benedict de Spinoza

'Spinoza (1632–77),' wrote Bertrand Russell, 'is the noblest and most lovable of the great philosophers. Intellectually, some others have surpassed him, but ethically he is supreme.'

Virgil in English

From Chaucer to Auden, Virgil is a defining presence in English poetry. Penguin Classics' new series, Poets in Translation, offers the best translations in English, through the centuries, of the major Classical and European poets.

What is Art? Leo Tolstoy

Tolstoy wrote prolifically in a series of essays and polemics on issues of morality, social justice and religion. These culminated in *What is Art?*, published in 1898, in which he rejects the idea that art reveals and reinvents through beauty.

An Autobiography Anthony Trollope

A fascinating insight into a writer's life, in which Trollope also recorded his unhappy youth and his progress to prosperity and social recognition.

READ MORE IN PENGUIN

A CHOICE OF CLASSICS

Aeschylus	**The Oresteian Trilogy**
	Prometheus Bound/The Suppliants/Seven against Thebes/The Persians
Aesop	**Fables**
Ammianus Marcellinus	**The Later Roman Empire (AD 354–378)**
Apollonius of Rhodes	**The Voyage of Argo**
Apuleius	**The Golden Ass**
Aristophanes	**The Knights/Peace/The Birds/The Assemblywomen/Wealth**
	Lysistrata/The Acharnians/The Clouds
	The Wasps/The Poet and the Women/ The Frogs
Aristotle	**The Art of Rhetoric**
	The Athenian Constitution
	De Anima
	Ethics
	Poetics
Arrian	**The Campaigns of Alexander**
Marcus Aurelius	**Meditations**
Boethius	**The Consolation of Philosophy**
Caesar	**The Civil War**
	The Conquest of Gaul
Catullus	**Poems**
Cicero	**Murder Trials**
	The Nature of the Gods
	On the Good Life
	Selected Letters
	Selected Political Speeches
	Selected Works
Euripides	**Alcestis/Iphigenia in Tauris/Hippolytus**
	The Bacchae/Ion/The Women of Troy/ Helen
	Medea/Hecabe/Electra/Heracles
	Orestes and Other Plays

READ MORE IN PENGUIN

A CHOICE OF CLASSICS

Hesiod/Theognis	**Theogony/Works and Days/Elegies**
Hippocrates	**Hippocratic Writings**
Homer	**The Iliad**
	The Odyssey
Horace	**Complete Odes and Epodes**
Horace/Persius	**Satires and Epistles**
Juvenal	**The Sixteen Satires**
Livy	**The Early History of Rome**
	Rome and Italy
	Rome and the Mediterranean
	The War with Hannibal
Lucretius	**On the Nature of the Universe**
Martial	**Epigrams**
Ovid	**The Erotic Poems**
	Heroides
	Metamorphoses
	The Poems of Exile
Pausanias	**Guide to Greece** (in two volumes)
Petronius/Seneca	**The Satyricon/The Apocolocyntosis**
Pindar	**The Odes**
Plato	**Early Socratic Dialogues**
	Gorgias
	The Last Days of Socrates (Euthyphro/ The Apology/Crito/Phaedo)
	The Laws
	Phaedrus and **Letters VII and VIII**
	Philebus
	Protagoras/Meno
	The Republic
	The Symposium
	Theaetetus
	Timaeus/Critias

READ MORE IN PENGUIN

A CHOICE OF CLASSICS

Plautus	**The Pot of Gold/The Prisoners/The Brothers Menaechmus/The Swaggering Soldier/Pseudolus**
	The Rope/Amphitryo/The Ghost/A Three-Dollar Day
Pliny	**The Letters of the Younger Pliny**
Pliny the Elder	**Natural History**
Plotinus	**The Enneads**
Plutarch	**The Age of Alexander** (Nine Greek Lives)
	The Fall of the Roman Republic (Six Lives)
	The Makers of Rome (Nine Lives)
	The Rise and Fall of Athens (Nine Greek Lives)
	Plutarch on Sparta
Polybius	**The Rise of the Roman Empire**
Procopius	**The Secret History**
Propertius	**The Poems**
Quintus Curtius Rufus	**The History of Alexander**
Sallust	**The Jugurthine War** and **The Conspiracy of Cataline**
Seneca	**Four Tragedies** and **Octavia**
	Letters from a Stoic
Sophocles	**Electra/Women of Trachis/Philoctetes/Ajax**
	The Theban Plays
Suetonius	**The Twelve Caesars**
Tacitus	**The Agricola** and **The Germania**
	The Annals of Imperial Rome
	The Histories
Terence	**The Comedies (The Girl from Andros/The Self-Tormentor/TheEunuch/Phormio/The Mother-in-Law/The Brothers)**
Thucydides	**The History of the Peloponnesian War**
Virgil	**The Aeneid**
	The Eclogues
	The Georgics
Xenophon	**Conversations of Socrates**
	A History of My Times
	The Persian Expedition

READ MORE IN PENGUIN

A CHOICE OF CLASSICS

Adomnan of Iona	**Life of St Columba**
St Anselm	**The Prayers and Meditations**
St Augustine	**Confessions**
	The City of God
Bede	**Ecclesiastical History of the English People**
Geoffrey Chaucer	**The Canterbury Tales**
	Love Visions
	Troilus and Criseyde
Marie de France	**The Lais of Marie de France**
Jean Froissart	**The Chronicles**
Geoffrey of Monmouth	**The History of the Kings of Britain**
Gerald of Wales	**History and Topography of Ireland**
	The Journey through Wales and **The Description of Wales**
Gregory of Tours	**The History of the Franks**
Robert Henryson	**The Testament of Cresseid and Other Poems**
Walter Hilton	**The Ladder of Perfection**
St Ignatius	**Personal Writings**
Julian of Norwich	**Revelations of Divine Love**
Thomas à Kempis	**The Imitation of Christ**
William Langland	**Piers the Ploughman**
Sir John Mandeville	**The Travels of Sir John Mandeville**
Marguerite de Navarre	**The Heptameron**
Christine de Pisan	**The Treasure of the City of Ladies**
Chrétien de Troyes	**Arthurian Romances**
Marco Polo	**The Travels**
Richard Rolle	**The Fire of Love**
François Villon	**Selected Poems**

READ MORE IN PENGUIN

A CHOICE OF CLASSICS

ANTHOLOGIES AND ANONYMOUS WORKS

The Age of Bede
Alfred the Great
Beowulf
A Celtic Miscellany
The Cloud of Unknowing and Other Works
The Death of King Arthur
The Earliest English Poems
Early Irish Myths and Sagas
Egil's Saga
English Mystery Plays
Eyrbyggja Saga
Hrafnkel's Saga and Other Stories
The Letters of Abelard and Heloise
Medieval English Lyrics
Medieval English Verse
Njal's Saga
Roman Poets of the Early Empire
Seven Viking Romances
Sir Gawain and the Green Knight

READ MORE IN PENGUIN

A CHOICE OF CLASSICS

Francis Bacon	**The Essays**
Aphra Behn	**Love-Letters between a Nobleman and His Sister**
	Oroonoko, The Rover and Other Works
George Berkeley	**Principles of Human Knowledge/Three Dialogues between Hylas and Philonous**
James Boswell	**The Life of Samuel Johnson**
Sir Thomas Browne	**The Major Works**
John Bunyan	**The Pilgrim's Progress**
Edmund Burke	**Reflections on the Revolution in France**
Frances Burney	**Evelina**
Margaret Cavendish	**The Blazing World and Other Writings**
William Cobbett	**Rural Rides**
William Congreve	**Comedies**
Thomas de Quincey	**Confessions of an English Opium Eater**
	Recollections of the Lakes and the Lake Poets
Daniel Defoe	**A Journal of the Plague Year**
	Moll Flanders
	Robinson Crusoe
	Roxana
	A Tour Through the Whole Island of Great Britain
Henry Fielding	**Amelia**
	Jonathan Wild
	Joseph Andrews
	The Journal of a Voyage to Lisbon
	Tom Jones
John Gay	**The Beggar's Opera**
Oliver Goldsmith	**The Vicar of Wakefield**
Lady Gregory	**Selected Writings**

READ MORE IN PENGUIN

A CHOICE OF CLASSICS

William Hazlitt	**Selected Writings**
George Herbert	**The Complete English Poems**
Thomas Hobbes	**Leviathan**
Samuel Johnson/	
James Boswell	**A Journey to the Western Islands of Scotland** and **The Journal of a Tour of the Hebrides**
Charles Lamb	**Selected Prose**
George Meredith	**The Egoist**
Thomas Middleton	**Five Plays**
John Milton	**Paradise Lost**
Samuel Richardson	**Clarissa**
	Pamela
Earl of Rochester	**Complete Works**
Richard Brinsley	
Sheridan	**The School for Scandal and Other Plays**
Sir Philip Sidney	**Selected Poems**
Christopher Smart	**Selected Poems**
Adam Smith	**The Wealth of Nations** (Books I–III)
Tobias Smollett	**The Adventures of Ferdinand Count Fathom**
	Humphrey Clinker
	Roderick Random
Laurence Sterne	**The Life and Opinions of Tristram Shandy**
	A Sentimental Journey Through France and Italy
Jonathan Swift	**Gulliver's Travels**
	Selected Poems
Thomas Traherne	**Selected Poems and Prose**
Henry Vaughan	**Complete Poems**

READ MORE IN PENGUIN

A CHOICE OF CLASSICS

Leopoldo Alas	**La Regenta**
Leon B. Alberti	**On Painting**
Ludovico Ariosto	**Orlando Furioso** (in 2 volumes)
Giovanni Boccaccio	**The Decameron**
Baldassar Castiglione	**The Book of the Courtier**
Benvenuto Cellini	**Autobiography**
Miguel de Cervantes	**Don Quixote**
	Exemplary Stories
Dante	**The Divine Comedy** (in 3 volumes)
	La Vita Nuova
Machado de Assis	**Dom Casmurro**
Bernal Díaz	**The Conquest of New Spain**
Carlo Goldoni	**Four Comedies (The Venetian Twins/The Artful Widow/Mirandolina/The Superior Residence)**
Niccolò Machiavelli	**The Discourses**
	The Prince
Alessandro Manzoni	**The Betrothed**
Emilia Pardo Bazán	**The House of Ulloa**
Benito Pérez Galdós	**Fortunata and Jacinta**
Giorgio Vasari	**Lives of the Artists** (in 2 volumes)

and

Five Italian Renaissance Comedies
   (Machiavelli/**The Mandragola**; Ariosto/**Lena**; Aretino/**The Stablemaster**; Gl'Intronati/**The Deceived**; Guarini/**The Faithful Shepherd**)
The Poem of the Cid
Two Spanish Picaresque Novels
   (Anon/**Lazarillo de Tormes**; de Quevedo/**The Swindler**)

READ MORE IN PENGUIN

A CHOICE OF CLASSICS

Basho	**The Narrow Road to the Deep North**
	On Love and Barley
Cao Xueqin	**The Story of the Stone** also known as **The Dream of The Red Chamber** (in five volumes)
Confucius	**The Analects**
Khayyam	**The Ruba'iyat of Omar Khayyam**
Lao Tzu	**Tao Te Ching**
Li Po/Tu Fu	**Poems**
Sarma	**The Pancatantra**
Sei Shonagon	**The Pillow Book of Sei Shonagon**
Somadeva	**Tales from the Kathasaritsagara**
Wang Wei	**Poems**
Yuan Qu and Others	**The Songs of the South**

ANTHOLOGIES AND ANONYMOUS WORKS

The Bhagavad Gita
Buddhist Scriptures
Chinese Love Poetry
The Dhammapada
Hindu Myths
The Koran
The Laws of Manu
Poems of the Late T'Ang
The Rig Veda
Speaking of Siva
Tales from the Thousand and One Nights
The Upanishads